Introduction to 64 Bit Assembly Programming for Linux and OS X

Ray Seyfarth

Ray Seyfarth
Hattiesburg, MS
USA

Seyfarth, Ray
64 Bit Assembly Language Programming for Linux and OS X
Includes index
ISBN-13: 978-1484921906
ISBN-10: 1484921909

Preface

The Intel CPU architecture has evolved over 3 decades from a 16 bit CPU with no memory protection, through a period with 32 bit processors with sophisticated architectures into the current series of processors which support all the old modes of operation in addition to a greatly expanded 64 bit mode of operation. Assembly textbooks tend to focus on the history and generally conclude with a discussion of the 32 bit mode. Students are introduced to the concepts of 16 bit CPUs with segment registers allowing access to 1 megabyte of internal memory. This is an unnecessary focus on the past.

With the x86-64 architecture there is almost a complete departure from the past. Segment registers are essentially obsolete and more register usage is completely general purpose, with the glaring exception of the repeat-string loops which use specific registers and have no operands. Both these changes contribute to simpler assembly language programming.

There are now 16 general purpose integer registers with a few specialized instructions. The archaic register stack of the 8087 has been superseded by a well-organized model providing 16 floating point registers with floating point instructions along with the SSE and AVX extensions. In fact the AVX extensions even allow a three operand syntax which can simplify coding even more.

Overall the x86-64 assembly language programming is simpler than its predecessors. The dominant mode of operation will be 64 bits within a few short years. Today most personal computers ship with 64 bit operating systems. In fact the latest versions of the Apple OS X operating system are only available in 64 bits, though Linux and Microsoft Windows still have 32 and 64 bit versions. The era of 32 bit CPUs and operating systems is nearly over. Together these trends indicate that it is time to teach 64 bit assembly language.

The focus in this textbook is on early hands-on use of 64 bit assembly programming. There is no 16 or 32 bit programming and the discussion of the history is focused on explaining the origin of the old register names and the few non-orthogonal features of the instruction set.

iii

The first version of this book discussed using the yasm assembler and the gdb debugger directly. Now the author provides a free integrated development environment named "ebe", which automates the process of using yasm. The ebe environment is a GUI program written in C++ using the Qt system and supports C, C++ and FORTRAN in addition to assembly language, though its purpose is to support assembly programming. There was a previous version of ebe written in Python, but the newer version offers many more features. The Qt version of ebe is available at `http://qtebe.sourceforge.net`.

This version of the book discusses assembly programming for both the Linux and OS X operating systems. Fortunately these two operating systems use the same function call protocol and discussing them both is convenient in one book. There is a companion book discussing assembly programming for Windows which uses a different function call interface. There is a discussion of the function call protocol differences for Linux, OS X and Windows, so having one of the two books should be sufficient for someone interested in programming on multiple operating systems.

Due to costs this book is printed in black and white. The pictures captured from ebe would have been prettier and perhaps more useful in color, but the cost of the book would have been roughly double the cost of a black and white version. The added utility of color is certainly not worth the extra cost. Generally the highlighted text in ebe is shown with a colored background while the printed version presents this text with a light gray background.

Most of the sample code execution in the first edition was illustrated using gdb. This function has largely been superseded with screen captures from ebe, though some use of gdb is still shown. It might be that some people would prefer using a text interface and blind programmers in particular might find a GUI interface to be a real inconvenience.

There are assignments using the computer from the very first chapter. Not every statement will be fully understood at this time, but the assignments are still possible.

The primary target for this book is beginning assembly language programmers and for a gentle introduction to assembly programming, students should study chapters 1, 2, 3, 5, 6, 7, 8, 9, 10 and 11. Chapter 4 on memory mapping is not critical to the rest of the book and can be skipped if desired.

Chapters 12 through 15 are significantly more in depth. Chapter 15 is about data structures in assembly and is an excellent adjunct to studying data structures in C/C++. The subject will be much clearer after exposure in assembly language.

The final four chapters focus on high performance programming, including discussion of SSE and AVX programming.

The author provides slides for classroom instruction along with sample code and errata at `http://rayseyfarth.com/asm`.

If you find errors in the book or have suggestions for improvement, please email the author as `ray.seyfarth@gmail.com`. Your suggestions will help improve the book and are greatly appreciated.

You may also email me with questions or suggestions about ebe. Your email will assist me with providing better on-line support and will help improve the quality of the software.

Thank you for buying the book and I hope you find something interesting and worthwhile inside.

Acknowledgements

No book is created in isolation. This book is certainly no exception. I am indebted to numerous sources for information and assistance with this book.

Dr. Paul Carter's PC assembly language book was used by this author to study 32 bit assembly language programming. His book is a free PDF file downloadable from his web site. This is a 195 page book which covers the basics of assembly language and is a great start at 32 bit assembly language.

While working on this book, I discovered a treatise by Drs. Bryant and O'Hallaron of Carnegie Mellon about how gcc takes advantage of the features of the x86-64 architecture to produce efficient code. Some of their observations have helped me understand the CPU better which assists with writing better assembly code. Programmers interested in efficiency should study their work.

I found the Intel manuals to be an invaluable resource. They provide details on all the instructions of the CPU. Unfortunately the documents cover 32 bit and 64 bit instructions together which, along with the huge number of instructions, makes it difficult to learn assembly programming from these manuals. I hope that reading this book will make a good starting point, but a short book cannot cover many instructions. I have selected what I consider the most important instructions for general use, but an assembly programmer will need to study the Intel manuals (or equivalent manuals from AMD).

I thank my friends Maggie and Tim Hampton for their editing contributions to the book.

I am indebted to my CSC 203 - Assembly Language class at the University of Southern Mississippi for their contributions to this book. Teaching 64 bit assembly language has uncovered a few mistakes and errors in the original Create Space book from July 2011. In particular I wish to thank Chris Greene, Evan Stuart, Brandon Wolfe and Zachary Dillon for locating errors in the book.

Thanks to Ken O'Brien for helping locate mistakes in the book. Thanks go to Christian Korn and Markus Bohm of Germany who have assisted with "debugging" this book. Thanks also to Francisco Perdomo of the Canary Islands for assistance. Carsten Hansen of Sweden has also assisted with debugging the book. David Langer has contributed some code comment repairs.

Thanks to Quentin Gouchet for locating several typos which had persisted for several years.

Thanks for Keiji Omori for pointing out that the stack size limits for Linux processes are now quite generous. At some point there was a hard kernel limit which could be changed by recompiling the kernel. Now it can be changed in /etc/security/limits.conf.

Thanks to Wendell Xe for offering suggestions for improving the book and also suggestions for ebe.

Last I thank my wife, Phyllis, and my sons, David and Adam, for their encouragement and assistance. Phyllis and Adam are responsible for the cover design for both this and the Create Space book.

Contents

Chapter 1
Introduction

This book is an introduction to assembly language programming for the x86-64 architecture of CPUs like the Intel Core processors and the AMD Athlon and Opteron processors. While assembly language is no longer widely used in general purpose programming, it is still used to produce maximum efficiency in core functions in scientific computing and in other applications where maximum efficiency is needed. It is also used to perform some functions which cannot be handled in a high-level language.

The goal of this book is to teach general principles of assembly language programming. It targets people with some experience in programming in a high level language (ideally C or C++), but with no prior exposure to assembly language.

Assembly language is inherently non-portable and this text focuses on writing code for the Linux and OS X operating systems, due to the free availability of excellent OS X compilers, assemblers and debuggers. The variants of the BSD operating system use the same function call protocol which makes it likely that this book would be adequate to BSD systems. (Minor alterations would be needed in the ebe program for BSD). The instructions are the same on x86-64 systems regardless of the operating system, though Windows uses a different function call protocol which is the reason for having a separate book. Differences between assembly programming for Windows systems will be detailed as the work unfolds

The primary goal of this text is to learn how to write functions callable from C or C++ programs. This focus should give the reader an increased understanding of how a compiler implements a high level language. This understanding will be of lasting benefit in using high level languages.

A secondary goal of this text is to introduce the reader to using SSE and AVX instructions. The coming trend is for the size of SIMD (Single Instruction Multiple Data) registers to increase and it generally requires assembly language to take advantage of the SIMD capabilities.

1

1.1 Why study assembly language?

In a time when the latest fads in programming tend to be object-oriented high-level languages implemented using byte-code interpreters, the trend is clearly to learn to write portable programs with high reliability in record time. It seems that worrying about memory usage and CPU cycles is a relic from a by-gone era. So why would anyone want to learn assembly language programming?

Assembly language programming has some of the worst "features" known in computing. First, assembly language is the poster child for non-portable code. Certainly every CPU has its own assembly language and many of them have more than one. The most common example is the Intel CPU family along with the quite similar AMD CPU collection. The latest versions of these chips can operate in 16 bit, 32 bit and 64 bit modes. In each of these modes there are differences in the assembly language. In addition the operating system imposes additional differences. Further the function call interface employed in x86-64 Linux and OS X systems OS X differs from that used in Microsoft Windows systems. Portability is difficult if not impossible in assembly language.

An even worse issue with assembly language programming is reliability. In modern languages like Java the programmer is protected from many possible problems like pointer errors. Pointers exist in Java, but the programmer can be blissfully unaware of them. Contrast this to assembly language where every variable access is essentially a pointer access. Furthermore high level language syntax resembles mathematical syntax, while assembly language is a sequence of individual machine instructions which bears no syntactic resemblance to the problem being solved.

Assembly language is generally accepted to be much slower to write than higher level languages. While experience can increase one's speed, it is probably twice as slow even for experts. This makes it more expensive to write assembly code and adds to the cost of maintenance.

So what is good about assembly language?

The typical claim is that assembly language is more efficient than high level languages. A skilled assembly language coder can write code which uses less CPU time and less memory than that produced by a compiler. However modern C and C++ compilers do excellent optimization and beginning assembly programmers are no match for a good compiler. The compiler writers understand the CPU architecture quite well. On the other hand an assembly programmer with similar skills can achieve remarkable results. A good example is the Atlas (Automatically Tuned Linear algebra Software) library which can achieve over 95% of the possible CPU performance. The Atlas matrix multiplication function is probably at least 4 times as efficient as similar code written well in C. So, while it is true that assembly language can offer performance benefits, it is unlikely to outperform C/C++ for most general purpose tasks. Furthermore it takes intimate knowledge of the CPU to achieve these gains. In this book we will point out some general strategies for writing efficient assembly programs.

One advantage of assembly language is that it can do things not possible in high level languages. Examples of this include handling hardware interrupts and managing memory mapping features of a CPU. These features are essential in an operating system, though not required for application programming.

So far we have seen that assembly language is much more difficult to use than higher level languages and only offers benefits in special cases to well-trained programmers. What benefit is there for most people?

The primary reason to study assembly language is to learn how a CPU works. This helps when programming in high level languages. Understanding how the compiler implements the features of a high level language can aid in selecting features for efficiency. More importantly understanding the translation from high level language to machine language is fundamental in understanding why bugs behave the way they do. Without studying assembly language, a programming language is primarily a mathematical concept obeying mathematical laws. Underneath this mathematical exterior the computer executes machine instructions which have limits and can have unexpected behavior. Assembly language skills can help in understanding this unexpected behavior and improve one's debugging skills.

1.2 What is a computer?

A computer is a machine for processing bits. A bit is an individual unit of computer storage which can take on 2 values: 0 and 1. We use computers to process information, but all the information is represented as bits. Collections of bits can represent characters, numbers, or any other information. Humans interpret these bits as information, while computers simply manipulate the bits.

The memory of a computer (ignoring cache) consists mainly of a relatively large amount of "main memory" which holds programs and data while programs are executing. There is also a relatively small collection of memory within the CPU chip called the "register set" of the computer.

The registers primarily function as a place to store intermediate values during calculations based on values from main memory.

Bytes

Modern computers access memory in 8 bit chunks. Each 8 bit quantity is called a "byte". The main memory of a computer is effectively an array of bytes with each byte having a separate memory address. The first byte address is 0 and the last address depends on the hardware and software in use.

A byte can be interpreted as a binary number. The binary number 01010101 equals the decimal number 85 (64+16+4+1). If this number is interpreted as a machine instruction the computer will push the value of the rbp register onto the run-time stack. The number 85 can also be interpreted as the upper case letter "U". The number 85 could be part of a larger number in the computer. The letter "U" could be part of a string in memory. It's all a matter of interpretation.

Program execution

A program in execution occupies a range of addresses for the instructions of the program. The following 12 bytes constitute a very simple program which simply exits (with status 5):

Address	Value
400080	184
400081	60
400082	0
400083	0
400084	0
400085	191
400086	5
400087	0
400088	0
400089	0
40008a	15
40008b	5

The addresses are listed in hexadecimal though they could have started with the equivalent decimal number 4194432. The hexadecimal values are more informative in this case, since there are numerous 0 values in the hexadecimal representation. This gives a clue to the way the operating system maps a program into memory. Pages of memory begin

4

with addresses with the rightmost 3 hexadecimal "digits" (also called nibbles) equal to 0, so the beginning of the 12 byte program is fairly close to the start of a page of memory.

1.3 Machine language

Each type of computer has a collection of instructions it can execute. These instructions are stored in memory and fetched, interpreted and executed during the execution of a program. The sequence of bytes (like the previous 12 byte program) is called a "machine language" program. It would be quite painful to use machine language. You would have to enter the correct bytes for each instruction of your program and you would need to know the addresses of all data used in your program. A more realistic program would have branching instructions. The address to branch to depends on where the computer loads your program into memory when it is executed. Furthermore the address to branch to can change when you add, delete or change instructions in your program.

The very first computers were programmed in machine language, but people soon figured out ways to make the task easier. The first improvement is to use words like mov to indicate the selection of a particular instruction. In addition people started using symbolic names to represent addresses of instructions and data in a program. Using symbolic names prevents the need to calculate addresses and insulates the programmer from changes in the source code.

1.4 Assembly language

Very early in the history of computing (1950s), programmers developed symbolic assembly languages. This rapidly replaced the use of machine language, eliminating a lot of tedious work. Machine languages are considered "first-generation" programming languages, while assembly languages are considered "second-generation".

Many programs continued to be written in assembly language after the invention of FORTRAN and COBOL ("third-generation" languages) in the late 1950s. In particular operating systems were typically nearly 100% assembly until the creation of C as the primary language for the UNIX operating system.

The source code for the 12 byte program from earlier is listed below:

```
;   Program: exit
;
;   Executes the exit system call
;
;   No input
;
;   Output: only the exit status
;           $? in the shell
;
        segment .text
        global    start
start:
        mov   eax,60   ; 60 is the exit syscall number
                       ; 0x2000001 for OS X
        mov   edi,5    ; the status value to return
        syscall        ; execute a system call
        end
```

You will observe the use of ";" to signal the start of comments in this program. Some of the comments are stand-alone comments and others are end-of-line comments. It is fairly common to place end-of-line comments on each assembly instruction.

Lines of assembly code consist of labels and instructions. A label is a string of letters, digits and underscore with the first character either a letter or an underscore. A label usually starts in column 1, but this is not required. A label establishes a symbolic name for the current point in the assembler. A label on a line by itself must have a colon after it, while the colon is optional if there is more to the line. It is probably safer to always use a colon after a label definition to avoid confusion.

Instructions can be machine instructions, macros or instructions to the assembler. Instructions usually are placed further right than column 1. Many people establish a pattern of starting all instructions in the same column. I suggest using indentation to represent the high level structure of code, though spacing constraints limit the indentation in the examples.

The statement "segment .text" is an instruction to the assembler itself rather than a machine instruction. This statement indicates that the data or instructions following it are to be placed in the .text segment or section. This is where the instructions of a program are located.

The statement "global start" is another instruction to the assembler called an assembler directive or a pseudo opcode (pseudo-op). This pseudo-op informs the assembler that the label start is to be made known to the linker when the program is linked. The start function is the most basic "entry point" for a Linux or OS X program. When the system runs a program it transfers control to the start function. In truth Linux programs start with _start and OS X programs start with start, but internally ebe has yasm include an assembly file, ebe.inc, which converts start to _start on Linux but leaves it alone on OS X. A typical C program has a main function which is called indirectly via a start function in the C library. This pattern of using _ as a prefix is reversed for all functions other than

6

start. The OS X gcc prefixes each function name with an underscore, but gcc under Linux leaves the names alone. This difference is also handled by the ebe.inc which allows the same source to be compiled under OS X and Linux.

The line beginning with start is a label. Since no code has been generated up to this point, the label refers to location 0 of the program's text segment.

The remaining lines use symbolic opcodes representing the 3 executable instructions in the program. The first instruction moves the constant 60 into register eax while the second moves the constant 5 into register edi. The final instruction generates a system call. The last line contains the end pseudo-op indicating the end of the assembly code. The behavior is the same under OS X though the system calls are different numbers.

1.5 Assembling and linking

We use the yasm assembler to produce an object file from an assembly source code file:

```
yasm -f elf64 -P ebe.inc -g dwarf2 -l exit.lst exit.asm
```

The yasm assembler is modeled after the nasm assembler. Yasm produces object code which works properly with the gdb and ddd debuggers, while nasm did not produce acceptable code for debugging during testing. The -f elf64 option selects a 64 bit output format which is compatible with Linux and gcc. The -P ebe.inc option tells yasm to prefix exit.asm with ebe.inc which handles the naming differences between Linux and OS X. Ebe will prepare a copy of ebe.inc in the same directory as the assembly file for each assembly. The -g dwarf2 option selects the dwarf2 debugging format, which is essential for use with a debugger. For OS X the equivalent option would be -g macho64. The -l exit.lst option asks for a listing file which shows the generated code in hexadecimal.

The yasm command produces an object file named exit.o, which contains the generated instructions and data in a form ready to link with other code from other object files or libraries. In the case of an assembly program with the start function the linking needs to be done with ld:

```
ld -o exit exit.o
```

The -o exit option gives a name to the executable file produced by ld. Without that option, ld produces a file named a.out. If the assembly program defines main rather than start, then the linking needs to be done using gcc:

```
gcc -o exit exit.o
```

In this case gcc will incorporate its own version of start and start will call main from start (or indirectly from start).

You can execute the program using:

```
./exit
```

1.6 Using ebe to run the program

To use ebe to assemble, link and run the program is considerably simpler. First start ebe by entering "ebe". This will create a window with several subwindows including a source code subwindow as shown in Figure 1.1 below. The various subwindows can be rearranged by dragging them by their title bars. They can be dropped on top of each other to create tabbed subwindows, they can be resized, they can be hidden and they can be dragged out of the main window to become stand-alone windows.

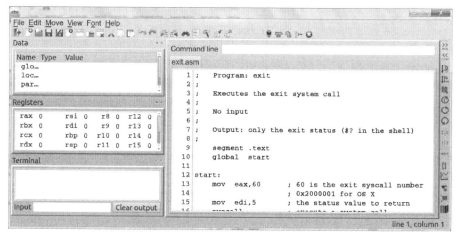

Figure 1.1 Exit program in ebe

For better visibility Figure 1.2 shows ebe without the register, data and terminal windows. Using the source code window you can enter the text shown and use the File menu to save the file as "exit.asm". To run the program simply click on the "Run button, the icon which looks like a green alien (or gray). There is an arrow pointing to the "Run" button. If there were any output from the program, it would be displayed in the terminal subwindow. After saving the file once, you can start ebe using "ebe exit.asm".

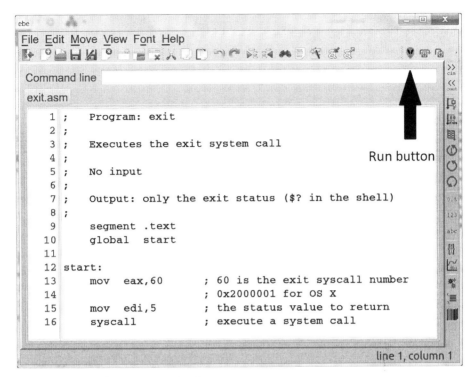

Figure 1.2. Exit program in ebe

More details on using ebe will be illustrated later and a chapter on ebe is included in the appendix. This is sufficient for the first chapter.

Exercises

1. Enter the assembly language program from this chapter and assemble and link it. Then execute the program from the command line and enter "echo $?". By convention in UNIX systems, a non-zero status from a program indicates an error. Change the program to yield a 0 status.

2. Modify the assembly program to define `main` rather than `start`. Assemble it and link it using ebe. What is the difference in size of the executables?

3. In C and many other languages, 0 means false and 1 (or non-zero) means true. In the shell 0 for the status of a process means success and non-zero means an error. Shell if statements essentially use 0 for true. Why did the writer of the first shell decide to use 0 for true?

Chapter 2
Numbers

All information in a computer is stored as collections of bits. These bits can be interpreted in a variety of ways as numbers. In this chapter we will discuss binary numbers, hexadecimal numbers, integers and floating point numbers.

2.1 Binary numbers

We are used to representing numbers in the decimal place-value system. In this representation, a number like 1234 means $10^3 + 2 * 10^2 + 3 * 10 + 4$. Similarly binary numbers are represented in a place-value system using 0 and 1 as the "digits" and powers of 2 rather than powers of 10.

Let's consider the binary number 10101111. This is an 8 bit number so the highest power of 2 is 2^7. So this number is

$$10101111 \quad = \quad 2^7 + 2^5 + 2^3 + 2^2 + 2 + 1$$
$$= \quad 128 + 32 + 8 + 4 + 2 + 1$$
$$= \quad 175$$

The bits of an 8 bit number are numbered from 0 to 7 with 0 being the least significant bit and 7 being the most significant bit

The number 175 has its bits defined below.

bit value	1	0	1	0	1	1	1	1
bit position	7	6	5	4	3	2	1	0

The conversion from binary to decimal is straightforward. It takes a little more ingenuity to convert from decimal to binary. Let's examine the number 741. The highest power of 2 less than (or equal to) 741 is $2^9 = 512$. So we have

$$741 \quad = \quad 512 + 229$$
$$= \quad 2^9 + 229$$

11

Now we need to work on 229. The highest power of 2 less than 229 is $2^7 = 128$. So we now have

$$741 \quad = \quad 512 + 128 + 101$$
$$= \quad 2^9 + 2^7 + 101$$

The process continues with 101. The highest power of 2 less than 101 is $2^6 = 64$. So we get

$$741 \quad = \quad 512 + 128 + 64 + 37$$
$$= \quad 2^9 + 2^7 + 2^6 + 37$$

Next we can find that 37 is greater than $2^5 = 32$, so

$$741 \quad = \quad 512 + 128 + 64 + 32 + 5$$
$$= \quad 2^9 + 2^7 + 2^6 + 2^5 + 5$$

Working on the 5 we see that

$$741 \quad = \quad 512 + 128 + 64 + 32 + 4 + 1$$
$$= \quad 2^9 + 2^7 + 2^6 + 2^5 + 2^2 + 1$$

Below is 741 expressed as a 16 bit integer.

bit value	1	0	1	1	1	0	0	1	0	1
bit position	9	8	7	6	5	4	3	2	1	0

A binary constant can be represented in the yasm assembler by appending "b" to the end of a string of 0's and 1's. So we could represent 741 as 1011100101b.

An alternative method for converting a decimal number to binary is by repeated division by 2. At each step, the remainder yields the next higher bit.

Let's convert 741 again.

division		quotient	remainder	binary number
741/2	=	370	1	1
370/2	=	185	0	01
185/2	=	92	1	101
92/2	=	46	0	0101
46/2	=	23	0	00101
23/2	=	11	1	100101
11/2	=	5	1	1100101
5/2	=	2	1	11100101
2/2	=	1	0	011100101
1/2	=	0	1	1011100101

The repeated division algorithm is easier since you don't have to identify (guess?) powers of 2 less than or equal to the number under question. It is also easy to program.

2.2 Hexadecimal numbers

Binary numbers are a fairly effective way of representing a string of bits, but they can get pretty tedious if the string is long. In a 64 bit computer it is fairly common to work with 64 bit integers. Entering a number as 64 bits followed by a "b" would be tough. Decimal numbers are a much more compact representation, but it is not immediately apparent what bits are 0's and 1's in a decimal number. Enter hexadecimal...

A hexadecimal number is a number in base 16. So we need "digits" from 0 to 15. The digits from 0-9 are just like in decimal. The digits from 10-15 are represented by the letters 'A' through 'F'. We can also use lower case letters. Fortunately both yasm and C/C++ represent hexadecimal numbers using the prefix 0x. You could probably use 0X but the lower case x tends to make the numbers more visually obvious.

Let's consider the value of 0xa1a. This number uses a which means 10, so we have

$$
\begin{aligned}
0xa1a &= 10 * 16^2 + 1 * 16 + 10 \\
&= 10 * 256 + 16 + 10 \\
&= 2586
\end{aligned}
$$

Converting a decimal number to hexadecimal follows a pattern like the one used before for binary numbers except that we have to find the highest power of 16 and divide by that number to get the correct "digit". Let's convert 40007 to hexadecimal. The first power of 16 to use is $16^3 = 4096$. $40007/4096 = 9$ with a remainder of 3143, so we have

$$40007 = 9 * 16^3 + 3143.$$

$3143/16^2 = 3143/256 = 12$ with a remainder of 71, so we get

$$40007 = 9 * 16^3 + 12 * 16^2 + 71.$$

$71/16 = 4$ with a remainder of 7, so the final result is

$$40007 = 9 * 16^3 + 12 * 16^2 + 4 * 16 + 7 = 0x9C47.$$

As with conversion to binary we can perform repeated division and build the number by keeping the remainders.

division		quotient	remainder	hexadecimal
40007/16	=	2500	7	0x7
2500/16	=	156	4	0x47
156/16	=	9	12	0x947
12/16	=	0	12	0xc947

Converting back and forth between decimal and binary or decimal and hexadecimal is a bit painful. Computers can do that quite handily, but why would you want to convert from decimal to hexadecimal? If you are entering a value in the assembler, simply enter it in the form which matches your interpretation. If you're looking at the number 1027 and need to use it in your program to perform arithmetic, enter it as a decimal number. If you want to represent some pattern of bits in the computer, then your choices are binary and hexadecimal. Binary is pretty obvious to use, but only for fairly short binary strings. Hexadecimal is more practical for longer binary strings.

The bottom line is conversion between binary and hexadecimal is all that one normally needs to do. This task is made easier since each hexadecimal "digit" represents exactly 4 bits (frequently referred to as a "nibble"). Consult the table below to convert between binary and hexadecimal.

Hex	Binary
0	0000
1	0001
2	0010
3	0011
4	0100
5	0101
6	0110
7	0111
8	1000
9	1001
10	1010
11	1011
12	1100
13	1101
14	1110
15	1111

Let's now consider converting 0x1a5b to binary. 1 = 0001, a = 1010, 5 = 0101 and b = 1011, so we get

0x1a5b = 0001 1010 0101 1011 = 0001101001011011b

Below 0x1a5b is shown with each bit position labeled:

Bit value	0	0	0	1	1	0	1	0	0	1	0	1	1	0	1	1
Bit position	15	14	13	12	11	10	9	8	7	6	5	4	3	2	1	0

The value of each bit position is 2 raised to that power. In the number above the leftmost 1 bit is in position 12, so it represents $2^{12} = 4096$. So the number is

$$2^{12} + 2^{11} + 2^9 + 2^6 + 2^4 + 2^3 + 2^1 + 2^0$$
$$4096 + 2048 + 512 + 64 + 16 + 8 + 2 + 1$$
$$6737$$

2.3 Integers

On the x86-64 architecture integers can be 1 byte, 2 bytes, 4 bytes, or 8 bytes in length. Furthermore for each length the numbers can be either signed or unsigned. Below is a table listing minimum and maximum values for each type of integer.

Variety	Bits	Bytes	Minimum	Maximum
unsigned	8	1	0	255
signed	8	1	-128	127
unsigned	16	2	0	65535
signed	16	2	-32768	32767
unsigned	32	4	0	4294967295
signed	32	4	-2147483648	2147483647
unsigned	64	8	0	18446744073709551615
signed	64	8	-9223372036854775808	9223372036854775807

Let's consider the maximum unsigned 16 bit integer. This maximum number is 16 bits all equal to 1 or 1111111111111111. The leftmost bit is bit 15 so its value is 2^{15}. Now suppose we add 1 to 1111111111111111. It's pretty clear that we will get a carry in every position and the result is 10000000000000000. This new number has 17 bits and the first bit position is 16, so we get

$$1111111111111111 + 1 = 2^{16}$$

Phrasing this more conveniently

$$1111111111111111 = 2^{16} - 1 = 65536 - 1 = 65535$$

Similarly the maximum unsigned 64 bit integer is $2^{64} - 1$ and the maximum signed 64 bit integer is $2^{63} - 1$. The range of 64 bit integers is large enough for most needs. Of course there are exceptions, like 20! = 51090942171709440000.

Unsigned integers are precisely the binary numbers discussed earlier. Signed integers are stored in a useful format called "two's complement". The first bit of a signed integer is the sign bit. If the sign bit is 0, the number is positive. If the sign bit is 1, the number is negative. The most obvious way to store negative numbers would be to use the remaining bits to store the absolute value of the number.

sign bit   value

31   0

Let's consider 8 bit signed integers and what we would get if we used the existing circuitry to add 2 such integers. Let's add -1 and 1. Well, if we store -1 with a sign bit and then the value we would get

$$
\begin{array}{rcl}
-1 & = & 10000001 \\
1 & = & 00000001 \\
\hline
-1+1 & = & 10000010
\end{array}
$$

Oops! We end up with -2 rather than 0.

Let's try storing 8 bit numbers as a sign bit and invert the bits for the absolute value part of the number:

$$
\begin{array}{rcl}
-1 & = & 11111110 \\
1 & = & 00000001 \\
\hline
-1+1 & = & 11111111
\end{array}
$$

Now this is interesting: the result is actually -0, rather than 0. This sounds somewhat hopeful. Let's try a different pair of numbers:

$$
\begin{array}{rcl}
-1 & = & 11111110 \\
4 & = & 00000100 \\
\hline
-1+4 & = & 00000010 = 2
\end{array}
$$

Too bad! It was close. What we need is to add one to the complemented absolute value for the number. This is referred to as "two's complement" arithmetic. It works out well using the same circuitry as for unsigned numbers and is mainly a matter of interpretation.

So let's convert -1 to its two's complement format.

```
       00000001 for the absolute value
       11111110 for the complement
       11111111 after adding 1
-1 =   11111111
```

Using two's complement numbers the largest negative 8 bit integer is 10000000. To convert this back, complement the number and add 1. This gives 01111111 + 1 = 10000000 = 128, so 10000000 = -128. You may have noticed in the table of minimums and maximums that the minimum values were all 1 larger in absolute value than the maximums. This is due to complementing and adding 1. The complement yields a string of 1's and adding 1 to that yields a single 1 with a bunch of 0's. The result is that the largest value for an n-bit signed integer is $2^{n-1} - 1$ and the smallest value is -2^{n-1}.

Now let's convert the number -750 to a signed binary number.

$$750 = 512 + 128 + 64 + 32 + 8 + 4 + 2 = 1011101110b$$

Now expressing this as a 16 bit binary number (with spaces to help keep track of the bits) we get 0000 0010 1110 1110. Next we invert the bits to get 1111 1101 0001 0001. Finally we add 1 to get -750 = 1111 1101 0001 0010 = 0xFD12.

16

Next let's convert the hexadecimal value 0xFA13 from a 16 bit signed integer to a decimal value. Start by converting to binary: 1111 1010 0001 0011. Then invert the bits: 0000 0101 1110 1100. Add 1 to get the 2's complement: 0000 0101 1110 1101. Convert this to decimal: 1024 + 256 + 128 + 64 + 32 + 8 + 4 + 1 = 1517, so 0xFA13 = -1517.

Let's add -750 and -1517 in binary:

```
    1111 1101 0001 0010
+   1111 1010 0001 0011
  ─────────────────────
  1 1111 0111 0010 0101
```

We can ignore the leading 1 bit (a result of a carry). The 16 bit sum is 1111 0111 0010 0101, which is negative. Inverting: 0000 1000 1101 1010. Next adding 1 to get the two's complement: 0000 1000 1101 1011. So the number is 2048 + 128 + 64 + 16 + 8 + 2 + 1 = 2267. So we have -750 + -1517 = -2267.

Binary addition

Performing binary addition is a lot like decimal addition. Let's add 2 binary numbers

```
    10001111
+   01011010
  ──────────
           1
```

The first pair of bits was easy. Adding the second pair of bits gives a value of 2, but 2 = 10b, so we place a 0 on the bottom and carry a 1

```
           1
    10001111
+   01011010
  ──────────
          01
```

We continue in the same way:

```
           1
    10001111
+   01011010
  ──────────
         001
```

```
           1
    10001111
+   01011010
  ──────────
        1001
```

```
            1
       10001111
     + 01011010
         01001

          . . .

       10001111
     + 01011010
       11101001
```

Binary multiplication

Binary multiplication is also much like decimal multiplication. You multiply one bit at a time of the second number by the top number and write these products down staggered to the left. Of course these "products" are trivial. You are multiplying by either 0 or 1. In the case of 0, you just skip it. For 1 bits, you simply copy the top number in the correct columns.

After copying the top number enough times, you add all the partial products. Here is an example:

```
           1010101
       x     10101
          1010101
        1010101
       11011111001
```

2.4 Floating point numbers

The x86-64 architecture supports 3 different varieties of floating point numbers: 32 bit, 64 bit and 80 bit numbers. These numbers are stored in IEEE 754 format

Below are the pertinent characteristics of these types:

Variety	Bits	Exponent	Exponent Bias	Fraction	Precision
float	32	8	127	23	7 digits
double	64	11	1023	52	16 digits
long double	80	15	16383	64	19 digits

The IEEE format treats these different length numbers in the same way, but with different lengths for the fields. In each format the highest order bit is the sign bit. A negative number has its sign bit set to 1 and

18

the remaining bits are just like the corresponding positive number. Each number has a binary exponent and a fraction. We will focus on the float type to reduce the number of bits involved.

31 30   23 22   0

The exponent for a float is an 8 bit field. To allow large numbers or small numbers to be stored, the exponent is interpreted as positive or negative. The actual exponent is the value of the 8 bit field minus 127. 127 is the "exponent bias" for 32 bit floating point numbers.

The fraction field of a float holds a small surprise. Since 0.0 is defined as all bits set to 0, there is no need to worry about representing 0.0 as an exponent field equal to 127 and fraction field set to all 0's. all other numbers have at least one 1 bit, so the IEEE 754 format uses an implicit 1 bit to save space. So if the fraction field is 00000000000000000000000, it is interpreted as 1.00000000000000000000000. This allows the fraction field to be effectively 24 bits. This is a clever trick made possible by making exponent fields of 0x00 and 0xFF special.

A number with exponent field equal to 0x00 is defined to be 0. Interestingly, it is possible to store a negative 0. An exponent of 0xFF is used to mean either negative or positive infinity. There are more details required for a complete description of IEEE 754, but this is sufficient for our needs.

To illustrate floating point data, consider the following assembly file, "fp.asm"

```
        segment .data
zero    dd      0.0
one     dd      1.0
neg1    dd      -1.0
a       dd      1.75
b       dd      122.5
d       dd      1.1
e       dd      10000000000.
```

This is not a program, it is simply a definition of 7 float values in the data segment. The dd command specifies a double word data item. Other options include db (data byte), dw (data word) and dq (data quad-word). A word is 2 bytes, a double word is 4 bytes and a quad-word is 8 bytes.

Now consider the listing file, "fp.lst", produced by executing the following command to assemble the file and produce a listing

```
yasm -f elf64 -g dwarf2 -l fp.lst fp.asm
```

Here are the contents of the listing:

```
1                              %line 1+1 fp.asm
2                              [section .data]
3 00000000 00000000           zero dd 0.0
```

19

```
4 00000004 0000803F        one  dd 1.0
5 00000008 000080BF        neg1 dd -1.0
6 0000000C 0000E03F        a    dd 1.75
7 00000010 0000F542        b    dd 122.5
8 00000014 CDCC8C3F        d    dd 1.1
9 00000018 F9021550        e    dd 10000000000.0
```

The listing has line numbers in the first column. Characters 3-10 (if not blank) are relative addresses in hexadecimal. Characters 12-19 (again, if not blank) are the assembled bytes of data. So we see that zero occupies bytes 0-3, one occupies bytes 4-7, etc. We can also examine the data produced from each variable definition.

The zero variable is stored as expected - all 0 bits. The other numbers might be a little surprising. Look at one - the bytes are backwards! Reverse them and you get 3F800000. The most significant byte is 3F. The sign bit is 0. The exponent field consists of the other 7 bits of the most significant byte and the first bit of the next byte. This means that the exponent field is 127 and the actual binary exponent is 0. The remaining bits are the binary fraction field all 0's. Thus the value is $1.0 * 2^0 = 1.0$.

There is only 1 negative value shown: -1.0. It differs in only the sign bit from 1.0.

You will notice that 1.75 and 122.5 have a significant number of 0's in the fraction field. This is because .75 and .5 are both expressible as sums of negative powers of 2.

$$0.75 = 0.5 + 0.25 = 2^{-1} + 2^{-2}$$

On the other hand 1.1 is a repeating sequence of bits when expressed in binary. This is somewhat similar to expressing 1/11 in decimal:

$$1/11 = 0.0909\overline{09}$$

Looking at 1.1 in the proper order 1.1 = 0x3F8CCCCD. The exponent is 0 and the fraction field in binary is 00011001100110011001101. It looks like the last bit has been rounded up and that the repeated pattern is 1100.

$$1.1_{10} = 1.0001100110011001\overline{1100}_2$$

Having seen that floating point numbers are backwards, then you might suspect that integers are backwards also. This is indeed true. Consider the following code which defines some 32 bit integers:

```
         segment data
zero     dd      0
one      dd      1
neg1     dd      -1
a        dd      175
b        dd      4097
d        dd      65536
e        dd      100000000
```

20

The associated listing file shows the bits generated for each number. The bytes are backwards. Notice that 4097 is represented as 0x01100000 in memory. The first byte is the least significant byte. We would prefer to consider this as 0x00001001, but the CPU stores least significant byte first.

```
1                                    %line 1+1 int.asm
2                                    [section .data]
3  00000000 00000000                 zero dd 0
4  00000004 01000000                 one dd 1
5  00000008 FFFFFFFF                 neg1 dd -1
6  0000000C AF000000                 a dd 175
7  00000010 01100000                 b dd 4097
8  00000014 00000100                 d dd 65536
9  00000018 00E1F505                 e dd 100000000
```

Converting decimal numbers to floats

Let's work on an example to see how to do the conversion. Let's convert -121.6875 to its binary representation.

First let's note that the sign bit is 1. Now we will work on 121.6875.

It's fairly easy to convert the integer portion of the number: 121 = 1111001b. Now we need to work on the fraction.

Let's suppose we have a binary fraction x = 0.abcdefgh, where the letters indicate either a 0 or a 1. Then 2*x= a.bcdefgh. This indicates that multiplying a fraction by 2 will expose a bit.

We have $2*0.6875 = 1.375$ so the first bit to the right of the binary point is 1. So far our number is 1111001.1b.

Next multiply the next fraction: $2*0.375 = 0.75$, so the next bit is 0. We have 1111001.10b.

Multiplying again: $2*.75 = 1.5$, so the next bit is 1. We now have 1111001.101b.

Multiplying again: $2*0.5 = 1$, so the last bit is 1 leaving the final 1111001.1011b.

So our number -121.6875 = -1111001.1011b. We need to get this into exponential notation with a power of 2.

$$121.6875 = -1111001.1011$$
$$= -1.1110011011 * 2^6$$

We now have all the pieces. The sign bit is 1, the fraction (without the implied 1) is 11100110110000000000000 and the exponent field is 127+6 = 133 = 10000101. So our number is

1 10000101 11100110110000000000000

21

Organized into nibbles, this is 1100 0010 1111 0011 0110 0000 0000 0000 or 0xc2f36000. Of course if you see this in a listing it will be reversed: 0060f3c2.

Converting floats to decimal

An example will illustrate how to convert a float to a decimal number. Let's work on the float value 0x43263000.

The sign bit is 0, so the number is positive. The exponent field is 010000110 which is 134, so the binary exponent is 7. The fraction field is 010 0110 0011 0000 0000 0000 0000, so the fraction with implied 1 is 1.01001100011.

$$1.01001100011_2 * 2^7 \quad = \quad 10100110.0011_2$$
$$= \quad 166 + 2^{-3} + 2^{-4}$$
$$= \quad 166 + 0.125 + 0.0625$$
$$= \quad 166.1875$$

Floating point addition

In order to add two floating point numbers, we must first convert the numbers to binary real numbers. Then we need to align the binary points and add the numbers. Finally we need to convert back to floating point.

Let's add the numbers 41.275 and 0.315. In hexadecimal these numbers are 0x4225199a and 0x3ea147ae. Now let's convert 0x4225199a to a binary number with a binary exponent. The exponent field is composed of the first two nibbles and a 0 bit from the next nibble. This is $10000100_2 = 132$, so the exponent is 132-127=5. The fractional part with the understood 1 bit is

$$1.01001010001100110011010_2$$

So we have

$$0x4225199a \quad = \quad 1.01001010001100110011010_2 * 2^5$$
$$= \quad 101001.010001100110011010_2$$

Similarly 0x3ea147ae has an exponent field of the first 2 nibbles and a 1 from the third nibble. So the exponent field is $01111101_2 = 125$ yielding an exponent of -2. The fractional part with the understood 1 bit is

$$1.01000010100011110101110_2$$

So we have

$$0\text{x}3\text{ea}147\text{ae} = 1.01000010100011110101110_2 * 2^{-2}$$

$$= 0.0101000010100011110101110_2$$

Now we can align the numbers and add

```
  101001.010001100110011010
+      0.0101000010100011110101110
  101001.1001011100001010010101110
```

Now we have too many bits to store in a 32 bit float. The rightmost 7 bits will be rounded (dropped in this case) to get

$$101001.100101110000101001_2 = 1.01001100101110000101001_2 * 2^5$$

So the exponent is 5 and the exponent field is again 132. Next we combine the sign bit, the exponent field and the fraction field (dropping the implied 1) bit and convert to hexadecimal

```
0   10000100    01001100101110000101001 sign exponent
fraction
0100 0010 0010 0110 0101 1100 0010 1001 organized as nibbles
  4    2    2    6    5    c    2    9   hexadecimal
```

So we determine that the sum is 0x42265c29 which is 41.59 (approximately).

You should be able to see that we lost some bits of precision on the smaller number. In an extreme case we could try to add 1.0 to a number like 10^{38} and have no effect.

Floating point multiplication

Floating point multiplication can be performed in binary much like decimal multiplication. Let's skip the floating point to/from binary conversion and just focus on the multiplication of 7.5 and 4.375. First observe that $7.5 = 111.1_2$ and $4.375 = 100.011_2$. Then we multiply binary numbers and place the binary point in the correct place in the product.

```
   111.1           1111
   100.011      * 100011
                   1111
                   1111
                1111
                1000001101
```

```
      100000.1101      placing binary point in product
```

So we have the product 32.8125 as expected.

2.5 Exploring with the bit bucket

One of the subwindows of the ebe program is called the "bit bucket". The purpose of the bit bucket is to explore fundamental bit operations. Figure 2.1 shows the bit bucket at the start of a decimal to binary conversion.

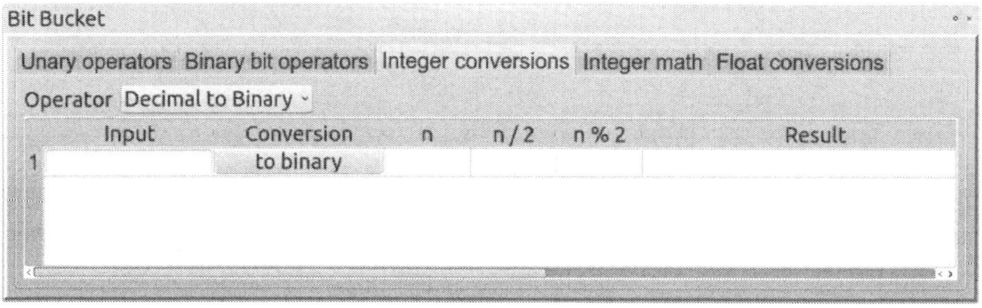

Figure 2.1 Bit bucket before decimal to binary conversion

There are 5 tabs which can be selected at the top of the bit bucket window, allowing you to explore unary operators, binary operators, integer conversions, integer math and float conversions. I have selected the integer conversions tab. Using the pull down list to the right of "Operator" I have chosen "Decimal to Binary". After selecting the conversion the table is cleared as you see it. There is a field for entering a number. In these fields in the bit bucket you can enter a hexadecimal number by using the prefix "0x" and you can also enter a binary number using the prefix "0b". After entering a number, you would step through the conversion by clicking on the "to binary" button. This button will move down the table through each step of the conversion.

Figure 2.2 shows the results from entering the number 131 and stepping through its conversion into binary.

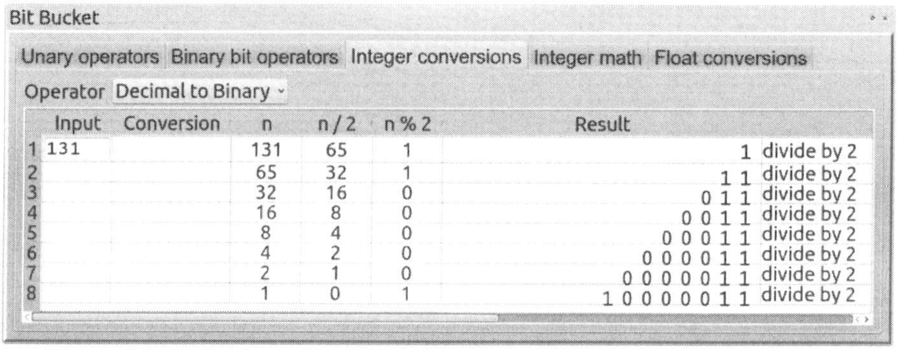

Figure 2.2 Bit bucket after converting 131 to binary

The bit bucket will help you explore the way that the computer represents and performs operations with numbers. There are conversions from decimal, binary and hexadecimal to the alternative forms. There are conversions for 32 bit floating point numbers in addition to integer conversions. All the arithmetic and bit operations on integers are also available for exploration.

Exercises

1. Convert the following integers to binary.
   - a. 37
   - b. 65
   - c. 350
   - d. 427

2. Convert the following 16 bit signed integers to decimal.
   - a. 0000001010101010b
   - b. 1111111111101101b
   - c. 0x0101
   - d. 0xffcc

3. Convert the following 16 bit unsigned integers to binary.
   - a. 0x015a
   - b. 0xfedc
   - c. 0x0101
   - d. 0xacdc

4. Convert the following numbers to 32 bit floating point.
   - a. 1.375
   - b. 0.041015625
   - c. -571.3125
   - d. 4091.125

5. Convert the following numbers from 32 bit floating point to decimal.
   - a. 0x3F82000
   - b. 0xBF82000
   - c. 0x4F84000
   - d. 0x3C86000

6. Perform the binary addition of the 2 unsigned integers below. Show each carry as a 1 above the proper position.

   $$0001001011001011$$
   $$+\ 1110110111101011$$

7. Perform the binary multiplication of the following unsigned binary numbers. Show each row where a 1 is multiplied times the top number. You may omit rows where a 0 is multiplied times the top

   $$1011001011$$
   $$\times\ \ \ \ 1101101$$

8. Write an assembly "program" (data only) defining data values using dw and dd for all the numbers in exercises 1-4.

Chapter 3
Computer memory

In this chapter we will discuss how a modern computer performs memory mapping to give each process a protected address space and how the Linux system manages the memory for a process. A practical benefit of this chapter is a discussion of how to examine memory using the gdb debugger and ebe.

3.1 Memory mapping

The memory of a computer can be considered an array of bytes. Each byte of memory has an address. The first byte is at address 0, the second byte at address 1, and so on until the last byte of the computer's memory.

In modern CPUs there are hardware mapping registers which are used to give each process a protected address space. This means that multiple people can each run a program which starts at address 0x4004c8 at the same time. These processes perceive the same "logical" addresses, while they are using memory at different "physical" addresses.

The hardware mapping registers on an x86-64 CPU can map pages of 2 different sizes - 4096 bytes and 2 megabytes. Linux, OS X and Windows all use 2 MB pages for the kernel and 4 KB pages for most other uses. All three operating systems allow user processes to use 2 MB pages. In some of the more recent CPUs there is also support for 1 GB pages.

The operation of the memory system is to translate the upper bits of the address from a process's logical address to a physical address. Let's consider only 4 KB pages. Then an address is translated based on the page number and the address within the page. Suppose a reference is made to logical address 0x4000002220. Since $4096 = 2^{12}$, the offset within the page is the right-most 12 bits (0x220). The page number is the rest of the bits (0x4000002). A hardware register (or multiple registers) translates this page number to a physical page address, let's say 0x780000000. Then the two addresses are combined to get the physical address 0x780000220.

Amazingly the CPU generally performs the translations without slowing down and this benefits the users in several ways. The most obvious benefit is memory protection. User processes are limited to reading and writing only their own pages. This means that the operating system is protected from malicious or poorly coded user programs. Also each user process is protected from other user processes. In addition to protection from writing, users can't read other users' data.

There are instructions used by the operating system to manage the hardware mapping registers. These instructions are not discussed in this book. Our focus is on programming user processes.

So why bother to discuss paging, if we are not discussing the instructions to manage paging? Primarily this improves one's understanding of the computer. When you write software which accesses data beyond the end of an array, you sometimes get a segmentation fault. However you only get a segmentation fault when your logical address reaches far enough past the end of the array to cause the CPU to reference a page table entry which is not mapped into your process.

3.2 Process memory model in Linux

In Linux memory for a process is divided into 4 logical regions: text, data, heap and stack. The stack is mapped to the highest address of a process and on x86-64 Linux this is 0x7fffffffffff or 131 TB. This address is selected based on the maximum number of bits allowed in logical addresses being 48 bits. This address is 47 bits of all 1 bits. The decision was made to not use bit 47, since canonical addresses have to extend bit 47 through bits 48-63.

In Figure 3.1 we see the arrangement of the various memory segments. At the lowest address we have the text segment (.text for yasm). This segment is shown starting at 0, though both start and main are at higher addresses. It appears that the lowest address in an x86-64 process is 0x400000. The text segment does not typically need to grow, so the data segment is placed immediately above the text segment. Above these two segments are the heap and stack segments.

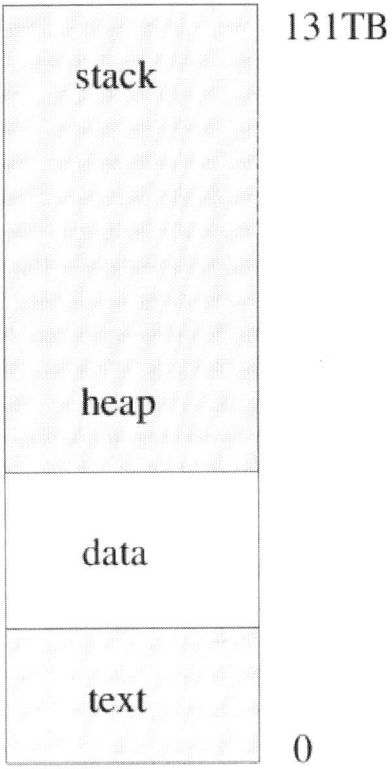

The data segment starts with the .data segment which contains initialized data. Above that is the .bss segment which stands for "block started by symbol". The .bss segment contains data which is statically allocated in a process, but is not stored in the executable file. Instead this data is allocated when the process is loaded into memory. The initial contents of the .bss segment are all 0 bits.

The heap is not really a heap in the sense discussed in a data structures course. Instead it is a dynamically resizable region of memory which is used to allocate memory to a process through

Figure 3.1 Process memory

functions like malloc in C and the new operator in C++. In x86-64 Linux this region can grow to very large sizes. The limit is imposed by the sum of physical memory and swap space.

The final segment of a process is the stack segment. This segment is restricted in size by the Linux kernel, typically to 16 megabytes. This is not a large amount of space, but as long as the programmer avoids putting large arrays on the stack it serves the purpose quite well of managing the run-time stack keeping track of function calls, parameters, local variables and return addresses. It is possible to change a user's hard limits by editing /etc/security/limits.conf. Within the hard limits set in limits.conf, a user can specify a new stack size limit using "ulimit s 20000" or whatever size is desired.

Given the top of the stack as 0x7fffffffffff and the stack size limited to 16 megabytes we see that the lowest valid stack address is 0x7fffff000000. The stack automatically grows when needed by the operating system responding to a page fault. The operating system recognizes the faulting address as being in the range from 0x7fffff000000 to 0x7fffffffffff, which is only used for the stack and allocates a new page of memory (4096 bytes) to the process.

This simple memory layout is not entirely accurate. There are shared object files which can be mapped into a process after the program is loaded which will result in regions in the heap range being used to store instructions and data. This region is also used for mapping shared memory regions into a process. Also to improve security some versions of Linux use somewhat random stack, data, and heap start addresses. On such systems the top of the stack would differ each time a program is executed though the address used will be close to 0x7fffffffffff. Likewise the address of main might vary each time a program is executed.

If you wish to examine the memory used by one of your processes, you can execute "cat /proc/999/maps" where 999 needs to be replaced by your process id. To see the memory used by your shell process enter

```
cat /proc/$$/maps
```

3.3 Process memory model in OS X

The layout of an OS X process is similar to a Linux process with one big difference. In OS X the lowest 4 GB of a processes virtual address space is mapped to what is called a "zero page". This covers the address range from 0x0 to 0xffffffff. The effect of this mapping is that any memory reference to a location in the zero page results in a segmentation fault. The purpose behind this decision is to limit the effect of truncated pointers, which might arise from moving the lower half of a 64 bit pointer into a register. It is better to have the program fail than to continue to execute after accessing the wrong section of memory.

This means that all addresses in the program are too big to fit in 32 bits. In particular this impacts assembly programming since function addresses are locations to branch to in memory won't fit in 32 bits. This matters since the address field for such instructions is 32 bits. To get around this problem coding in OS X is done using "rip relative" addressing. This means that addresses stored in instructions are relative to the current value of the instruction pointer register, rip.

It is generally possible for all the instructions and static data for a program to fit in less than 2GB of memory. This allows Linux to essentially use 32 bit addressing for code and static data and OS X to use 32 bit relative addressing for the same purposes.

3.4 Memory example

Here is a sample assembly program, "memory.asm" with several memory items defined:

```
        segment .data
a       dd      4
b       dd      4.4
c       times   10 dd 0
d       dw      1, 2
e       db      0xfb
f       db      "hello world", 0

        segment .bss
g       resd    1
h       resd    10
i       resb    100

        segment .text
        global  main    ; tell linker about main
main:
        push    rbp        ; set up a stack frame
        mov     rbp, rsp   ; rbp points to stack frame
        sub     rsp, 16    ; leave some room for locals
                           ; rsp on a 16 byte boundary
        xor     eax, eax   ; rax = 0 for return value
        leave              ; undo stack frame changes
        ret
```

After assembling the program we get the following listing file:

```
 1                              %line 1+1 memory.asm
 2                              [section .data]
 3 00000000 04000000         a dd 4
 4 00000004 CDCC8C40         b dd 4.4
 5 00000008 00000000<rept>   c times 10 dd 0
 6 00000030 01000200         d dw 1, 2
 7 00000034 FB               e db 0xfb
 8 00000035 68656C6C6F20776F72-  f db  "hello world", 0
 9 00000035 6C6400
10
11                              [section .bss]
12 00000000 <gap>            g resd 1
13 00000004 <gap>            h resd 10
14 0000002C <gap>            i resb 100
15
16                              [section .text]
17                              [global main]
18                              main:
19 00000000 55                 push rbp
20 00000001 4889E5             mov rbp, rsp
21 00000004 4883EC10           sub rsp, 16
22 00000008 31C0               xor eax, eax
23 0000000A C9                 leave
24 0000000B C3                 ret
```

You can see from the listing the relative addresses of the defined data elements. In the data section we have a double word (4 bytes) named a at location 0. Notice that the bytes of a are reversed compared to what you might prefer.

Following a is a double word defined as a floating point value named b at relative address 4. The bytes for b are also reversed. Consider it as 0x408ccccd. Then the sign bit is 0, the exponent field is the rightmost 7

31

bits of the "first" byte, 0x40, with the leftmost bit of the next byte, 0x8c. So the exponent field is 0x81 = 129, which is a binary exponent of 2. The fraction field (with the implied initial 1 bit) is 0x8ccccd. So b = 1.0001100110011001100101 * 2^3 = 4.4.

The next data item is the array c defined with the times pseudo-op which has 10 double word locations. The relative location for c is 8 and c consists of 40 bytes, so the next item after c is at relative address 48 or 0x30.

Following c is the length 2 array d with values 1 and 2. Array d is of type word so each value is 2 bytes. Again you can see that the bytes are reversed for each word of d.

The next data item is the byte variable e with initial value 0xfb. After e is the byte array f which is initialized with a string. Notice that I have added a terminal null byte explicitly to f. Strings in yasm do not end in null bytes.

After the data segment I have included a bss segment with 3 variables. These are listed with their relative addresses as part of the bss segment. After linking the bss data items will be loaded into memory beginning with g defined by the resd op-code which means "reserve" double word. With resd the number 1 means 1 double word. The next bss item is h which has 10 reserved double words. The last bss item is i which has 100 reserved bytes. All these data items are shown in the listing with addresses relative to the start of the bss segment. They will all have value 0 when the program starts.

3.5 Examining memory with ebe

In this section we will give a brief introduction to examining memory with ebe. We will show how to start the memory program with a breakpoint so that we can examine the variables defined in the program.

Setting a breakpoint

A breakpoint is a marker for an instruction which is used by a debugger to stop the execution of a program when that instruction is reached. The general pattern for debugging is to set a breakpoint and then run the program. The program will run until the breakpoint is reached and stop without executing that instruction.

Ebe uses the line number column to the left of the source code to indicate breakpoints. Left clicking on one of the line numbers will set (or clear if already set) a breakpoint on that line of code. Ebe indicates the existence of a breakpoint by coloring that line number with a red background.

The picture below shows the ebe source window with the memory program with a breakpoint set on line 17. The breakpoint is shown with a gray background in the printed book. Also this picture has been updated with an arrow pointing to the ebe "Run" button.

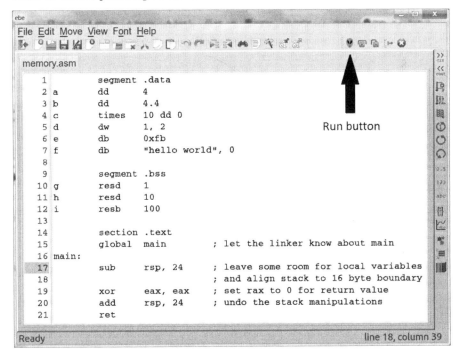

Running a program and viewing a variable

Having set the breakpoint on line 17, if we now click on the "Run" button (the alien icon pointed to by the arrow) the program will be assembled, linked and executed. It will stop execution with the "sub rsp, 24" instruction as the next instruction to execute. The source window will indicate the next line to execute by giving that line a blue-green background (gray in the illustration).

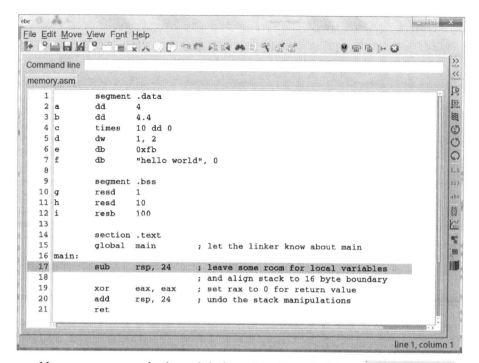

```
ebe
File  Edit  Move  View  Font  Help

Command line

memory.asm
    1              segment .data
    2  a           dd      4
    3  b           dd      4.4
    4  c           times   10 dd 0
    5  d           dw      1, 2
    6  e           db      0xfb
    7  f           db      "hello world", 0
    8
    9              segment .bss
   10  g           resd    1
   11  h           resd    10
   12  i           resb    100
   13
   14              section .text
   15              global  main        ; let the linker know about main
   16  main:
   17              sub     rsp, 24     ; leave some room for local variables
   18                                  ; and align stack to 16 byte boundary
   19              xor     eax, eax    ; set rax to 0 for return value
   20              add     rsp, 24     ; undo the stack manipulations
   21              ret

                                                              line 1, column 1
```

Now you can mark the a label on line 2 and right-click. Then ebe will popup a menu which will allow you to do one of a few options.

Undo
Redo
Cut
Copy
Paste
Define variable

Choose the "Define variable" option to popup a form allowing you to define how to display the data for the variable a:

There is no need to alter the name and address fields of the form. However the name field can be changed to any string you prefer and the address field could be altered. It could be handy to enter a hexadecimal address, but ebe has other ways to define variables based on hexadecimal addresses. Ebe doesn't really have access to data types and sizes like it would for a C program, but it attempts to guess the type and sizes. I have clicked on the triangle to the right of the "Format" label and

Define Variable

Name	a
Address	&a
type	int
Format	Decimal
array variable ☐	
First	0
Last	0
OK	Cancel

selected "Decimal" for the format. The format choices are Decimal, Hexadecimal, Floating point, String and String array. I also selected "4" for the "Size" field since a was defined using "dd". The size choices are 8, 4, 2 and 1. You can also click the "array variable" checkbox and select first and last indexes for the variable which operate like C arrays with 0 being the first index. After clicking on "OK" the popup form will go away and ebe will display variable a in the data window. It will refresh the value of a after each step of execution so you can monitor its value as the program executes.

Name	Type	Value
˅ globals		
ˎ stack	unsigned long *	0x00002aaaaaff5ec5 0x0000000000000000 …
locals		
parameters		
˅ user-defined		
a	int	4

You will note that the data window also shows the top part of the stack in hexadecimal. This is quite useful and normally hexadecimal is a good choice for the stack. You can alter the format, size and first and last indexes for any non-stack variable by right clicking on the name of a variable. This will popup a form which will allow you to edit or delete a variable. Editing will then popup the same form used when the variable was created.

I have continued on to display all the variables in "memory.asm". I chose last index 9 for c which is an array of 10 double words. I chose size 2 for d and 1 for e. For f I chose the "String" format which is a little special. This is a C string which is simply an array of characters ending with a 0 byte. The size for a string doesn't matter, but I left it as 8. You can see in the figure below that the variables in the bss segment are all 0's.

Name	Type	Value
˅ user-defined		
a	int	4
b	float	4.4
ˎ c[0:9]	int	0 0 0 0 0 0 0 0 0 0
ˎ d[0:1]	short	1 2
e	unsigned char	0xfb
ˎ f[0:1]	char	"hello world"
g	int	0
ˎ h[0:9]	int	0 0 0 0 0 0 0 0 0 0
ˎ i[0:9]	int	0 0 0 0 0 0 0 0 0 0

3.6 Examining memory with gdb

Using ebe is probably sufficient for most debugging, but it can occasionally be useful to understand gdb commands. In particular you can use the ebe console window to enter a gdb command from within ebe. The console window shows all the gdb commands used by ebe, so this could help discover how to use gdb directly.

In this section we will focus on using the gdb print (abbreviated as p) and examine (abbreviated as x) commands. Print is a simple command which can print some data values and is versatile enough to print various forms of C expressions. Examine is strictly for printing data from memory and is quite useful for printing arrays of various types.

Printing with gdb

The format for the p command is either "p expression" or "p/FMT expression" where FMT is a single letter defining the format of data to print. The format choices are

letter	format
d	decimal
x	hexadecimal
t	binary
u	unsigned
f	floating point
i	instruction
c	character
s	string
a	address

Let's see a few commands in action in gdb. Note the gdb prompt is "(gdb)" and commands to gdb have been displayed in bold font.

```
(gdb) p a
$32 = 4
(gdb) p/a &a
$33 = 0x601018 <a>
(gdb) p b
$34 = 1082969293
(gdb) p/f b
$35 = 4.4000001
(gdb) p/a &b
$36 = 0x60101c <b>
(gdb) p/x &b
$37 = 0x60101c
(gdb) p/a &c
$39 = 0x601020 <c>
(gdb) p/a &d
$40 = 0x601048 <d>
(gdb) p/a &e
$41 = 0x60104c <e>
(gdb) p/a &f
$42 = 0x60104d <f>
(gdb) p/a &g
$43 = 0x601070 <g>
(gdb) p/a &h
```

```
$45 = 0x601074 <h>
(gdb) p/a &i
$46 = 0x60109c <i>
```

We see that gdb handles a perfectly. It gets the type right and the
length since it defaults to decimal format and 4 byte integers. It needs the
/f option to print b correctly. Notice that a is located at address 0x601018
which is 24 bytes after the start of a page in memory. Despite the fact that
a is the first item of data it does not start at the beginning of a page of
memory. gdb will prohibit accessing memory before a, though there is no
hardware restriction to the previous 24 bytes. We see that the data
segment variables are placed in memory one after another until f which
starts at 0x60104d and extends to 0x601058. There is a gap until the bss
segment which starts with g at address 0x601070. The bss data items are
placed back to back in memory with no gaps.

Examining memory

Notice that there are no length specifiers with p. If you want to print
doubles in memory it could be done with some mental gymnastics with p.
The examine command handles this job readily.

The format for examine is x/NFS address where N is a number of
items to print (default 1), F is a single letter format as used in the print
command and S is the size of each memory location. Unfortunately gdb
picked some size letters which conflict with some of the size options in
yasm. Here are the size options:

letter	size	bytes
b	byte	1
h	halfword	2
w	word	4
g	giant	8

Here are some examples of examining memory:

```
(gdb) x/w &a
0x601018 <a>:        0x4
(gdb) x/fw &b
0x60101c <b>:        4.4000001
(gdb) x/fg &b
0x60101c <b>:        5.3505792317228316e-315
(gdb) x/10dw &c
0x601020 <c>:        0     0     0     0
0x601030 <c+16>:     0     0     0     0
0x601040 <c+32>:     0     0
(gdb) x/2xh &d
0x601048 <d>:        0x0001 0x0002
(gdb) x/12cb &f
0x60104d <f>:        104 'h' 101 'e' 108 'l' 108 'l' 111 'o'
                     32 ' ' 119 'w' 111 'o'
```

37

```
0x601055 <f+8>:      114 'r' 108 'l' 100 'd' 0 '000'
(gdb) x/s &f
0x60104d <f>:        "hello world"
```

Things match what you expect if you use the correct format and size. I
first printed b with the correct size and then with the giant size (8 bytes).
Gdb interpreted 8 bytes of memory starting at the address of b as a double
getting the wrong exponent and fraction. The use of the count field is quite
useful for dumping memory.

Exercises

1. Write a data-only program like the one in this chapter to define an array of 10 8 byte integers in the data section, an array of 5 2 byte integers in the bss section, and a string terminated by 0 in the data section. Use gdb's examine command to print the 8 byte integers in hexadecimal, the 2 byte integers as unsigned values, and the string as a string.

2. Assuming that the stack size limit is 16MB, about how large can you declare an array of doubles inside a C++ function. Do not use the keyword static.

3. Find out the stack size limit using the ulimit command in bash. If bash is not your shell, simply type in bash to start a sub-shell.

4. Print the value of rsp in gdb. How many bits are required to store this value?

Chapter 4
Memory mapping in 64 bit mode

In this chapter we discuss the details of how virtual addresses are translated to physical addresses in the x86-64 architecture. Some of the data for translation is stored in the CPU and some of it is stored in memory.

4.1 The memory mapping register

The CPU designers named this register "Control Register 3" or just CR3. A simplified view of CR3 is that it is a pointer to the top level of a hierarchical collection of tables in memory which define the translation from virtual addresses (the addresses your program sees) to physical addresses. The CPU retains quite a few page translations internally, but let's consider first how the CPU starts all this translation process.

Somewhere in the kernel of the operating system, an initial hierarchy of the translation tables is prepared and CR3 is filled with the address of the top level table in the hierarchy. This table is given the illustrious name "Page Map Level 4" or PML4. When the CPU is switched to using memory mapping on the next memory reference it uses CR3 to fetch entries from PML4.

4.2 Page Map Level 4

A virtual address can be broken into fields like this:

63 48	47 39	38 30	29 21	20 12	11 0
unused	PML4 index	page directory pointer index	page directory index	page table index	page offset

Here we see that a virtual or logical address is broken into 6 fields. The top-most 16 bits are ignored. They are supposed to be a sign extension of bit 47, but they are not part of the address translation. In fact bit 47 is left as 0 in user processes Linux and OS X so bits 47-63 are all 0's. In both operating systems bits 47-63 are all 1 for kernel addresses. We will focus on user process memory management. Following the unused bits are four 9 bit fields which undergo translation and finally a 12 bit page offset. The result of the translation process will be a physical address like 0x7f88008000 which is combined with the offset (let's say it was 0x1f0) to yield a physical address of 0x7f880081f0.

Pages of memory are $2^{12} = 4096$ bytes, so the 12 bit offset makes sense. What about those 9 bit fields? Well, addresses are 8 bytes so you can store 512 addresses in a page and $512 = 2^9$, so 9 bit fields allow storing each of the 4 types of mapping tables in a page of memory.

Bits 47-39 of a virtual address are used as an index into the PML4 table. The PML4 table is essentially an array of 512 pointers (256 would be enough for user processes since bit 47 is 0). These pointers point to pages of memory, so the rightmost 12 bits of each pointer can be used for other purposes like indicating whether an entry is valid or not. Generally not all entries in the PML4 will be valid.

Let's suppose that CR3 has the physical address 0x4ffff000. Then let's suppose that bits 47-39 of our sample address are 0x001, then we would have an array in memory at 0x4ffff000 and we would access the second entry (index 1) to get the address of a page directory pointer table: 0x3467000.

PML4 at 0x4ffff000

0	0x3466000
1	0x3467000
2	0x3468000
...	. . .
511	unused

41

4.3 Page Directory Pointer Table

The next level in the memory translation hierarchy is the collection of page directory pointer tables. Each of these tables is also an array of 512 pointers. These pointers are to page directory tables. Let's assume that our sample address has the value 0x002 for bits 38-30. Then the computer will fetch the third entry of the page directory pointer table to lead next to a page directory table at address 0x3588000.

Page Directory Pointer
Table at 0x3467000

0	0x3587000
1	unused
2	0x3588000
...	. . .
511	unused

4.4 Page Directory Table

The third level in the memory translation hierarchy is the collection of page directory tables. Each of these tables is an array of 512 pointers, which point to page tables. Let's assume that our sample address has the value 0x000 for bits 29-21. Then the computer will fetch the first entry of the page directory table to lead next to a page table at address 0x3678000

Page Directory
Table at 0x3588000

0	0x3678000
1	0x3679000
2	unused
...	. . .
511	unused

4.5 Page Table

The fourth and last level in the memory translation hierarchy is the collection of page tables. Again each of these tables is an array of 512 pointers to pages. Let's assume that our sample address has the value 0x1ff for bits 20-12. Then the computer will fetch the last entry of the page table to lead next to a page at address 0x5799000.

	Page Table at 0x3678000
0	0x5788000
1	0x5789000
2	0x578a000
...	. . .
511	0x5799000

After using 4 tables we reach the address of the page of memory which was originally referenced. Then we can or in the page offset (bits 11-0) of the original - say 0xfa8. This yields a final physical address of 0x5799fa8.

4.6 Large pages

The normal size page is 4096 bytes. The CPU designers have added support for large pages using three levels of the existing translation tables. By using 3 levels of tables, there are $9 + 12 = 21$ bits left for the within page offset field. This makes large pages $2^{21} = 2097152$ bytes.

Some of the latest CPUs support pages using 2 levels of page tables which results in having pages of size 2^{30} which is 1 GB. These huge pages will be popular for applications requiring large amounts of RAM like database management systems and virtual machine emulators.

4.7 CPU Support for Fast Lookups

This process would be entirely too slow if done every time by traversing through all these tables. Instead whenever a page translation has been performed, the CPU adds this translation into a cache called a "Translation Lookaside Buffer" or TLB. Then hopefully this page will be used many times without going back through the table lookup process.

A TLB operates much like a hash table. It is presented with a virtual page address and produces a physical page address or failure within roughly 1 / 2 of a clock cycle. In the case of a failure the memory search takes from 10 to 100 cycles. Typical miss rates are from 0.01% to 1%.

Clearly there is a limit to the number of entries in the TLB for a CPU. The Intel Core 2 series has a total of 16 entries in a level 1 TLB and 256 entries in a level 2 TLB. The Core i7 has 64 level 1 TLB entries and 512 level 2 entries. The AMD Athlon II CPU has 1024 TLB entries.

Given the relatively small number of TLB entries in a CPU it seems like it would be a good idea to migrate to allocating 2 MB pages for programs. Linux supports the use of 2 MB pages through its HUGETLB option. It requires adjusting the system parameters and allocating shared memory regions using the SHM_HUGETLB option. This could improve the performance of processes using large arrays. OS X and Windows also support 2 MB pages.

Exercises

1. Suppose you were given the opportunity to redesign the memory mapping hierarchy for a new CPU. We have seen that 4 KB pages seem a little small. Suppose you made the pages $2^{17} = 131072$ bytes. How many 64 bit pointers would fit in such a page?

2. How many bits would be required for the addressing of a page table?

3. How would you break up the bit fields of virtual addresses?

4. Having much larger pages seems desirable. Let's design a memory mapping system with pages of $2^{20} = 1048576$ bytes but use partial pages for memory mapping tables. Design a system with 3 levels of page mapping tables with at least 48 bits of usable virtual address space.

5. Suppose a virtual memory address is 0x123456789012. Divide this address into the 4 different page table parts and the within page offset.

6. Suppose a virtual memory address is 0x123456789012. Suppose this happens to be an address within a 2MB page. What is the within page offset for this address? Write an assembly language program to compute the cost of electricity for a home. The cost per kilowatt hour will be an integer number of pennies stored in a memory location. The kilowatt hours used will also be an integer stored in memory. The bill amount will be $5.00 plus the cost per kilowatt hour times the number of kilowatt hours over 1000. You can use a conditional move to set the number of hours over 1000 to 0 if the number of hours over 1000 is negative. Move the number of dollars into one memory location and the number of pennies into another.

Chapter 5
Registers

Computer memory is essentially an array of bytes which software uses for instructions and data. While the memory is relatively fast, there is a need for a small amount of faster data to permit the CPU to execute instructions faster. A typical computer executes at 3 GHz and many instructions can execute in 1 cycle. However for an instruction to execute the instructions and any data required must be fetched from memory. One fairly common form of memory has a latency of 6 nanoseconds, meaning the time lag between requesting the memory and getting the data. This 6 nanoseconds would equal 18 CPU cycles. If the instructions and data were all fetched from and stored in memory there would probably be about 18 nanoseconds required for common instructions. 18 nanoseconds is time enough for 54 instructions at 1 instruction per cycle. There is clearly a huge need to avoid using the relatively slow main memory.

One type of faster memory is cache memory, which is perhaps 10 times as fast as main memory. The use of cache memory can help address the problem, but it is not enough to reach the target of 1 instruction per CPU cycle. A second type of faster memory is the CPU's registers. Cache might be several megabytes, but the CPU has only a few registers. However the registers are accessible in roughly one half of a CPU cycle or less. The use of registers is essential to achieving high performance. The combination of cache and registers provides roughly half a modern CPU's performance. The rest is achieved with pipelining and multiple execution units. Pipelining means dividing instructions into multiple steps and executing several instructions simultaneously though each at different steps. Pipelining and multiple execution units are quite important but these features are not part of general assembly language programming, while registers are a central feature.

The x86-64 CPUs have 16 general purpose 64 bit registers and 16 modern floating point registers. These floating point registers are either 128 or 256 bits depending on the CPU model and can operate on multiple integer or floating point values. There is also a floating point register stack which we will not use in this book. The CPU has a 64 bit instruction pointer register (rip) which contains the address of the next instruction to execute. There is also a 64 bit flags register (rflags). There are additional registers which we probably won't use. Having 16 registers means that a register's "address" is only 4 bits. This makes instructions using registers much smaller than instructions using only memory addresses.

The 16 general purpose registers are 64 bit values stored within the CPU. Software can access the registers as 64 bit values, 32 bit values, 16 bit values and 8 bit values. Since the CPU evolved from the 8086 CPU, the registers have evolved from 16 bit registers to 32 bit registers and finally to 64 bit registers.

On the 8086 registers were more special purpose than general purpose:

ax - accumulator for numeric operations

bx - base register (array access)

cx - count register (string operations)

dx - data register item si - source index

di - destination index

bp - base pointer (for function frames)

sp - stack pointer

In addition the 2 halves of the first 4 registers can be accessed using al for the low byte of ax, ah for the high byte of ax, and bl, bh, cl, ch, dl and dh for the halves of bx, cx and dx.

When the 80386 CPU was designed the registers were expanded to 32 bits and renamed as eax, ebx, ecx, edx, esi, edi, ebp, and esp. Software could also use the original names to access to lower 16 bits of each of the registers. The 8 bit registers were also retained without allowing direct access to the upper halves of the registers.

For the x86-64 architecture the registers were expanded to 64 bits and 8 additional general purpose registers were added. The names used to access the 64 bit registers are rax, rbx, rcx, rdx, rsi, rdi, rbp, and rsp for the compatible collection and r8-r15 for the 8 new registers. As you might expect you can still use ax to access the lowest word of the rax register along with eax to access the lower half of the register. Likewise the other 32 bit and 16 bit register names still work in 64 bit more. You can also access registers r8-r15 as byte, word, or double word registers by appending b, w or d to the register name.

The rflags register is a 64 bit register, but currently only the lower 32 bits are used, so it is generally sufficient to refer to eflags. In addition the flags register is usually not referred to directly. Instead conditional instructions are used which internally access 1 or more bits of the flags register to determine what action to take.

Moving data seems to be a fundamental task in assembly language. In the case of moving values to/from the integer registers, the basic command is mov. It can move constants, addresses and memory contents into registers, move data from 1 register to another and move the contents of a register into memory.

5.1 Observing registers in ebe

One of the windows managed by ebe is the register window. After each step of program execution ebe obtains the current values of the general purpose registers and displays them in the register window. Similarly ebe displays the floating point registers in the floating point register window. Below is a sample of the register window.

```
Registers                                                                    ▪ ▪
  rax  0x400c00            rsi  0x7fffffffeb38   r8   0x400c9a   r12  0x4009d0
  rbx  0x0                 rdi  0x1              r9   0x0        r13  0x7fffffffeb30
  rcx  0xffffffffffffffff  rbp  0x0             r10  0x1        r14  0x0
  rdx  0x7fffffffeb48      rsp  0x7fffffffea58  r11  0x246      r15  0x0
  rip  0x400c00          eflags  PF ZF IF
```

You can select a different format for the registers by right clicking on the name of a register. This will popup a list of choices. You can choose either decimal or hexadecimal format for that register or for all the general purpose registers. You can see below the general purpose registers, the instruction pointer register (rip) and the flags register (eflags). For simplicity the set bits of eflags are displayed by their acronyms. Here the parity flag (PF), the zero flag (ZF) and the interrupt enable flag (IF) are all set.

5.2 Moving a constant into a register

The first type of move is to move a constant into a register. A constant is usually referred to as an immediate value It consists of some bytes stored as part of the instruction. Immediate operands can be 1, 2 or 4 bytes for most instructions. The mov instruction also allows 8 byte immediate values.

```
        mov     rax, 100
        mov     eax, 100
```

Surprisingly, these two instructions have the same effect - moving the value 100 into rax. Arithmetic operations and moves with 4 byte register references are zero-extended to 8 bytes. The program shown below in ebe illustrates the mov instruction moving constants into register rax.

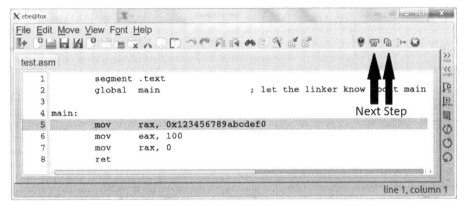

There has been a breakpoint set on line 5 and the program has been run by clicking the "Run" button. At this point the first mov has not been executed. You can advance the program by clicking on either "Next" or "Step" (highlighted with arrows in the picture). The difference is that "Step" will step into a function if a function call is made, while "Next" will execute the highlighted statement and advance to the next statement in the same function. The effect is the same in this code and here is the source window and the register window after executing the first mov:

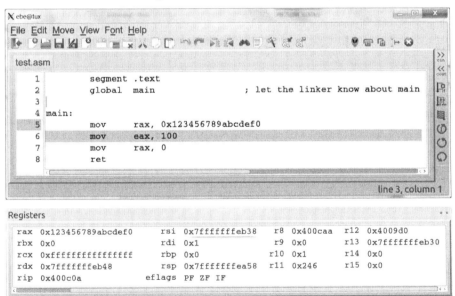

You can observe that the value 0x123456789abcdef0 has been placed into rax and that clearly the next mov has not been executed. There is little value in repeatedly displaying the source window but here is the register window after executing the mov at line 6:

Registers					
rax 100	rsi 0x7fffffffeb38	r8 0x400caa	r12 0x4009d0		
rbx 0x0	rdi 0x1	r9 0x0	r13 0x7fffffffeb30		
rcx 0xffffffffffffffff	rbp 0x0	r10 0x1	r14 0x0		
rdx 0x7fffffffeb48	rsp 0x7fffffffea58	r11 0x246	r15 0x0		
rip 0x400c0f	eflags PF ZF IF				

For convenience the display format for rax has been switched to decimal and you can observe that "mov eax, 100" results in moving 100 into the lower half of rax and 0 into the upper half.

The same operations can be done directly in gdb. Below is a gdb session illustrating moving constants. All the user inputs are in bold face to distinguish them from the text printed by gdb. Note also that gdb issues "(gdb)" for its prompt.

```
(gdb) list 5,7
5               mov        rax, 0x123456789abcdef0
6               mov        eax, 100
7               mov        rax, 0
(gdb) break 5
Breakpoint 1 at 0x400508: file test.asm,line 5
(gdb) run
Starting program: /home/seyfarth/asm/test
Breakpoint 1, main () at test.asm:5
5                  mov        rax, 0x123456789abcdef0
(gdb) nexti
6                  mov        eax, 100
(gdb) print/x $rax
$1 = 0x123456789abcdef0
(gdb) nexti
7                  mov        rax, 0
(gdb) print/x $rax
$2 = 0x64
```

You can see that the gdb prompt is (gdb). The first command entered is "list 5,7". This command lists line 5 through 7 of the source file. You can abbreviate "list" as "l".

The next command is "break 5", which sets a break point at line 5. "break" can be abbreviated as "b". A break point is a statement which will not be executed when the program in executed. Instead the control will be passed back to the debugger. After issuing the "run" command the debugger starts running the program, processing instructions until it reaches line 5. It breaks there without executing that instruction.

The next command is "nexti" which means execute the next instruction and return to the debugger. "nexti" can be abbreviated as "ni". After executing that mov, the value of register rax is printed in hexadecimal. "print" can be abbreviated as "p". The purpose of loading the large value is to place non-zero bits in the top half of rax.

You can follow the sequence of statements and observe that moving 100 into eax will clear out the top half of rax. It turns out that a 32 bit constant is stored in the instruction stream for the mov which moves 100. Also the instruction to move into eax is 1 byte long and the move into rax is 3 bytes long. The shorter instruction is preferable. You might be tempted to move 100 into al, but this instruction does not clear out the rest of the register.

5.3 Moving values from memory to registers

In order to move a value from memory into a register, you must use the address of the value. Consider the program shown below

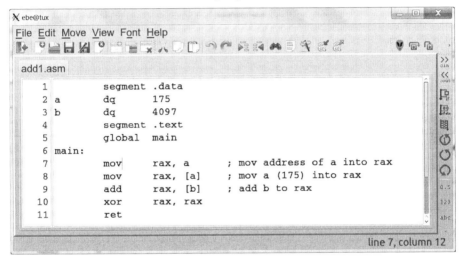

The label a is will be replaced by the address of a if included in an instruction under Linux. OS X uses relative addressing and a will be replaced by its address relative to register rip. The reason is that OS X addresses are too big to fit in 32 bits. In fact yasm will not allow moving an address under OS X. The alternative is to use the lea (load effective address) instruction which will be discussed later. Consider the following statement in the .text section.

```
mov     rax, a
```

The instruction has a 32 bit constant field which is replaced with the address of a when the program is executed on Linux. When tested, the rax register receives the value 0x602088 as shown below:

```
rax  0x602088              rsi  0x7fffffffeb38    r8  0x400caa
rbx  0x0                   rdi  0x1               r9  0x0
rcx  0xffffffffffffffff    rbp  0x0               r10 0x1
rdx  0x7fffffffeb48        rsp  0x7fffffffea58    r11 0x246
rip  0x400c07            eflags PF ZF IF
```

The proper syntax to get the value of a, 175, is from line 8 of the program and also below:

```
mov     rax, [a]
```

The meaning of an expression in square brackets is to use that expression as a memory address and to load or store from that address. In this case it loads the value from the address represented by a. This is basically a different instruction from the other mov. The other is "load constant" and the latest one is "load from memory".

After executing line 8 we see that rax has the value 175. In the register display below I have used a decimal format to make the effect more obvious.

```
rax  175                   rsi  0x7fffffffeb38    r8  0x400caa
rbx  0x0                   rdi  0x1               r9  0x0
rcx  0xffffffffffffffff    rbp  0x0               r10 0x1
rdx  0x7fffffffeb48        rsp  0x7fffffffea58    r11 0x246
rip  0x400c0f            eflags PF ZF IF
```

In line 9 of the program I have introduced the add instruction to make things a bit more interesting. The effect of line 9 is to add the contents of b, 4097, to rax. The result of the add instruction is shown below:

```
rax  4272                  rsi  0x7fffffffeb38    r8  0x400caa
rbx  0x0                   rdi  0x1               r9  0x0
rcx  0xffffffffffffffff    rbp  0x0               r10 0x1
rdx  0x7fffffffeb48        rsp  0x7fffffffea58    r11 0x246
rip  0x400c17            eflags AF IF
```

You will notice that my main routine calls no other function. Therefore there is no need to establish a stack frame and no need to force the stack pointer to be a multiple of 16.

Below is the result of running this program in gdb:

```
(gdb) b 7
Breakpoint 1 at 0x4004c0: file add1.asm, line 7.
(gdb) r
```

```
Starting program: /home/seyfarth/asm/add1
Breakpoint 1, main () at add1.asm:7
7            mov     rax, a      ; mov address of a to rax
(gdb) n
8            mov     rax, [a]    ; mov a (175) into rax
(gdb) p/x $rax
$1 = 0x601018
(gdb) n
9            add     rax, [b]    ; add b to rax
(gdb) p $rax
$2 = 175
(gdb) n
10           xor     rax, rax
(gdb) p $rax
$3 = 4272
(gdb) p a+b
$4 = 4272
```

It can be slightly confusing running gdb since it always prints the line which will be the one next to execute. For example right after it printed line 8, I printed rax which contained the value placed in it from the last executed instruction (from line 7). Ebe is more obvious if you remember that the highlighted line is the next one to execute.

We see that the correct sum is placed in rax by the add instruction. We also see that gdb knows about the labels in the code. It can print a and b, and can even compute their sum. Unfortunately the code produced by yasm does not inform gdb of the data types, so gdb assumes that the variables are double word integers. Still, this ability to print arithmetic expressions can be quite convenient.

There are other ways to move data from memory into a register, but this is sufficient for simpler programs. The other methods involve storing addresses in registers and using registers to hold indexes or offsets in arrays.

You can also move integer values less than 8 bytes in size into a register. If you specify an 8 bit register such as al or a 16 bit register such as ax, the remaining bits of the register are unaffected. However it you specify a 32 bit register such as eax, the remaining bits are set to 0. This may or may not be what you wish.

Alternatively you can use move and sign extend (movsx) or move and zero extend (movzx) to control the process. In these cases you would use the 64 bit register as a destination and add a length qualifier to the instruction. There is one surprise - a separate instruction to move and sign extend a double word: movsxd. Here are some examples:

```
movsx  rax, byte [data]  ; move byte, sign extend
movzx  rbx, word [sum]   ; move word, zero extend
movsxd rcx, dword [count]; move dword, sign extend
```

53

5.4 Moving values from a register to memory

Moving data from a register to memory is very similar to moving from memory to a register - you simply swap the operands so that the memory address is on the left (destination).

```
mov     [sum], rax
```

Below is a program which adds 2 numbers from memory and stores the sum into a memory location named sum:

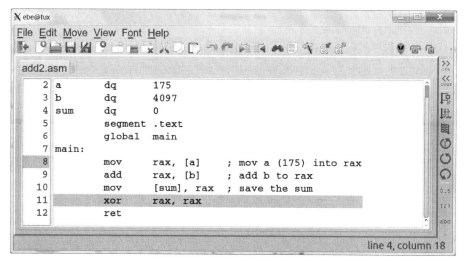

The source window shows line 11 highlighted which means that the mov instruction saving the sum has been executed. You can see that there is a breakpoint on line 8 and clearly the "Run" button was used to start the program and "Next" was clicked 3 times. Below is the data for the program:

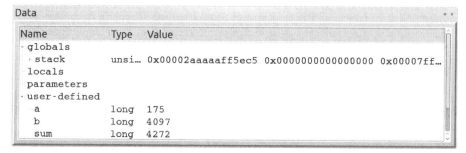

5.5 Moving data from one register to another

Moving data from one register to another is done as you might expect - simply place 2 register names as operands to the mov instruction.

```
mov     rbx, rax    ; move value in rax to rbx
```

Below is a program which moves the value of a into rax and then moves the value into rbx so that the value can be used to compute a+b and also a-b.

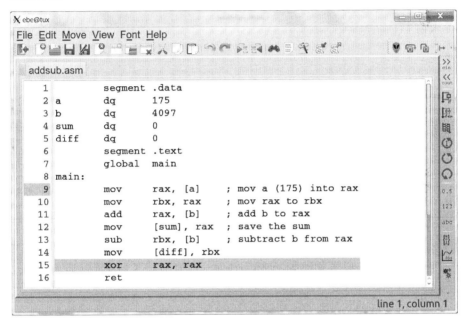

You can see that there is a breakpoint on line 8 and that line 15 is the next to be executed. This program introduces the sub instruction which subtracts one value from another. In this case it subtracts the value from memory location b from rbx with the difference being placed in rbx.

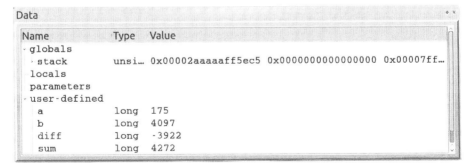

It might be a little interesting to note the value of eflags shown in the registers for the addition and subtraction program. You will see SF in

55

the flag values which stands for "sign flag" and indicates that the last
instruction which modified the flags, sub, resulted in a negative value.

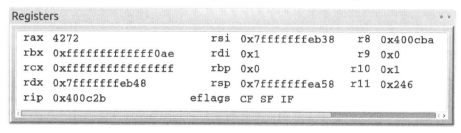

```
Registers                                                              ◇ ✕

  rax  4272                  rsi  0x7fffffffeb38    r8  0x400cba
  rbx  0xffffffffffffff0ae   rdi  0x1               r9  0x0
  rcx  0xffffffffffffffff    rbp  0x0               r10 0x1
  rdx  0x7fffffffeb48        rsp  0x7fffffffea58    r11 0x246
  rip  0x400c2b              eflags  CF SF IF

◇                                                                  ‹ ›
```

Exercises

1. Write an assembly program to define 4 integers in the .data section. Give two of these integers positive values and 2 negative values. Define one of your positive numbers using hexadecimal notation. Write instructions to load the 4 integers into 4 different registers and add them with the sum being left in a register. Use gdb or ebe to single-step through your program and inspect each register as it is modified.

2. Write an assembly program to define 4 integers - one each of length 1, 2, 4 and 8 bytes. Load the 4 integers into 4 registers using sign extension for the shorter values. Add the values and store the sum in a memory location.

3. Write an assembly program to define 3 integers of 2 bytes each. Name these a, b and c. Compute and save into 4 memory locations a+b, a-b, a+c and a-c.

Chapter 6
A little bit of math

So far the only mathematical operations we have discussed are integer addition and subtraction. With negation, addition, subtraction, multiplication and division it is possible to write some interesting programs. For now we will stick with integer arithmetic.

6.1 Negation

The neg instruction performs the two's complement of its operand, which can be either a general purpose register or a memory reference. You can precede a memory reference with a size specifier from the following table:

Specifier	Size in bytes
byte	1
word	2
dword	4
qword	8

The neg instruction sets the sign flag (SF) if the result is negative and the zero flag (ZF) if the result is 0, so it is possible to do conditional operations afterwards.

The following code snippet illustrates a few variations of neg:

```
neg    rax        ; negate the value in rax
neg    dword [x] ; negate 4 byte int at x
neg    byte [x]  ; negate byte at x
```

6.2 Addition

Integer addition is performed using the add instruction. This instruction has 2 operands: a destination and a source. As is typical for the x86-64 instructions, the destination operand is first and the source operand is second. It adds the contents of the source and the destination and stores the result in the destination.

The source operand can be an immediate value (constant) of 32 bits, a memory reference or a register. The destination can be either a memory reference or a register. Only one of the operands may be a memory reference. This restriction to at most one memory operand is another typical pattern for the x86-64 instruction set.

The add instruction sets or clears several flags in the rflags register based on the results of the operation. These flags can be used in conditional statements following the add. The overflow flag (OF) is set if the addition overflows. The sign flag (SF) is set to the sign bit of the result. The zero flag (ZF) is set if the result is 0. Some other flags are set related to performing binary-coded-decimal arithmetic.

There is no special add for signed numbers versus unsigned numbers since the operations are the same. The same is true for subtraction, though there are special signed and unsigned instructions for division and multiplication.

There is a special increment instruction (inc), which can be used to add 1 to either a register or a memory location.

Below is a sample program with some add instructions. You can see that there is a breakpoint on line 8. It is a little surprising that when you click on the "Run" button, the next line to execute is line 10. The reason for this is that lines 8 and 9 establish a "stack frame" which is used in gdb to keep track of which function is being executed. Gdb doesn't want to break in the middle of the instructions which establish the stack frame for a function, since commands related to local variables would be incorrect until the frame is complete. Line 10 is a fairly common operation to prepare some space for local variables on the stack. These 3 instructions are so common that there is a leave instruction which can undo the effect of them to prepare for returning from a function.

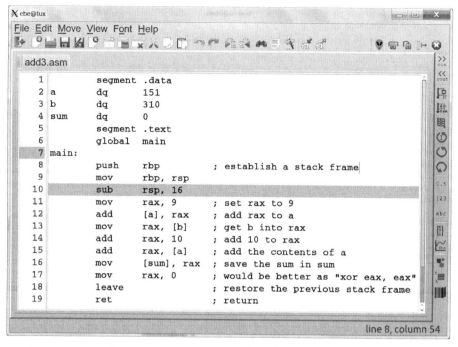

Next we see the registers and data for the program after executing lines 10 through 12.

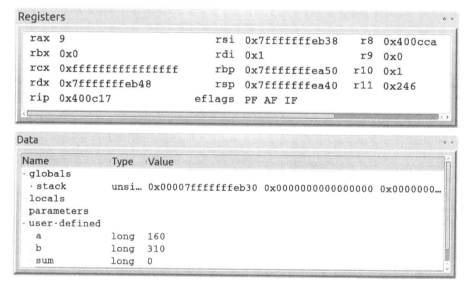

You can see that the sum computed on line 12 has been stored in memory in location a.

Below we see the registers and data after executing lines 13 through 16. This starts by moving b (310) into rax. Then it adds 10 to rax to get 320. After adding a (160) we get 480 which is stored in sum.

Registers

rax	480	rsi	0x7fffffffeb38	r8	0x400cca
rbx	0x0	rdi	0x1	r9	0x0
rcx	0xffffffffffffffff	rbp	0x7fffffffea50	r10	0x1
rdx	0x7fffffffeb48	rsp	0x7fffffffea40	r11	0x246
rip	0x400c33	eflags	IF		

Data

Name	Type	Value
globals		
stack	unsi…	0x00007fffffffeb30 0x0000000000000000 0x0000000…
locals		
parameters		
user-defined		
a	long	160
b	long	310
sum	long	480

Below is a gdb session illustrating this program.

```
(gdb) b 11
Breakpoint 1 at 0x4004c8: file add3.asm,line 11
(gdb) run
Starting program: /home/seyfarth/asm/add3

Breakpoint 1, main ( at add3.asm:11
11        mov    rax, 9    ; set rax to 9
(gdb) ni
12        add    [a], rax  ; add rax to a
(gdb) p $rax
$1 = 9
(gdb) ni
13        mov    rax, [b]  ; get b into rax
(gdb) p a
$2 = 160
(gdb) ni
14        add    rax, 10   ; add 10 to rax
(gdb) p $rax
$3 = 310
(gdb) ni
15        add    rax, [a]  ; add contents of a
(gdb) p $rax
$4 = 320
(gdb) ni
16        mov    [sum], rax ; save sum in sum
(gdb) p $rax
$5 = 480
(gdb) ni
17            mov    rax, 0
(gdb) p sum
$6 = 480
```

6.3 Subtraction

Integer subtraction is performed using the sub instruction. This instruction has 2 operands: a destination and a source. It subtracts the contents of the source from the destination and stores the result in the destination.

The operand choices follow the same pattern as add. The source operand can be an immediate value (constant) of 32 bits, a memory reference or a register. The destination can be either a memory reference or a register. Only one of the operands can be a memory reference.

The sub instruction sets or clears the overflow flag (OF), the sign flag (SF), and the zero flag (ZF) like add. Some other flags are set related to performing binary-coded-decimal arithmetic.

As with addition there is no special subtract for signed numbers versus unsigned numbers.

There is a decrement instruction (dec) which can be used to decrement either a register or a value in memory.

Below is a program with some sub instructions. You can see that the program has a breakpoint on line 8 and that gdb has stopped execution just after establishing the stack frame. Near the end this program uses "xor rax, rax" as an alternative method for setting rax (the return value for the function) to 0. This instruction is a 3 byte instruction. The same result can be obtained using "xor eax, eax" using 2 bytes which can reduce memory using. Both alternatives will execute in 1 cycle, but using fewer bytes may be faster due to using fewer bytes of instruction cache.

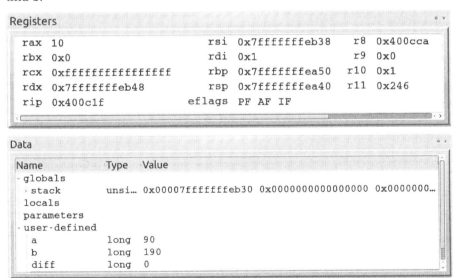

```
X ebe@tux                                                    _ □ X

File  Edit  Move  View  Font  Help
  ⬦  ⬦ ⬛⬛⬛⬛ ⬦ ⬦ ⬦ ⬦ x ⬦ ⬦⬦ ⬦ ⬦ ⬦⬦⬦⬦ ⬦ ⬦ ⬦⬦ ⬦         ⬦ ⬦ ⬦ ⬦ ⬦

 sub.asm                                                           >>
                                                                   cin
    1           segment  .data                                     <<
    2  a        dq       100                                       cout
    3  b        dq       200
    4  diff     dq       0
    5           segment  .text
    6           global   main
    7  main:
    8           push     rbp
    9           mov      rbp, rsp
   10           sub      rsp, 16
   11           mov      rax, 10
   12           sub      [a], rax   ; subtract 10 from a
   13           sub      [b], rax   ; subtract 10 from b
   14           mov      rax, [b]   ; move b into rax
   15           sub      rax, [a]   ; set rax to b-a
   16           mov      [diff], rax ; move the difference to diff
   17           xor      rax, rax   ; was "mov   rax, 0"
   18           leave
   19           ret

                                                  line 5, column 22
```

The next two figures show the registers and data for the program after
executing lines 11 through 13 which subtract 10 from memory locations a
and b.

```
Registers                                                       ◦ x

 rax  10                   rsi  0x7fffffffeb38   r8  0x400cca
 rbx  0x0                  rdi  0x1              r9  0x0
 rcx  0xffffffffffffffff   rbp  0x7fffffffea50   r10 0x1
 rdx  0x7fffffffeb48       rsp  0x7fffffffea40   r11 0x246
 rip  0x400c1f           eflags PF AF IF
```

```
Data                                                            ◦ x

Name            Type  Value
- globals
  ⟩ stack       unsi… 0x00007fffffffeb30 0x0000000000000000 0x0000000…
  locals
  parameters
- user-defined
    a           long  90
    b           long  190
    diff        long  0
```

Next we see the results of executing lines 14 through 16, which stores
b-a in diff.

Registers

rax	100	rsi	0x7fffffffeb38	r8	0x400cca
rbx	0x0	rdi	0x1	r9	0x0
rcx	0xffffffffffffffff	rbp	0x7fffffffea50	r10	0x1
rdx	0x7fffffffeb48	rsp	0x7fffffffea40	r11	0x246
rip	0x400c37	eflags	IF		

Data

Name	Type	Value
globals		
stack	unsi…	0x00007fffffffeb30 0x0000000000000000 0x0000000…
locals		
parameters		
user-defined		
a	long	90
b	long	190
diff	long	100

Here is a gdb session illustrating the same program:

```
(gdb) b 11
Breakpoint 1 at 0x4004c8: file sub.asm, line 11
(gdb) run
Starting program: /home/seyfarth/asm/sub

Breakpoint 1, main ( at sub.asm:11
11      mov   rax, 10
(gdb) ni
12         sub   [a], rax    ; subtract 10 from a
(gdb) p $rax
$1 = 10
(gdb) ni
13         sub   [b], rax    ; subtract 10 from b
(gdb) p a
$2 = 90
(gdb) ni
14      mov   rax, [b]    ; move b into rax
(gdb) p b
$3 = 190
(gdb) ni
15         sub   rax, [a]    ; set rax to b-a
(gdb) p $rax
$4 = 190
(gdb) ni
16      mov   [diff], rax ; move difference to diff
(gdb) p $rax
$5 = 100
(gdb) ni
17      mov      rax, 0
(gdb) p diff
$6 = 100
```

6.4 Multiplication

Multiplication of unsigned integers is performed using the mul instruction, while multiplication of signed integers is done using imul. The mul instruction is fairly simple, but we will skip it in favor of imul.

The imul instruction, unlike add and sub, has 3 different forms. One form has 1 operand (the source operand), a second has 2 operands (source and destination) and the third form has 3 operands (destination and 2 source operands).

One operand imul

The 1 operand version multiples the value in rax by the source operand and stores the result in rdx:rax. The source could be a register or a memory reference. The reason for using 2 registers is that multiplying two 64 bit integers yields a 128 bit result. Perhaps you are using large 64 bit integers and need all 128 bits of the product. Then you need this instruction. The low order bits of the answer are in rax and the high order bits are in rdx.

```
imul   qword [data]; multiply rax by data
mov    [high], rdx ; store top of product
mov    [low], rax  ; store bottom of product
```

Note that yasm requires the quad-word attribute for the source for the single operand version which uses memory. It issued a warning during testing, but did the correct operation.

Here is a sample program which uses the single operand version of imul to illustrate a product which requires both rax and rdx.

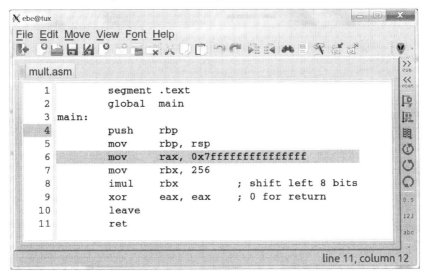

65

The mov in line 6 fills rax with a number composed of 63 bits equal to 1 and a 0 for the sign bit. This is the largest 64 bit signed integer, $2^{63} - 1$. The imul instruction in line 8 will multiply this large number by 256. Note that multiplying by a power of 2 is the same as shifting the bits to the left, in this case by 8 bits. This will cause the top 8 bits of rax to be placed in rdx and 8 zero bits will be introduced in the right of rax.

Here are the registers before imul:

```
Registers                                                          ◦ ×

rax  9223372036854775807      rsi  0x7fffffffeb38     r8  0x400caa
rbx  0x100                    rdi  0x1                r9  0x0
rcx  0xffffffffffffffff       rbp  0x7fffffffea50     r10 0x1
rdx  0x7fffffffeb48           rsp  0x7fffffffea50     r11 0x246
rip  0x400c15              eflags  PF ZF IF
```

and then after imul:

```
Registers                                                          ◦ ×

rax  -256                     rsi  0x7fffffffeb38     r8  0x400caa
rbx  0x100                    rdi  0x1                r9  0x0
rcx  0xffffffffffffffff       rbp  0x7fffffffea50     r10 0x1
rdx  0x7f                     rsp  0x7fffffffea50     r11 0x246
rip  0x400c18              eflags  CF PF SF IF OF
```

Two and three operand imul

Quite commonly 64 bit products are sufficient and either of the other forms will allow selecting any of the general purpose registers as the destination register.

The two-operand form allows specifying the source operand as a register, a memory reference or an immediate value. The source is multiplied times the destination register and the result is placed in the destination.

```
imul    rax, 100    ; multiply rax by 100
imul    r8, [x]     ; multiply r8 by x
imul    r9, r10     ; multiply r9 by r10
```

The three-operand form is the only form where the destination register is not one of the factors in the product. Instead the second operand, which is either a register or a memory reference, is multiplied by the third operand which must be an immediate value.

```
imul    rbx, [x], 100 ; store 100*x in rbx
imul    rdx, rbx, 50  ; store 50*rbx in rdx
```

66

The carry flag (CF) and the overflow flag (OF) are set when the product exceeds 64 bits (unless you explicitly request a smaller multiply). The zero flag and sign flags are undefined, so testing for a zero, positive or negative result requires an additional operation.

Testing for a Pythagorean triple

Below is shown a program which uses imul, add and sub to test whether 3 integers, a, b, and c, form a Pythagorean triple. If so, then $a^2 + b^2 = c^2$.

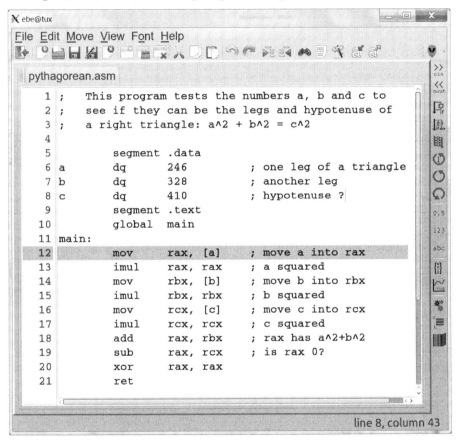

```
 1 ;    This program tests the numbers a, b and c to
 2 ;    see if they can be the legs and hypotenuse of
 3 ;    a right triangle: a^2 + b^2 = c^2
 4
 5        segment .data
 6 a      dq      246         ; one leg of a triangle
 7 b      dq      328         ; another leg
 8 c      dq      410         ; hypotenuse ?
 9        segment .text
10        global  main
11 main:
12        mov     rax, [a]    ; move a into rax
13        imul    rax, rax    ; a squared
14        mov     rbx, [b]    ; move b into rbx
15        imul    rbx, rbx    ; b squared
16        mov     rcx, [c]    ; move c into rcx
17        imul    rcx, rcx    ; c squared
18        add     rax, rbx    ; rax has a^2+b^2
19        sub     rax, rcx    ; is rax 0?
20        xor     rax, rax
21        ret
```

line 8, column 43

You can see that there is a breakpoint on line 12 and the next line to execute is 12. After clicking on "Next" line 12 will be executed and you can see that the value of a is placed in rax.

```
rax  246                    rsi  0x7fffffffeb28   r8  0x400cba   r12
rbx  0                      rdi  0x1              r9  0x0        r13
rcx  -1                     rbp  0x0             r10  0x1        r14
rdx  0x7fffffffeb38         rsp  0x7fffffffea48  r11  0x246      r15
rip  0x400c08             eflags  PF ZF IF
```

Next rax is multiplied by itself to get a^2 in rax.

```
rax  60516                  rsi  0x7fffffffeb28   r8  0x400cba   r12
rbx  0                      rdi  0x1              r9  0x0        r13
rcx  -1                     rbp  0x0             r10  0x1        r14
rdx  0x7fffffffeb38         rsp  0x7fffffffea48  r11  0x246      r15
rip  0x400c0c             eflags  IF
```

Line 14 moves the value of b into rbx.

```
rax  60516                  rsi  0x7fffffffeb28   r8  0x400cba   r12
rbx  328                    rdi  0x1              r9  0x0        r13
rcx  -1                     rbp  0x0             r10  0x1        r14
rdx  0x7fffffffeb38         rsp  0x7fffffffea48  r11  0x246      r15
rip  0x400c14             eflags  IF
```

Then rbx is multiplied by itself to get b^2 in rbx.

```
rax  60516                  rsi  0x7fffffffeb28   r8  0x400cba   r12
rbx  107584                 rdi  0x1              r9  0x0        r13
rcx  -1                     rbp  0x0             r10  0x1        r14
rdx  0x7fffffffeb38         rsp  0x7fffffffea48  r11  0x246      r15
rip  0x400c18             eflags  IF
```

Line 16 moves the value of c into rcx.

```
rax  60516                  rsi  0x7fffffffeb28   r8  0x400cba   r12
rbx  107584                 rdi  0x1              r9  0x0        r13
rcx  410                    rbp  0x0             r10  0x1        r14
rdx  0x7fffffffeb38         rsp  0x7fffffffea48  r11  0x246      r15
rip  0x400c20             eflags  IF
```

Then rcx is multiplied by itself to get c^2 in rcx.

```
rax  60516              rsi  0x7fffffffeb28    r8   0x400cba    r12
rbx  107584             rdi  0x1               r9   0x0         r13
rcx  168100             rbp  0x0               r10  0x1         r14
rdx  0x7fffffffeb38     rsp  0x7fffffffea48    r11  0x246       r15
rip  0x400c24           eflags  IF
```

Line 18 adds rbx to rax so rax holds $a^2 + b^2$.

```
rax  168100             rsi  0x7fffffffeb28    r8   0x400cba    r12
rbx  107584             rdi  0x1               r9   0x0         r13
rcx  168100             rbp  0x0               r10  0x1         r14
rdx  0x7fffffffeb38     rsp  0x7fffffffea48    r11  0x246       r15
rip  0x400c27           eflags  IF
```

Finally line 19 subtracts rcx from rax. After this rax holds $a^2 + b^2 - c^2$. If the 3 numbers form a Pythagorean triple then rax must be 0. You can see that rax is 0 and also that the zero flag (ZF) is set in eflags.

```
rax  0                  rsi  0x7fffffffeb28    r8   0x400cba    r12
rbx  107584             rdi  0x1               r9   0x0         r13
rcx  168100             rbp  0x0               r10  0x1         r14
rdx  0x7fffffffeb38     rsp  0x7fffffffea48    r11  0x246       r15
rip  0x400c2a           eflags  PF ZF IF
```

If we used a few more instructions we could test to see if ZF were set and print a success message.

6.5 Division

Division is different from the other mathematics operations in that it returns 2 results: a quotient and a remainder. The idiv instruction behaves a little like the inverse of the single operand imul instruction in that it uses rdx:rax for the 128 bit dividend.

The idiv instruction uses a single source operand which can be either a register or a memory reference. The unsigned division instruction div operates similarly on unsigned numbers. The dividend is the two registers rdx and rax with rdx holding the most significant bits. The quotient is stored in rax and the remainder is stored in rdx.

The `idiv` instruction does not set any status flags, so testing the results must be done separately.

Below is a program which illustrates the `idiv` instruction. You can see that a breakpoint was placed on line 8 and the program was started using the "Run" button.

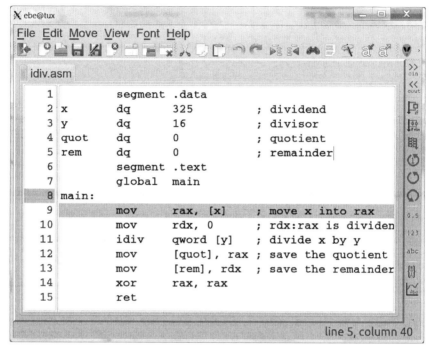

Next we see the registers after loading x into `rax` and zeroing out `rdx`.

The next display shows the changes to `rax` and `rdx` from executing the `idiv` instruction. The quotient is 20 and the remainder is 5 since $325 = 20 * 16 + 5$.

The final display shows the variables after executing lines 12 and 13.

Name	Type	Value
˅ user-defined		
quot	long	20
rem	long	5
x	long	325
y	long	16

6.6 Conditional move instructions

There are a collection of conditional move instructions which can be used profitably rather than using branching. Branching causes the CPU to perform branch prediction which will be correct sometimes and incorrect other times. Incorrect predictions slow down the CPU dramatically by interrupting the instruction pipeline, so it is worthwhile to learn to use conditional move instructions to avoid branching in simple cases.

The conditional move instructions have operands much like the mov instruction. There are a variety of them which all have the same 2 operands as mov, except that there is no provision for immediate operands.

instruction	effect
cmovz	move if result was zero
cmovnz	move if result was not zero
cmovl	move if result was negative
cmovle	move if result was negative or zero
cmovg	move if result was positive
cmovge	move if result was positive or zero

There are lot more symbolic patterns which have essentially the same meaning, but these are an adequate collection. These all operate by testing for combinations of the sign flag (SF) and the zero flag (ZF).

The following code snippet converts the value in rax to its absolute value:

```
mov     rbx, rax  ; save original value
neg     rax       ; negate rax
cmovl   rax, rbx  ; replace rax if negative
```

The code below loads a number from memory, subtracts 100 and replaces the difference with 0 if the difference is negative:

```
mov     rbx, 0    ; set rbx to 0
mov     rax, [x]  ; get x from memory
```

```
sub     rax, 100  ; subtract 100 from x
cmovl   rax, rbx  ; set rax to 0 if x-100 was negative
```

6.7 Why move to a register?

Both the add and sub instructions can operate on values stored in memory. Alternatively you could explicitly move the value into a register, perform the operation and then move the result back to the memory location. In this case it is 1 instruction versus 3. It seems obvious that 1 instruction is better.

Now if the value from memory is used in more than 1 operation, it might be faster to move it into a register first. This is a simple optimization which is fairly natural. It has the disadvantage of requiring the programmer to keep track of which variables are in which registers. If this code is not going to be executed billions of times, then the time required will probably not matter. In that case don't overwhelm yourself with optimization tricks. Also if the 2 uses are more than a few instructions apart, then keep it simple.

Exercises

1. Write an assembly language program to compute the distance squared between 2 points in the plane identified as 2 integer coordinates each, stored in memory.

   Remembe the Pythagoran Theorem!

2. If we could do floating point division, this exercise would have you compute the slope of the line segment connecting 2 points. Instead you are to store the difference in x coordinates in 1 memory location and the difference in y coordinates in another. The input points are integers stored in memory. Leave register rax with the value 1 if the line segment is vertical (infinite or undefined slope) and 0 if it is not. You should use a conditional move to set the value of rax.

3. Write an assembly language program to compute the average of 4 grades. Use memory locations for the 4 grades. Make the grades all different numbers from 0 to 100. Store the average of the 4 grades in memory and also store the remainder from the division in memory.

Chapter 7
Bit operations

A computer is a machine to process bits. So far we have discussed using bits to represent numbers. In this chapter we will learn about a handful of computer instructions which operate on bits without any implied meaning for the bits like signed or unsigned integers.

Individual bits have the values 0 and 1 and are frequently interpreted as false for 0 and true for 1. Individual bits could have other interpretations. A bit might mean male or female or any assignment of an entity to one of 2 mutually exclusive sets. A bit could represent an individual cell in Conway's game of Life.

Sometimes data occurs as numbers with limited range. Suppose you need to process billions of numbers in the range of 0 to 15. Then each number could be stored in 4 bits. Is it worth the trouble to store your numbers in 4 bits when 8 bit bytes are readily available in a language like C++? Perhaps not if you have access to a machine with sufficient memory. Still it might be nice to store the numbers on disk in half the space. So you might need to operate on bit fields.

7.1 Not operation

The not operation is a unary operation, meaning that it has only 1 operand. The everyday interpretation of not is the opposite of a logical statement. In assembly language we apply not to all the bits of a word. C has two versions of not, "!" and "~". "!" is used for the opposite of a true or false value, while "~" applies to all the bits of a word. It is common to distinguish the two nots by referring to "!" as the "logical" not and "~" as the "bit-wise" not. We will use "~" since the assembly language not instruction inverts each bit of a word. Here are some examples, illustrating the meaning of not (pretending the length of each value is as shown).

```
~0 == 1
~1 == 0
~10101010b == 01010101b
~0xff00 == 0x00ff
```

The not instruction has a single operand which serves as both the source and the destination. It can be applied to bytes, words, double words and quad-words in registers or in memory. Here is a code snippet illustrating its use.

```
mov    rax, 0
not    rax        ; rax == 0xffffffffffffffff
mov    rdx, 0     ; preparing for divide
mov    rbx, 15    ; will divide by 15 (0xf)
div    rbx        ; unsigned divide
                  ; rax == 0x1111111111111111
not    rax        ; rax == 0xeeeeeeeeeeeeeeee
```

Let's assume that you need to manage a set of 64 items. You can associate each possible member of the set with 1 bit of a quad-word. Using not will give you the complement of the set.

7.3 And operation

The and operation is also applied in programming in 2 contexts. First it is common to test for both of 2 conditions being true - && in C. Secondly you can do an and operation of each pair of bits in 2 variables - & in C. We will stick with the single & notation, since the assembly language and instruction matches the C bit-wise and operation.

Here is a truth table for the and operation:

&	0	1
0	0	0
1	0	1

Applied to some bit fields we get:

```
11001100b & 00001111b == 00001100b
11001100b & 11110000b == 11000000b
0xabcdefab & 0xff == 0xab
0x0123456789 & 0xff00ff00ff == 0x0100450089
```

You might notice that the examples illustrate using & as a bit field selector. Wherever the right operand has a 1 bit, the operation selected the bit from the left operand. You could say the same thing about the left operand, but in these examples the right operand has more obvious "masks" used to select bits.

Below is a code snippet illustrating the use of the and instruction:

```
mov     rax, 0x12345678
mov     rbx, rax
and     rbx, 0xf        ; rbx has nibble 0x8
mov     rdx, 0          ; prepare to divide
mov     rcx, 16         ; by 16
idiv    rcx             ; rax has 0x1234567
and     rax, 0xf        ; rax has nibble 0x7
```

It is a little sad to use a divide just to shift the number 4 bits to the right, but shift operations have not been discussed yet.

Using sets of 64 items you can use and to form the intersection of 2 sets. Also you can use and and not to form the difference of 2 sets, since $A - B = A \cap \bar{B}$.

7.3 Or operation

The or operation is the final bit operation with logical and bit-wise or meanings. First it is common to test for either (or both) of 2 conditions being true - || in C. Secondly you can do an or operation of each pair of bits in 2 variables - | in C. We will stick with the single | notation, since the assembly language or instruction matches the bit-wise or operation.

You need to be aware that the "or" of everyday speech is commonly used to mean 1 or the other but not both. When someone asks you if you want of cup of "decaf" or "regular", you probably should not answer "Yes". The "or" of programming means one or the other or both.

Here is a truth table for the or operation:

|	0	1
0	0	1
1	1	1

Applied to some bit fields we get:

```
11001100b | 00001111b == 11001111b
11001100b | 11110000b == 11111100b
0xabcdefab | 0xff == 0xabcdefff
0x0123456789 | 0xff00ff00ff == 0xff23ff67ff
```

You might notice that the examples illustrate using | as a bit setter. Wherever the right operand has a 1 bit, the operation sets the corresponding bit of the left operand. Again, since or is commutative, we could say the same thing about the left operand, but the right operands have more obvious masks.

Here is a code snippet using the or instruction to set some bits:

```
mov     rax, 0x1000
or      rax, 1          ; make the number odd
or      rax, 0xff00     ; set bits 15-8 to 1
```

76

Using sets of 64 items you can use or to form the union of 2 sets.

7.4 Exclusive or operation

The final bit-wise operation is exclusive-or. This operation matches the everyday concept of 1 or the other but not both. The C exclusive-or operator is "^".

Here is a truth table for the exclusive-or operation:

^	0	1
0	0	1
1	1	0

From examining the truth table you can see that exclusive-or could also be called "not equals". In my terminology exclusive-or is a "bit-flipper". Consider the right operand as a mask which selects which bits to flip in the left operand. Consider these examples:

```
00010001b ^ 00000001b == 00010000b
01010101b ^ 11111111b == 10101010b
01110111b ^ 00001111b == 01111000b
0xaaaaaaaa ^ 0xffffffff == 0x55555555
0x12345678 ^ 0x12345678 == 0x00000000
```

The x86-64 exclusive-or instruction is named xor. The most common use of xor is as an idiom for setting a register to 0. This is done because moving 0 into a register requires 7 bytes for a 64 bit register, while xor requires 3 bytes. You can get the same result using the 32 bit version of the intended register which requires only 2 bytes for the instruction.

Observe some uses of xor:

```
mov     rax, 0x1234567812345678
xor     eax, eax            ; set to 0
mov     rax, 0x1234
xor     rax, 0xf            ; change to 0x123b
```

You can use xor to form the symmetric difference of 2 sets. The symmetric difference of 2 sets is the the elements which are in one of the 2 sets but not both. If you don't like exclusive-or, another way to compute this would be using $A \Delta B = (A \cup B) \cap \overline{A \cap B}$. Surely you like exclusive-or.

7.5 Shift operations

In the code example for the and instruction I divided by 16 to achieve the effect of converting 0x12345678 into 0x1234567. This effect could have been obtained more simply by shifting the register's contents to the right

4 bits. Shifting is an excellent tool for extracting bit fields and for building values with bit fields.

In the x86-64 architecture there are 4 varieties of shift instructions: shift left (shl), shift arithmetic left (sal), shift right (shr), and shift arithmetic right (sar). The shl and sal shift left instructions are actually the same instruction. The sar instruction propagates the sign bit into the newly vacated positions on the left which preserves the sign of the number, while shr introduces 0 bits from the left.

15															0
1	0	1	0	1	1	0	0	1	0	1	1	0	1	1	0

0	1	0	1	0	1	1	0	0	1	0	1	1	0	1	1

0	0	1	0	1	0	1	1	0	0	1	0	1	1	0	1

0	0	0	1	0	1	0	1	1	0	0	1	0	1	1	0

There are 2 operands for a shift instruction. The first operand is the register or memory location to shift and the second is the number of bits to shift. The number to shift can be 8, 16, 32 or 64 bits in length. The number of bits can be an immediate value or the cl register. There are no other choices for the number of bits to shift.

C contains a shift left operator (<<) and a shift right operator (>>). The decision of logical or arithmetic shift right in C depends on the data type being shifted. Shifting a signed integer right uses an arithmetic shift.

Here are some examples of shifting:

```
10101010b >> 2 == 00101010b
10011001b << 4 == 100110010000b
0x12345678 >> 4 == 0x01234567
0x1234567 << 4 == 0x12345670
0xabcd >> 8 == 0x00ab
```

To extract a bit field from a word, you first shift the word right until the right most bit of the field is in the least significant bit position (bit 0) and then "and" the word with a value having a string of 1 bits in bit 0 through n-1 where n is the number of bits in the field to extract. For example to extract bits 4-7, shift right four bits, and then and with 0xf.

To place some bits into position, you first need to clear the bits and then "or" the new field into the value. The first step is to build the mask with the proper number of 1's for the field width starting at bit 0. Then shift the mask left to align the mask with the value to hold the new field. Negate the mask to form an inverted mask. And the value with the inverted mask to clear out the bits. Then shift the new value left the proper number of bits and or this with the value.

Now consider the following program which extracts a bit field and then replaces a bit field.

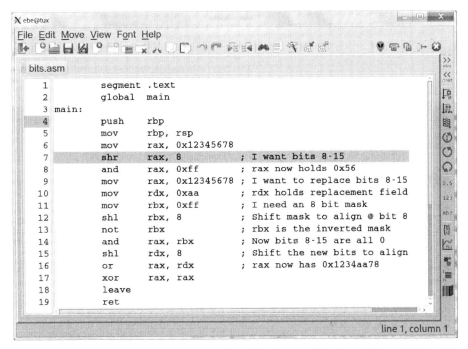

```
      segment .text
      global  main
main:
      push    rbp
      mov     rbp, rsp
      mov     rax, 0x12345678
      shr     rax, 8          ; I want bits 8-15
      and     rax, 0xff       ; rax now holds 0x56
      mov     rax, 0x12345678 ; I want to replace bits 8-15
      mov     rdx, 0xaa       ; rdx holds replacement field
      mov     rbx, 0xff       ; I need an 8 bit mask
      shl     rbx, 8          ; Shift mask to align @ bit 8
      not     rbx             ; rbx is the inverted mask
      and     rax, rbx        ; Now bits 8-15 are all 0
      shl     rdx, 8          ; Shift the new bits to align
      or      rax, rdx        ; rax now has 0x1234aa78
      xor     rax, rax
      leave
      ret
```

The program was started with a breakpoint on line 4 and I used "Next" until line 6 was executed which placed 0x12345678 into rax.

Registers

rax	0x12345678	rsi	0x7fffffffeb38	r8	0x400cca
rbx	0x0	rdi	0x1	r9	0x0
rcx	0xffffffffffffff…	rbp	0x7fffffffea50	r10	0x1
rdx	0x7fffffffeb48	rsp	0x7fffffffea50	r11	0x246
rip	0x400c0b	eflags	PF ZF IF		

The first goal is to extract bits 8-15. We start by shifting right 8 bits. This leave the target bits in bits 0-7 of rax.

Registers

rax	0x123456	rsi	0x7fffffffeb38	r8	0x400c
rbx	0x0	rdi	0x1	r9	0x0
rcx	0xffffffffffffffff	rbp	0x7fffffffea50	r10	0x1
rdx	0x7fffffffeb48	rsp	0x7fffffffea50	r11	0x246
rip	0x400c0f	eflags	PF IF		

Next we must get rid of bits 8-63. The easiest way to do this is to and with 0xff.

79

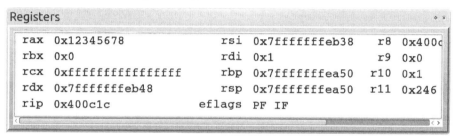

```
Registers                                                                    ◇ ✕
  rax  0x56                      rsi  0x7ffffffffeb38    r8   0x400c
  rbx  0x0                       rdi  0x1                r9   0x0
  rcx  0xffffffffffffffff        rbp  0x7ffffffffea50    r10  0x1
  rdx  0x7ffffffffeb48           rsp  0x7ffffffffea50    r11  0x246
  rip  0x400c15                  eflags  PF IF
```

The next goal is to replace bits 8-15 of 0x12345678 with 0xaa yielding 0x1234aa78. We start by moving 0x12345678 into rax.

```
Registers                                                                    ◇ ✕
  rax  0x12345678                rsi  0x7ffffffffeb38    r8   0x400c
  rbx  0x0                       rdi  0x1                r9   0x0
  rcx  0xffffffffffffffff        rbp  0x7ffffffffea50    r10  0x1
  rdx  0x7ffffffffeb48           rsp  0x7ffffffffea50    r11  0x246
  rip  0x400c1c                  eflags  PF IF
```

The second step is to get the value 0xaa into rdx.

```
Registers                                                                    ◇ ✕
  rax  0x12345678                rsi  0x7ffffffffeb38    r8   0x400c
  rbx  0x0                       rdi  0x1                r9   0x0
  rcx  0xffffffffffffffff        rbp  0x7ffffffffea50    r10  0x1
  rdx  0xaa                      rsp  0x7ffffffffea50    r11  0x246
  rip  0x400c23                  eflags  PF IF
```

We need a mask to clear out bits 8-15. We start building the mask by placing 0xff into rbx.

```
Registers                                                                    ◇ ✕
  rax  0x12345678                rsi  0x7ffffffffeb38    r8   0x400c
  rbx  0xff                      rdi  0x1                r9   0x0
  rcx  0xffffffffffffffff        rbp  0x7ffffffffea50    r10  0x1
  rdx  0xaa                      rsp  0x7ffffffffea50    r11  0x246
  rip  0x400c2a                  eflags  PF IF
```

Then we shift rbx left 8 positions to align the mask with bits 8-15. We could have started with 0xff00.

Registers   ◊ ×

rax 0x12345678   rsi 0x7fffffffeb38   r8 0x400c
rbx 0xff00   rdi 0x1   r9 0x0
rcx 0xffffffffffffffff   rbp 0x7fffffffea50   r10 0x1
rdx 0xaa   rsp 0x7fffffffea50   r11 0x246
rip 0x400c2e   eflags PF IF

The final preparation of the mask is to complement all the bits with
not. We could have started with 0xffffffffffff00ff, but that would
require some counting and is not as generally useful.

Registers   ◊ ×

rax 0x12345678   rsi 0x7fffffffeb38   r8 0x400c
rbx 0xffffffffffff00ff   rdi 0x1   r9 0x0
rcx 0xffffffffffffffff   rbp 0x7fffffffea50   r10 0x1
rdx 0xaa   rsp 0x7fffffffea50   r11 0x246
rip 0x400c31   eflags PF IF

Using and as a bit selector we select each bit of rax which has a
corresponding 1 bit in rbx.

Registers   ◊ ×

rax 0x12340078   rsi 0x7fffffffeb38   r8 0x400c
rbx 0xffffffffffff00ff   rdi 0x1   r9 0x0
rcx 0xffffffffffffffff   rbp 0x7fffffffea50   r10 0x1
rdx 0xaa   rsp 0x7fffffffea50   r11 0x246
rip 0x400c34   eflags PF IF

Now we can shift 0xaa left 8 positions to align with bits 8-15.

Registers   ◊ ×

rax 0x12340078   rsi 0x7fffffffeb38   r8 0x400c
rbx 0xffffffffffff00ff   rdi 0x1   r9 0x0
rcx 0xffffffffffffffff   rbp 0x7fffffffea50   r10 0x1
rdx 0xaa00   rsp 0x7fffffffea50   r11 0x246
rip 0x400c38   eflags PF IF

Having cleared out bits 8-15 of rax, we now complete the task by or'ing
rax and rdx.

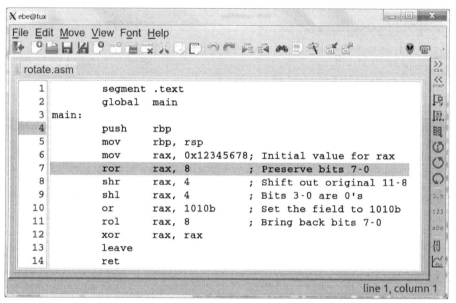

```
Registers                                                    ◊ ×

rax  0x1234aa78            rsi  0x7fffffffeb38    r8   0x400c
rbx  0xffffffffffff00ff    rdi  0x1               r9   0x0
rcx  0xffffffffffffffff    rbp  0x7fffffffea50    r10  0x1
rdx  0xaa00                rsp  0x7fffffffea50    r11  0x246
rip  0x400c3b              eflags PF IF
```

The x86-64 instruction set also includes rotate left (rol) and rotate right (ror) instructions. These could be used to shift particular parts of a bit string into proper position for testing while preserving the bits. After rotating the proper number of bits in the opposite direction, the original bit string will be left in the register or memory location.

The rotate instructions offer a nice way to clear out some bits. The code below clears out bits 11-8 of rax and replaces these bits with 1010b.

```
X ebe@tux                                          _  □  ×

File  Edit  Move  View  Font  Help

[toolbar icons]

rotate.asm

 1          segment  .text
 2          global   main
 3  main:
 4          push     rbp
 5          mov      rbp, rsp
 6          mov      rax, 0x12345678; Initial value for rax
 7          ror      rax, 8        ; Preserve bits 7-0
 8          shr      rax, 4        ; Shift out original 11-8
 9          shl      rax, 4        ; Bits 3-0 are 0's
10          or       rax, 1010b    ; Set the field to 1010b
11          rol      rax, 8        ; Bring back bits 7-0
12          xor      rax, rax
13          leave
14          ret

                                              line 1, column 1
```

Observe that a breakpoint has been placed on line 4 and the program run and stepped to line 7. In the register display below we see that 0x12345678 has been placed in rax.

```
Registers                                                    ◊ ×

rax  0x12345678            rsi  0x7fffffffeb38    r8   0x400c
rbx  0x0                   rdi  0x1               r9   0x0
rcx  0xffffffffffffffff    rbp  0x7fffffffea50    r10  0x1
rdx  0x7fffffffeb48        rsp  0x7fffffffea50    r11  0x246
rip  0x400c0b              eflags PF ZF IF
```

Executing the rotate instruction on line 7 moves the 0x78 byte in rax to the upper part of the register.

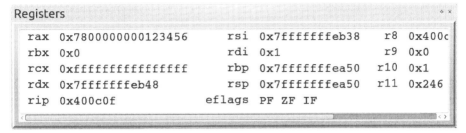

Next the shift instruction on line 8 wipes out bits 3-0 (original 11-8).

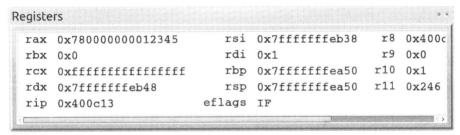

The shift instruction on line 9 introduces four 0 bits into rax.

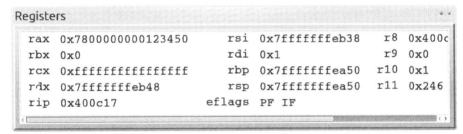

Now the or instruction at line 10 places 1010b into bits 3-0.

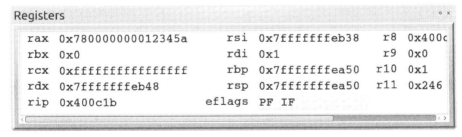

Finally the rotate left instruction at line 11 realigns all the bits as they were originally.

```
rax  0x12345a78            rsi  0x7ffffffeb38      r8   0x400c
rbx  0x0                   rdi  0x1                r9   0x0
rcx  0xffffffffffffffff    rbp  0x7ffffffea50      r10  0x1
rdx  0x7ffffffeb48         rsp  0x7ffffffea50      r11  0x246
rip  0x400c1f              eflags  PF IF OF
```

Interestingly C provides shift left (<<) and shift right (>>) operations, but does not provide a rotate operation. So a program which does a large amount of bit field manipulations might be better done in assembly. On the other hand a C struct can have bit fields in it and thus the compiler can possibly use rotate instructions with explicit bit fields.

7.6 Bit testing and setting

It takes several instructions to extract or insert a bit field. Sometimes you need to extract or insert a single bit. This can be done using masking and shifting as just illustrated. However it can be simpler and quicker to use the bit test instruction (bt) and either the bit test and set instruction (bts) or the bit test and reset instruction (btr).

The bt instruction has 2 operands. The first operand is a 16, 32 or 64 bit word in memory or a register which contains the bit to test. The second operand is the bit number from 0 to the number of bits minus 1 for the word size which is either an immediate value or a value in a register. The bt instructions set the carry flag (CF) to the value of the bit being tested.

The bts and btr instructions operate somewhat similarly. Both instructions test the current bit in the same fashion as bt. They differ in that bts sets the bit to 1 and btr resets (or clears) the bit to 0.

One particular possibility for using these instructions is to implement a set of fairly large size where the members of the set are integers from 0 to $n - 1$ where n is the universe size. A membership test translates into determining a word and bit number in memory and testing the correct bit in the word. Following the bt instruction the setc instruction can be used to store the value of the carry flag into an 8 bit register. There are setCC instructions for each of the condition flags in the eflags register. Insertion into the set translates into determining the word and bit number and using bts to set the correct bit. Removal of an element of the set translates into using btr to clear the correct bit in memory.

In the code below we assume that the memory for the set is at a memory location named set and that the bit number to work on is in register rax. The code preserves rax and performs testing, insertion and removal.

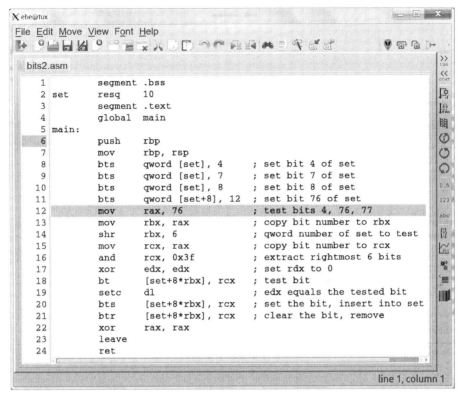

```
                segment  .bss
  2 set         resq     10
  3             segment  .text
  4             global   main
  5 main:
  6             push     rbp
  7             mov      rbp, rsp
  8             bts      qword [set], 4        ; set bit 4 of set
  9             bts      qword [set], 7        ; set bit 7 of set
 10             bts      qword [set], 8        ; set bit 8 of set
 11             bts      qword [set+8], 12     ; set bit 76 of set
 12             mov      rax, 76               ; test bits 4, 76, 77
 13             mov      rbx, rax              ; copy bit number to rbx
 14             shr      rbx, 6                ; qword number of set to test
 15             mov      rcx, rax              ; copy bit number to rcx
 16             and      rcx, 0x3f             ; extract rightmost 6 bits
 17             xor      edx, edx              ; set rdx to 0
 18             bt       [set+8*rbx], rcx      ; test bit
 19             setc     dl                    ; edx equals the tested bit
 20             bts      [set+8*rbx], rcx      ; set the bit, insert into set
 21             btr      [set+8*rbx], rcx      ; clear the bit, remove
 22             xor      rax, rax
 23             leave
 24             ret
```

Lines 8 through 11 set bits 4, 7, 8 and 76 in the array set. To set bit 76, we use [set+8] in the instruction to reference the second quad-word of the array. You will also notice the use of set+8*rbx in lines 18, 20 and 21. Previously we have used a variable name in brackets. Now we are using a variable name plus a constant or plus a register times 8. The use of a register times 8 allows indexing an array of 8 byte quantities. The instruction format includes options for multiplying an index register by 2, 4 or 8 to be added to the address specified by set. Use 2 for a word array, 4 for a double word array and 8 for a quad-word array. Register rbx holds the quad-word index into the set array.

Operating on the quad-word of the set in memory as opposed to moving to a register is likely to be the fastest choice, since in real code we will not need to test, insert and then remove in 1 function call. We would do only one of these operations.

Here we trace through the execution of this program. We start by observing the set array in hexadecimal at the breakpoint on line 12. We set bits 4, 7, 8 and 76. Setting bit 4 yields 0x10, setting bit 7 yields 0x90 and setting bit 8 yields 0x190. Bit 76 is bit 12 of the second quad-word in the array and yields 0x1000.

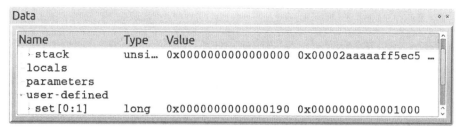

Data

Name	Type	Value	
› stack	unsi...	0x0000000000000000 0x00002aaaaaff5ec5 ...	
locals			
parameters			
˅ user-defined			
› set[0:1]	long	0x0000000000000190 0x0000000000001000	

Next lines 12 and 13 move 76 into `rax` and `rbx`.

Registers

rax	76	rsi	0x7fffffffeb38	r8	0x400cfa
rbx	76	rdi	0x1	r9	0x0
rcx	0xffffffffffffffff	rbp	0x7fffffffea50	r10	0x1
rdx	0x7fffffffeb48	rsp	0x7fffffffea50	r11	0x246
rip	0x400c36	eflags	PF ZF IF		

Shifting the bit number (76) right 6 bits will yield the quad-word number of the array. This works since $2^6 = 64$ and quad-words hold 64 bits. This shift leaves a 1 in `rbx`.

Registers

rax	76	rsi	0x7fffffffeb38	r8	0x400cfa
rbx	1	rdi	0x1	r9	0x0
rcx	0xffffffffffffffff	rbp	0x7fffffffea50	r10	0x1
rdx	0x7fffffffeb48	rsp	0x7fffffffea50	r11	0x246
rip	0x400c3a	eflags	IF		

We make another copy of the bit number in `rcx`.

Registers

rax	76	rsi	0x7fffffffeb38	r8	0x400cfa	r12
rbx	1	rdi	0x1	r9	0x0	r13
rcx	76	rbp	0x7fffffffea50	r10	0x1	r14
rdx	0x7fffffffeb48	rsp	0x7fffffffea50	r11	0x246	r15
rip	0x400c3d	eflags	IF			

The bit number and'ed with 0x3f will extract the rightmost 6 bits of the bit number. This will be the bit number of the quad-word containing the bit.

```
Registers                                                              ◇ ×
  rax  76              rsi  0x7fffffffeb38    r8   0x400cfa    r12
  rbx  1               rdi  0x1               r9   0x0         r13
  rcx  12              rbp  0x7fffffffea50    r10  0x1         r14
  rdx  0x7fffffffeb48  rsp  0x7fffffffea50    r11  0x246       r15
  rip  0x400c41      eflags  PF IF
```

Next we use xor to zero out rdx.

```
Registers                                                              ◇ ×
  rax  76            rsi  0x7fffffffeb38    r8   0x400cfa    r12
  rbx  1             rdi  0x1               r9   0x0         r13
  rcx  12            rbp  0x7fffffffea50    r10  0x1         r14
  rdx  0             rsp  0x7fffffffea50    r11  0x246       r15
  rip  0x400c43    eflags  PF ZF IF
```

Line 18 tests the bit we wish to test from the array. You will notice that the carry flag (CF) is set.

```
Registers                                                              ◇ ×
  rax  76            rsi  0x7fffffffeb38    r8   0x400cfa    r12
  rbx  1             rdi  0x1               r9   0x0         r13
  rcx  12            rbp  0x7fffffffea50    r10  0x1         r14
  rdx  0             rsp  0x7fffffffea50    r11  0x246       r15
  rip  0x400c4c    eflags  CF PF ZF IF
```

Line 19 uses the setc instruction to set dl which is now a 1 since 76 was in the set.

```
Registers                                                              ◇ ×
  rax  76            rsi  0x7fffffffeb38    r8   0x400cfa    r12
  rbx  1             rdi  0x1               r9   0x0         r13
  rcx  12            rbp  0x7fffffffea50    r10  0x1         r14
  rdx  1             rsp  0x7fffffffea50    r11  0x246       r15
  rip  0x400c4f    eflags  CF PF ZF IF
```

Line 20 sets the bit in the set.

Line 21 clears the bit (reset), effectively removing 76 from the set.

7.7 Extracting and filling a bit field

To extract a bit field you need to shift the field so that its least significant bit is in position 0 and then bit mask the field with an and operation with the appropriate mask. Let's suppose we need to extract bits 51-23 from a quad-word stored in a memory location. Then, after loading the quad-word, we need to shift it right 23 bits to get the least significant bit into the proper position. The bit field is of length 29. The simplest way to get a proper mask (29 bits all 1) is using the value 0x1fffffff. Seven f's is 28 bits and the 1 gives a total of 29 bits. Here is the code to do the work:

```
mov    rax, [sample]    ; move qword into rax
shr    rax, 23          ; align bit 23 at 0
and    rax, 0x1fffffff  ; select 29 low bits
mov    [field], rax     ; save the field
```

Of course it could be that the field width is not a constant. In that case you need an alternative. One possibility is to generate a string of 1 bits based on knowing that $2^n - 1$ is a string of n 1 bits. You can generate 2^n by shifting 1 to the left n times or use bts. Then you can subtract 1 using dec.

Another way to extract a bit field is to first shift left enough bits to clear out the bits to the left of the field and then shift right enough bits to wipe out the bits to the right of the field. This will be simpler when the field position and width are variable. To extract bits 51-23, we start by shifting left 12 bits. Then we need to shift right 35 bits. In general if the field is bits m through n where m is the higher bit number, we shift left $63 - m$ and then shift right $n + (63 - m)$.

```
mov   rax, [sample]  ; move qword into rax
shl   rax, 12        ; wipe out higher bits
shr   rax, 35        ; align the bit field
mov   [field], rax   ; save the field
```

Now suppose we wish to fill in bits 51-23 of sample with the bits in field. The easy method is to rotate the value to align the field, shift right and then left to clear 29 bits, or in the field, and then rotate the register to get the field back into bits 23-51. Here is the code:

```
mov   rax, [sample]  ; move qword into rax
ror   rax, 23        ; align bit 23 at 0
shr   rax, 29        ; wipe out 29 bits
shl   rax, 29        ; align bits again
or    rax, [field]   ; trust field is 29 bits
rol   rax, 23        ; realign the bit fields
mov   [sample], rax  ; store fields in memory
```

Exercises

1. Write an assembly program to count all the 1 bits in a byte stored in memory. Use repeated code rather than a loop.

2. Write an assembly program to swap 2 quad-words in memory using xor. Use the following algorithm:

   ```
   a = a ∧ b
   b = a ∧ b
   a = a ∧ b
   ```

3. Write an assembly program to use 3 quad-words in memory to represent 3 sets: A, B and C. Each set will allow storing set values 0-63 in the corresponding bits of the quad-word. Perform these steps:

   ```
   insert 0 into A
   insert 1 into A
   insert 7 into A
   insert 13 into A
   insert 1 into B
   insert 3 into B
   insert 12 into B
   store A union B into C
   store A intersect B into C
   store A - B into C
   remove 7 from C
   ```

4. Write an assembly program to move a quad-word stored in memory into a register and then compute the exclusive-or of the 8 bytes of the word. Use either ror or rol to manipulate the bits of the register so that the original value is retained.

5. Write an assembly program to dissect a double stored in memory. This is a 64 bit floating point value. Store the sign bit in one memory location. Store the exponent after subtracting the bias value into a second memory location. Store the fraction field with the implicit 1 bit at the front of the bit string into a third memory location.

6. Write an assembly program to perform a product of 2 float values using integer arithmetic and bit operations. Start with 2 float values in memory and store the product in memory.

Chapter 8
Branching and looping

So far we have not used any branching statements in our code. Using the conditional move instructions added a little flexibility to the code while preserving the CPU's pipeline contents. We have seen that it can be tedious to repeat instructions to process each byte in a quad-word or each bit in a byte. In the next chapter we will work with arrays. It would be fool-hardy to process an array of 1 million elements by repeating the instructions. It might be possible to do this, but it would be painful coping with variable sized arrays. We need loops.

In many programs you will need to test for a condition and perform one of 2 actions based on the results. The conditional move is efficient if the 2 actions are fairly trivial. If each action is several instructions long, then we need a conditional jump statement to branch to one alternative while allowing the CPU to handle the second alternative by not branching. After completing the second alternative we will typically need to branch around the code for the first alternative. We need conditional and unconditional branch statements.

8.1 Unconditional jump

The unconditional jump instruction (jmp) is the assembly version of the goto statement. However there is clearly no shame in using jmp. It is a necessity in assembly language, while goto can be avoided in higher level languages.

The basic form of the jmp instruction is

    jmp   label

where label is a label in the program's text segment. The assembler will generate a rip relative jump instruction, meaning that the flow of control will transfer to a location relative to the current value of the instruction pointer. The simplest relative jump uses an 8 bit signed immediate value and is encoded in 2 bytes. This allows jumping forwards or backwards about 127 bytes. The next variety of relative jump in 64 bit mode uses a 32 bit signed immediate value and requires a total of 5 bytes. Fortunately the assembler figures out which variety it can use and chooses the shorter form. The programmer simply specifies a label.

The effect of the jmp statement is that the CPU transfers control to the instruction at the labeled address. This is generally not too exciting except when used with a conditional jump. However, the jmp instruction can jump to an address contained in a register or memory location. Using a conditional move one could manage to use an unconditional jump to an address contained in a register to implement a conditional jump. This isn't sensible, since there are conditional jump statements which handle this more efficiently.

There is one more possibility which is more interesting - implementing a switch statement. Suppose you have a variable i which is known to contain a value from 0 to 2. Then you can form an array of instruction addresses and use a jmp instruction to jump to the correct section of code based on the value of i. Here is an example:

```
        segment .data
switch:
        dq      main.case0
        dq      main.case1
        dq      main.case2
i:      dq      2
        segment .text
        global  main
main:
        mov     rax, [i]        ; move i to rax
        jmp     [switch+rax*8]  ; switch ( i )
.case0:
        mov     rbx, 100        ; go here if i == 0
        jmp     .end
.case1:
        mov     rbx, 101        ; go here if i == 1
        jmp     .end
.case2:
        mov     rbx, 102        ; go here if i == 2
.end:
        xor     eax, eax
        ret
```

In this code we have used a new form of label with a dot prefix. These labels are referred to as "local" labels. They are defined within the range of enclosing regular labels. Basically the local labels could be used for all labels inside a function and this would allow using the same local labels in multiple functions. Also we used main.case0 outside of main to refer to the .case0 label inside main.

From this example we see that an unconditional jump instruction can be used to implement some forms of conditional jumps. Though conditional jumps are more direct and less confusing, in larger switch statements it might be advantageous to build an array of locations to jump to.

8.2 Conditional jump

To use a conditional jump we need an instruction which can set some flags. This could be an arithmetic or bit operation. However doing a subtraction just to learn whether 2 numbers are equal might wipe out a needed value in a register. The x86-64 CPU provides a compare instruction (cmp) which subtracts its second operand from its first and sets flags without storing the difference.

There are quite a few conditional jump instructions with the general pattern:

```
jcc     label  ; jump to location
```

The CC part of the instruction name represents any of a wide variety of condition codes. The condition codes are based on specific flags in eflags such as the zero flag, the sign flag, and the carry flag. Below are some useful conditional jump instructions.

instruction	meaning	aliases	flags
jz	jump if zero	je	ZF=1
jnz	jump if not zero	jne	ZF=0
jg	jump if > 0	jnle	ZF=0 and SF=0
jge	jump if ≥ 0	jnl	SF=0
jl	jump if > 0	jnge js	SF=1
jle	jump if ≤ 0	jng	ZF=1 or SF=1
jc	jump if carry	jb jnae	CF=1
jnc	jump if not carry	jnb jae	

It is possible to generate "spaghetti" code using jumps and conditional jumps. It is probably best to stick with high level coding structures translated to assembly language. The general strategy is to start with C code and translate it to assembly. The rest of the conditional jump section discusses how to implement C if statements.

Simple if statement

Let's consider how to implement the equivalent of a C simple if statement. Suppose we are implementing the following C code:

```
if ( a < b ) {
    temp = a;
    a = b;
```

```
;          b = temp;
           }
```

Then the direct translation to assembly language would be

```
;          if ( a < b ) {
           mov    rax, [a]
           mov    rbx, [b]
           cmp    rax, rbx
           jge    in_order
;            temp = a;
             mov   [temp],   rax
;            a = b;
             mov   [a], rbx
;            b = temp
             mov   [b], rax
;          }
in_order:
```

The most obvious pattern in this code is the inclusion of C code as comments. It can be hard to focus on the purpose of individual assembly statements. Starting with C code which is known to work makes sense. Make each C statement an assembly comment and add assembly statements to achieve each C statement after the C statement. Indenting might help a little though the indentation pattern might seem a little strange.

You will notice that the if condition was less than, but the conditional jump used greater than or equal to. Perhaps it would appeal to you more to use jnl rather than jge. The effect is identical but the less than mnemonic is part of the assembly instruction (with not). You should select the instruction name which makes the most sense to you.

If/else statement

It is fairly common to do 2 separate actions based on a test. Here is a simple C if statement with an else clause:

```
       if ( a < b ) {
           max = b;
       } else {
           max = a;
       }
```

This code is simple enough that a conditional move statement is likely to be a faster solution, but nevertheless here is the direct translation to assembly language:

```
;          if ( a < b ) {
           mov    rax, [a]
           mov    rbx, [b]
           cmp    rax, rbx
           jnl    else ;
             max = b;
             mov   [max], rbx
```

94

```
             jmp    endif
;       } else {
else:
;              max = a;
               mov    [max], rax

;       }
endif:
```

If/else-if/else statement

Just as in C/C++ you can have an if statement for the else clause, you can continue to do tests in the else clause of assembly code conditional statements. Here is a short if/else-if/else statement in C:

```
if ( a < b ) {
    result = 1;
} else if ( a > c ) {
    result = 2;
} else {
    result = 3;
}
```

This code is possibly a good candidate for 2 conditional move statements, but simplicity is bliss. Here is the assembly code for this:

```
;       if ( a < b ) {
        mov    rax, [a]
        mov    rbx, [b]
        cmp    rax, rbx
        jnl    else_if
;            result = 1;
             mov    qword [result], 1
             jmp    endif
;       } else if ( a > c ) {
else_if:
        mov    rcx, [c]
        cmp    rax, rcx
        jng    else
;            result = 2;
             mov    qword [result], 2
             jmp    endif
;       } else {
else:
;            result = 3;
             mov    qword [result], 3
;       }
endif:
```

It should be clear that an arbitrary sequence of tests can be used to simulate multiple else-if clauses in C.

8.3 Looping with conditional jumps

The jumps and conditional jumps introduced so far have been jumping forward. By jumping backwards, it is possible to produce a variety of loops. In this section we discuss `while` loops, `do-while` loops and counting loops. We also discuss how to implement the effects of C's `continue` and `break` statements with loops.

While loops

The most basic type of loop is possibly the `while` loop. It generally looks like this in C:

```
while ( condition ) {
    statements;
}
```

C `while` loops support the `break` statement which gets out of the loop and the `continue` statement which immediately goes back to the top of the loop. Structured programming favors avoiding `break` and `continue`. However they can be effective solutions to some problems and, used carefully, are frequently clearer than alternatives based on setting condition variables. They are substantially easier to implement in assembly than using condition variables and faster.

Counting 1 bits in a memory quad-word

The general strategy is to shift the bits of a quad-word 1 bit at a time and add bit 0 of the value at each iteration of a loop to the sum of the 1 bits. This loop needs to be done 64 times. Here is the C code for the loop:

```
sum = 0;
i = 0;
while ( i < 64 ) {
    sum += data & 1;
    data = data >> 1;
    i++;
}
```

The program below implements this loop with only the minor change that values are in registers during the execution of the loop. It would be pointless to store these values in memory during the loop. The C code is shown as comments which help explain the assembly code.

```
        segment .data ; long data;
data    dq      0xfedcba9876543210 ; long sum;
sum     dq      0
        segment .text
        global  main
```

```
;   int main()  ;  {
main:
        push    rbp
        mov     rbp, rsp
        sub     rsp, 16

;       int i;                  in register rcx
;       Register usage
;
;       rax: bits being examined
;       rbx: carry bit after bt, setc
;       rcx: loop counter i, 0-63
;       rdx: sum of 1 bits

        mov     rax, [data]
        xor     ebx, ebx
;       i = 0;
        xor     ecx, ecx
;       sum = 0;
        xor     edx, edx
;       while ( i < 64 ) {
while:
        cmp     rcx, 64
        jnl     end_while
;           sum += data & 1;
        bt      rax, 0
        setc    bl
        add     edx, ebx
;           data >>= 1;
        shr     rax, 1
;           i++;
        inc     rcx
;       }
        jmp     while
end_while:
        mov     [sum], rdx
        xor     eax, eax
        leave
        ret
```

The first instruction of the loop is cmp which is comparing i (rcx) versus 64. The conditional jump selected, jnl, matches the inverse of the C condition. Hopefully this is less confusing than using jge. The last instruction of the loop is a jump to the first statement of the loop. This is the typical translation of a while loop.

Coding this in C and running

```
gcc -O3 -S countbits.c
```

yields an assembly language file named countbits.s which is unfortunately not quite matching our yasm syntax. The assembler for gcc, gas, uses the AT&T syntax which differs from the Intel syntax used by yasm. Primarily the source and destination operands are reversed and some slight changes are made to instruction mnemonics. You can also use

```
gcc -O3 -S -masm=intel countbits.c
```

to request that gcc create an assembly file in Intel format which is very close to the code in this book. Here is the loop portion of the program produced by gcc;

```
        mov     rax, QWORD PTR data[rip]
        mov     ecx, 64
        xor     edx, edx
  .L2:
        mov rsi, rax
        sar     rax
        and     esi, 1
        add rdx, rsi
        sub     ecx, 1
        jne     .L2
```

You will notice that the compiler eliminated one jump instruction by shifting the test to the end of the loop. Also the compiler did not do a compare instruction. In fact it discovered that the counting up to 64 of i was not important. Only the number of iterations mattered, so it decremented down from 64 to 0. Thus it was possible to do a conditional jump after the decrement. Overall the compiler generated a loop with 6 instructions, while the hand-written assembly loop used 8 instructions. As stated in the introduction a good compiler is hard to beat. You can learn a lot from studying the compiler's generated code. If you are interested in efficiency you may be able to do better than the compiler. You could certainly copy the generated code and do exactly the same, but if you can't improve on the compiler's code then you should stick with C.

There is one additional compiler option, -funroll-all-loops which tends to speed up code considerably. In this case the compiler used more registers and did 8 iterations of a loop which added up 8 bits in each iteration. The compiler did 8 bits in 24 instructions where before it did 1 bit in 6 instructions. This is about twice as fast. In addition the instruction pipeline is used more effectively in the unrolled version, so perhaps this is 3 times as fast.

Optimization issues like loop unrolling are highly dependent on the CPU architecture. Using the CPU in 64 bit mode gives 16 general-purpose registers while 32 bit mode gives only 8 registers. Loop unrolling is much easier with more registers. Other details like the Intel Core i series processors' use of a queue of micro-opcodes might eliminate most of the effect of loops interrupting the CPU pipeline. Testing is required to see what works best on a particular CPU.

Do-while loops

We saw in the last section that the compiler converted a while loop into a do-while loop. The while structure translates directly into a conditional jump at the top of the loop and an unconditional jump at the bottom of the loop. It is always possible to convert a loop to use a conditional jump at the bottom.

A C do-while loop looks like

```
do {
    statements;
} while ( condition );
```

A do-while always executes the body of the loop at least once.

Let's look at a program implementing a search in a character array, terminated by a 0 byte. We will do an explicit test before the loop to not execute the loop if the first character is 0. Here is the C code for the loop:

```
i = 0;
c = data[i];
if ( c != 0 ) {
    do {
        if ( c == x ) break;
        i++;
        c = data[i];
    } while ( c != 0 );
}
n = c == 0 ? -1 : i;
```

Here's an assembly implementation of this code:

```
        SECTION .data
data    db       "hello world", 0
n       dq       0
needle:
        db       'w'
        SECTION .text
        global  main
main:
        push    rbp
        mov     rbp, rsp
        sub     rsp, 16

;       Register usage
;
;
;       rax: c, byte of data array
;       bl:  x, byte to search for
;       rcx: i, loop counter, 0-63

        mov     bl, [needle]
;       i = 0;
        xor     ecx, ecx
;       c = data[i];
        mov     al, [data+rcx]
;       if ( c != 0 ) {
        cmp     al, 0
        jz      end_if
;           do {
do_while:
;               if ( c == x ) break;
        cmp     al, bl
        je      found
;               i++;
        inc     rcx
```

99

```
;               c = data[i];
        mov     al, [data+rcx];
;           } while ( c != 0 );
        cmp     al, 0
        jnz     do_while
;       }
end_if:
;       n = c == 0 ? -1 : i;
        mov     rcx, -1 ; c == 0 if you reach here
found:
        mov     [n], rcx
;       return 0;
        xor     eax, eax
        leave
        ret
```

The assembly code (if stripped of the C comments) looks simpler than the C code. The C code would look better with a `while` loop. The conditional operator in C was not necessary in the assembly code, since the conditional jump on finding the proper character jumps past the movement of -1 to `rcx`.

It might seem rational to try to use more structured techniques, but the only reasons to use assembly are to improve efficiency or to do something which can't be done in a high level language. Bearing that in mind, we should try to strike a balance between structure and efficiency.

Counting loops

The normal counting loop in C is the `for` loop, which can be used to implement any type of loop. Let's assume that we wish to do array addition. In C we might use

```
for ( i = 0; i < n; i++ ) {
    c[i] = a[i] + b[i];
}
```

Translated into assembly language this loop might be

```
        mov     rdx, [n]
        xor     ecx, ecx
for:    cmp     rcx, rdx
        je      end_for
        mov     rax, [a+rcx*8]
        add     rax, [b+rcx*8]
        mov     [c+rcx*8], rax
        inc     rcx
        jmp     for
end_for:
```

Once again it is possible to do a test on `rdx` being 0 before executing the loop. This could allow the compare and conditional jump statements to be placed at the end of the loop. However it might be easier to simply translate C statements without worrying about optimizations until you improve your assembly skills. Perhaps you are taking an assembly class. If so, does performance affect your grade? If not, then keep it simple.

8.4 Loop instructions

There is a loop instruction along with a couple of variants which operate by decrementing the rcx register and branching until the register reaches 0. Unfortunately, it is about 4 times faster to subtract 1 explicitly from rcx and use jnz to perform the conditional jump. This speed difference is CPU specific and only true for a trivial loop. Generally a loop will have other work which will take more time than the loop instruction. Furthermore the loop instruction is limited to branching to a 8 bit immediate field, meaning that it can branch backwards or forwards about 127 bytes. All in all, it doesn't seem to be worth using.

Despite the forgoing tale of gloom, perhaps you still wish to use loop. Consider the following code which looks in an array for the right-most occurrence of a specific character:

```
        mov    ecx, [n]
more:   cmp    [data+rcx-1],al
        je     found
        loop   more
found:  sub    ecx, 1
        mov    [loc], ecx
```

8.5 Repeat string (array) instructions

The x86-64 repeat instruction (rep) repeats a string instruction the number of times specified in the count register (rcx). There are a handful of variants which allow early termination based on conditions which may occur during the execution of the loop. The repeat instructions allow setting array elements to a specified value, copying one array to another, and finding a specific value in an array.

String instructions

There are a handful of string instructions. The ones which step through arrays are suffixed with b, w, d or q to indicate the size of the array elements (1, 2, 4 or 8 bytes).

The string instructions use registers rax, rsi and rdi for special purposes. Register rax or its sub-registers eax, ax and al are used to hold a specific value. Resister rsi is the source address register and rdi is the destination address. None of the string instructions need operands.

All of the string operations working with 1, 2 or 4 byte quantities are encoded in 1 byte, while the 8 byte variants are encoded as 2 bytes. Combined with a 1 byte repeat instruction, this effectively encodes some fairly simple loops in 2 or 3 bytes. It is hard to beat a repeat.

The string operations update the source and/or destination registers after each use. This updating is managed by the direction flag (DF). If DF is 0 then the registers are increased by the size of the data item after each use. If DF is 1 then the registers are decreased after each use.

Move

The movsb instruction moves bytes from the address specified by rsi to the address specified by rdi. The other movs instructions move 2, 4 or 8 byte data elements from [rsi] to [rdi]. The data moved is not stored in a register and no flags are affected. After each data item is moved, the rdi and rsi registers are advanced 1, 2, 4 or 8 bytes depending on the size of the data item.

Below is some code to move 100000 bytes from one array to another:

```
lea     rsi, [source]
lea     rdi, [destination]
mov     rcx, 100000
rep     movsb
```

Store

The stosb instruction moves the byte in register al to the address specified by rdi. The other variants move data from ax, eax or rax to memory. No flags are affected. A repeated store can fill an array with a single value. You could also use stosb in non-repeat loops taking advantage of the automatic destination register updating.

Here is some code to fill an array with 1000000 double words all equal to 1:

```
mov     eax, 1
mov     ecx, 1000000
lea     rdi, [destination]
rep     stosd
```

Load

The lodsb instruction moves the byte from the address specified by rsi to the al register. The other variants move more bytes of data into ax, eax or rax. No flags are affected. Repeated loading seems to be of little use. However you can use lods instructions in other loops taking advantage of the automatic source register updating.

Here is a loop which copies data from 1 array to another removing characters equal to 13:

```
        lea    rsi, [source]
        lea    rdi, [destination]
        mov    ecx, 1000000
more: lodsb
        cmp    al, 13
        je     skip
        stosb
skip: sub     ecx, 1
        jnz    more
end
```

Scan

The scasb instruction searches through an array looking for a byte matching the byte in al. It uses the rdi register. Here is an implementation of the C strlen function:

```
        segment .text
        global  strlen
strlen:
        cld                 ; prepare to increment rdi
        mov    rcx, -1 ; maximum iterations
        xor    al, al  ; will scan for 0
        repne  scasb    ; repeatedly scan for 0
        mov    rax, -2 ; start at -1
                        ; end 1 past the end
        sub    rax, rcx
        ret
```

The function starts by setting rcx to -1, which would allow quite a long repeat loop since the code uses repne to loop. It would decrement rcx about 2^{64} times in order to reach 0. Memory would run out first.

It just so happens that the Linux C ABI places the first parameter to a function in rdi, so strlen starts with the proper address set for the scan. The standard way to return a value is to place it in rax, so we place the length there.

Compare

The cmpsb instruction compares values of 2 arrays. Typically it is used with repe which will continue to compare values until either the count in ecx reaches 0 or two different values are located. At this point the comparison is complete.

This is almost good enough to write a version of the C strcmp function, but strcmp expects strings terminated by 0 and lengths are not usually known for C strings. It is good enough for memcmp:

```
        segment .text
        global  memcmp
memcmp: mov     rcx, rdx
        repe    cmpsb    ; compare until end or difference
        cmp    rcx, 0
        jz     equal    ; reached the end
        movzx  eax, byte [rdi-1]
        movzx  ecx, byte [rsi-1]
```

```
        sub     rax, rcx
        ret
equal:  xor     eax, eax
        ret
```

In the memcmp function the repeat loop advances the rdi and rsi registers one too many times. Thus there is a ‑1 in the move and zero extend instructions to get the 2 bytes. Subtraction is sufficient since memcmp returns 0, a positive or a negative value. It was designed to be implemented with a subtraction yielding the return value. The first 2 parameters to memcmp are rdi and rsi with the proper order.

Set/clear direction

The clear direction cld instruction clears the direction flag to 0, which means to process increasing addresses with the string operations. The set direction std instruction sets the direction flag to 1. Programmers are supposed to clear the direction flag before exiting any function which sets it.

Exercises

1. Write an assembly program to compute the dot product of 2 arrays, i.e.

$$p = \sum_{i=0}^{n-1} a_i * b_i$$

   Your arrays should be double word arrays in memory and the dot product should be stored in memory.

2. Write an assembly program to compute Fibonacci numbers storing all the computed Fibonacci numbers in a quad-word array in memory. Fibonacci numbers are defined by

   ```
   fib(0) = 0
   fib(1) = 1
   fib(i) = fib(i-1) + fib(i-2) for i > 1
   ```

   What is the largest i for which you can compute `fib(i)`?

3. Write an assembly program to sort an array of double words using bubble sort. Bubble sort is defined as

   ```
   do {
       swapped = false;
       for ( i = 0; i < n-1; i++ ) {
           if ( a[i] > a[i+1] } {
               swap a[i] and a[i+1]
               swapped = true;
           }
       }
   } while ( swapped );
   ```

4. Write an assembly program to determine if a string stored in memory is a palindrome. A palindrome is a string which is the same after being reversed, like "refer". Use at least one repeat instruction.

5. Write an assembly program to perform a "find and replace" operation on a string in memory. Your program should have an input array and an output array. Make your program replace every occurrence of "amazing" with "incredible".A Pythagorean triple is a set of three integers a, b and c such that $a^2 + b^2 = c^2$. Write an assembly program to determine if an integer, c stored in memory has 2 smaller integers a and b making the 3 integers a Pythagorean triple. If so, then place a and b in memory.

Chapter 9
Functions

In this chapter we will discuss how to write assembly functions which can be called from C or C++ and how to call C functions from assembly. Since the C or C++ compiler generally does a very good job of code generation, it is usually not important to write complete programs in assembly. There might be a few algorithms which are best done in assembly, so we might write 90% of a program in C or C++ and write a few functions in assembly language.

It is also useful to call C functions from assembly. This gives your assembly programs full access to all C libraries. We will use scanf to input values from stdin and we will use printf to print results. This will allow us to write more useful programs.

9.1 The stack

So far we have had little use for the run-time stack, but it is an integral part of using functions. We stated earlier that the stack extends to the highest possible address: 0x7fffffffffff. This is not quite true. Inspection of the memory map using "cat /proc/$$/maps" shows the top stack address is 0x7fffa6b79000 for my bash process and different values for other processes always matching the pattern 0x7fffxxxxx000. Perhaps this is a result of "stack randomization" which is an attempt to avoid rogue code which modifies stack values.

Items are pushed onto the stack using the push instruction. The effect of push is to subtract 8 from the stack pointer rsp and then place the value being pushed at that address. Initially the stack pointer would be set to 0x7ffffffff000 (or some address ending in 000) by the operating system when a process is started. On the first push, rsp would be decreased to 0x7fffffffeff8 and an 8 byte value would be placed in bytes 0x7fffffffeff8 through 0x7fffffffefff.

Many different values are pushed onto the stack by the operating system. These include the environment (a collection of variable names and values defining things like the search path) and the command line parameters for the program.

Values can be removed from the stack using the pop instruction. pop operates in the reverse pattern of push. It moves the value at the location specified by the stack pointer (rsp) to a register or memory location and then adds 8 to rsp.

You can push and pop smaller values than 8 bytes, at some peril. It works as long as the stack remains bounded appropriately for the current operation. So if you push a word and then push a quad-word, the quad-word push may fail. It is simpler to push and pop only 8 byte quantities.

9.2 Call instruction

The assembly instruction to call a function is call. A typical use would be like

```
call    my_function
```

The operand my_function is a label in the text segment of a program. The effect of the call instruction is to push the address of the instruction following the call onto the stack and to transfer control to the address associated with my_function. The address pushed onto the stack is called the "return address". Another way to implement a call would be

```
        push    next_instruction
        jmp     my_function
next_instruction:
```

While this does work, the call instruction has more capability which we will generally ignore.

Ebe shows the top of the stack (normally 6 values) as your program executes. Below are the top 3 quad-words on the stack upon entry to main in an assembly program. Immediately preceding this register display was a call instruction to call main.

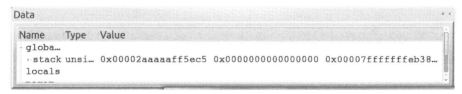

The first item on the stack is the return address, 0x2aaaaaff5ec5. Normal text segment addresses tend to be a little past 0x400000 in Linux programs as illustrated by rip in the register display below taken from

108

the same program when it enters main. The return address is an address in a shared object library, probably in the function __libc_start_main in libc.so. The same pattern occurs with OS X though the code addresses are larger numbers (bit 32 is set with addresses like 0x100400c06).

```
Registers                                                          ⌖ ⌄ ×
  rax  0x400c06              rsi  0x7fffffffeb38    r8   0x400c9a
  rbx  0x0                   rdi  0x1               r9   0x0
  rcx  0xffffffffffffffff    rbp  0x0               r10  0x1
  rdx  0x7fffffffeb48        rsp  0x7fffffffea58    r11  0x246
  rip  0x400c06           eflags  PF ZF IF
```

9.3 Return instruction

To return from a function you use the ret instruction. This instruction pops the address from the top of the stack and transfers control to that address. In the previous example next_instruction is the label for the return address.

Below is shown a very simple program which illustrates the steps of a function call and return. The first instruction in main is a call to the doit function.

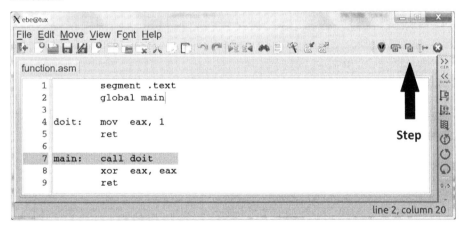

You can see that there is a breakpoint on line 7 and the call to doit has not yet been made. I have added an arrow pointing to the "Step" button which is immediately to the right of the "Next" button. In the register display below you can see that rip is 0x400c06.

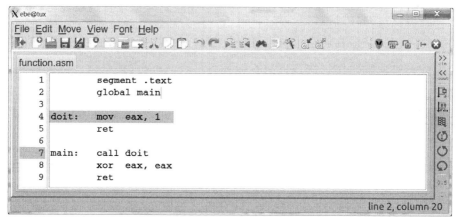

Previously we have used the "Next" button to execute the current instruction. However, if we use "Next" now, the debugger will execute the doit call and control will be returned after the function returns and the highlighted line will be line 8. In order to study the function call, I have clicked on "Step" which will step into the doit function.

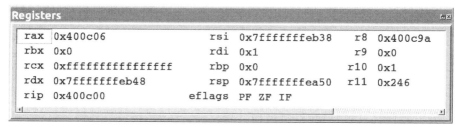

Now we see that the next instruction to execute is on line 4. It is instructive to view the registers at this point and the stack.

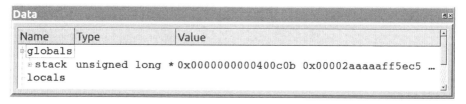

You can see that rip is now 4004c0 which is at a lower address than the call at line 7.

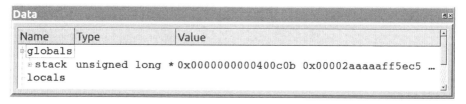

110

From the variable display we see that the first item on the stack is 4004cb which is the return address. After using "Step" two more times the debugger executes the return from doit. Below are the registers after executing the return.

rax	0x1	rsi	0x7fffffffeb38	r8	0x400c9a
rbx	0x0	rdi	0x1	r9	0x0
rcx	0xffffffffffffffff	rbp	0x0	r10	0x1
rdx	0x7fffffffeb48	rsp	0x7fffffffea58	r11	0x246
rip	0x400c0b	eflags	PF ZF IF		

Here we see that rip is now 0x4004cb which was the value placed on the stack by the call to doit.

9.4 Function parameters and return value

Most function have parameters which might be integer values, floating point values, addresses of data values, addresses of arrays, or any other type of data or address. The parameters allow us to use a function to operate on different data with each call. In addition most functions have a return value which is commonly an indicator of success or failure.

X86-64 Linux uses a function call protocol called the "System V Application Binary Interface" or System V ABI. The Apple Mac OS/X using x86-64 processing mode also uses the System V ABI, so the information in this book applies to Linux and to the Mac. Unfortunately Windows uses a different protocol called the "Microsoft x64 Calling Convention". In both protocols some of the parameters to functions are passed in registers. Linux allows the first 6 integer parameters to be passed in registers, while Windows allows the first 4 (using different registers). Linux and OS X allow the first 8 floating point parameters to be passed in floating pointer registers xmm0-xmm7, while Windows allows the first 4 floating point parameters to be passed in registers xmm0-xmm3.

Linux, OS X and Windows use register rax for integer return values and register xmm0 for floating point return values.

Both Linux and Windows expect the stack pointer to be maintained on 16 byte boundaries in memory. This means that the hexadecimal value for rsp should end in 0. The reason for this requirement is to allow local variables in functions to be placed at 16 byte alignments for SSE and AVX instructions. Executing a call would then decrement rsp leaving it ending with an 8. Conforming functions should either push something or subtract from rsp to get it back on a 16 byte boundary. It is common for a function to push rbp as part of establishing a stack frame which re-establishes the 16 byte boundary for the stack. If your function calls any external function, it seems wise to stick with the 16 byte bounding requirement.

The first 6 integer parameters in a function under Linux and OS X are passed in registers rdi, rsi, rdx, rcx, r8 and r9, while Windows uses rcx, rdx, r8 and r9 for the first 4 integer parameters. If a function requires more parameters, they are pushed onto the stack in reverse order.

Functions like scanf and printf which have a variable number of parameters pass the number of floating point parameters in the function call using the rax register.

For 32 bit programs the protocol is different. Registers r8-r15 are not available, so there is not much value in passing function parameters in registers. These programs use the stack for all parameters.

We are finally ready for "Hello World!"

```
        section .data
msg: db      "Hello world!",0x0a,0
        section .text
        global  main
        extern  printf
main:
        push    rbp
        mov     rbp, rsp
        lea     rdi, [msg] ; parameter 1 for printf
        xor     eax, eax   ; 0 floating point parameters
        call    printf
        xor     eax, eax   ; return 0
        pop     rbp
        ret
```

We use the "load effective address" instruction (lea) to load the effective address of the message to print with printf into rdi. This could also be done with mov, but lea allows specifying more items in the brackets so that we could load the address of an array element. Furthermore, under OS X mov will not allow you to move an address into a register. There the problem is that static addresses for data have values which exceed the capacity of 32 bit pointers and the constant field of the mov instruction is 32 bits. The easy assessment is to use lea to load addresses.

Interestingly when the system starts a program in _start (or simply start in OS X) the parameters to start are pushed onto the stack. However, the parameters to main are in registers like any other C function.

9.5 Stack frames

One of the most useful features of the gdb debugger is the ability to trace backwards through the stack functions which have been called using command bt or backtrace. To perform this trick each function must keep a pointer in rbp to a 2 quad-word object on the stack identifying the previous value of rbp along with the return address. You might notice the sequence "push rbp; mov rbp, rsp" in the hello world program. The first instruction pushes rbp immediately below the return address. The second instruction makes rbp point to that object.

Assuming all functions obey this rule of starting with the standard 2 instructions, there will be a linked list of objects on the stack - one for each function invocation. The debugger can traverse through the list to identify the function (based on the location of the return address) called and use other information stored in the executable to identify the line number for this return address.

These 2 quad-word objects are simple examples of "stack frames". In functions which do not call other functions (leaf functions), the local variables for the function might all fit in registers. If there are too many local variables or if the function calls other functions, then there might need to be some space on the stack for these local variables. To allocate space for the local variables, you simply subtract from rsp. For example to leave 32 bytes for local variables in the stack frame do this:

```
push    rbp
mov     rbp, rsp
sub     rsp, 32
```

Be sure to subtract a multiple of 16 bytes to avoid possible problems with stack alignment.

To establish a stack frame, you use the following 2 instructions at the start of a function:

```
push    rbp
mov     rbp, rsp
```

The effect of the these 2 instructions and a possible subtraction from rsp can be undone using

```
leave
```

just before a ret instruction. For a leaf function there is no need to do the standard 2 instruction prologue and no need for the leave instruction. They can also be omitted in general though it will prevent gdb from being able to trace backwards though the stack frames.

When you have local variables in the stack frame it makes sense to access these variables using names rather than adding 8 or 16 to rsp. This can be done by using yasm's equ pseudo-op. The following sets up symbolic names for 0 and 8 for two local variables.

```
x       equ     0
y       equ     8
```

Now we can easily save 2 registers in x and y prior to a function call using

```
mov     [rsp+x], r8
mov     [rsp+y], r9
```

With any function protocol you must specify which registers must be preserved in a function. For the System V ABI (Linux and OS X), registers rbx, rbp and r12-15 must be preserved, while the Windows calling convention requires that registers rbx, rbp, rsi, rdi and r12-15 must be preserved.

Function to print the maximum of 2 integers

The program listed below calls a function named print_max to print the maximum of 2 longs passed as parameters. It calls printf so it uses the extern pseudo-op to inform yasm and ld that printf will be loaded from a library.

```
      segment .text
      global  main
      extern  printf
; void print_max ( long a, long b )
; {
a     equ  0
b     equ  8
print_max:
      push rbp;          ; normal stack frame
      mov  rbp, rsp
      sub  rsp, 32       ; leave space for a, b and max
;     int max;
max equ   16
      mov  [rsp+a], rdi ; save a
      mov  [rsp+b], rsi ; save b
;     max = a;
      mov  [rsp+max], rdi
;     if ( b > max ) max = b;
      cmp  rsi, rdi
      jng  skip
      mov  [rsp+max], rsi
skip:
;     printf ( "max(%ld,%ld) = %ldn", a, b, max );
      segment .data
fmt db    'max(%ld,%ld) = %ld',0xa,0
      segment .text
      lea  rdi, [fmt]
      mov  rsi, [rsp+a]
      mov  rdx, [rsp+b]
      mov  rcx, [rsp+max]
      xor  eax, eax      ; 0 floating point parameters
```

```
    call printf
; }
    leave
    ret
main:
    push rbp
    mov  rbp, rsp
;   print_max ( 100, 200 );
    mov  rdi, 100    ; first parameter
    mov  rsi, 200    ; second parameter
    call print_max
    xor  eax, eax    ; to return 0
    leave
    ret
```

In main you first see the standard 2 instructions to establish a stack frame. There are no local variables in main, so there is no need to subtract anything from rsp. On the other hand the print_max function has 2 parameters and 1 local variable. The required space is 24 bytes, which is rounded up the next multiple of 16. It would be possible avoid storing these variables in memory, but it would be more confusing and less informative.

Immediately after the comment for the heading for print_max, I have 2 equates to establish offsets on the stack for a and b. After the comment for the declaration for max, I have an equate for it too.

Before doing any of the work of print_max I have 2 mov instructions to save a and b onto the stack. Both variables will be parameters to the printf call, but they will be the second and third parameters so they will need to be different registers at that point.

The computation for max is done using the stack location for max rather than using a register. It would have been possible to use rcx which is the register for max in the printf call, but would be less clear and the goal of this code is to show how to handle parameters and local variables to functions simply.

The call to printf requires a format string which should be in the data segment. It would be possible to have a collection of data prior to the text segment for the program, but it is nice to have the definition of the format string close to where it is used. It is possible to switch back and forth between the text and data segments, which seems easier to maintain.

9.6 Recursion

One of the fundamental problem solving techniques in computer programming is recursion. A recursive function is a function which calls itself. The focus of recursion is to break a problem into smaller problems.

Frequently these smaller problems can be solved by the same function. So you break the problem into smaller problems repeatedly and eventually you reach such a small problem that it is easy to solve. The easy to solve problem is called a "base case". Recursive functions typically start by testing to see if you have reached the base case or not. If you have reached the base case, then you prepare the easy solution. If not you break the problem into sub-problems and make recursive calls. As you return from recursive calls you assemble solutions to larger problems from solutions to smaller problems.

Recursive functions generally require stack frames with local variable storage for each stack frame. Using the complete stack frame protocol can help in debugging.

Using the function call protocol it is easy enough to write recursive functions. As usual, recursive functions test for a base case prior to making a recursive call.

The factorial function can be defined recursively as

$$f(n) = \begin{cases} 1 & \text{if } n \leq 1 \\ n * f(n-1) & \text{if } n < 1 \end{cases}$$

Here is a program to read an integer n, compute n! recursively and print n!.

```
        segment .data
x       dq          0
scanf_format:
        db      "%ld",0
printf_format:
        db      "fact(%ld) = %ld",0x0a,0

        segment .text
        global  main            ; tell world about main
        global  fact            ; tell world about fact
        extern  scanf           ; resolve scanf and
        extern  printf          ; printf from libc
main:
        push    rbp
        mov     rbp, rsp
        lea     rdi, [scanf_format] ; set arg 1
        lea     rsi, [x]    ; set arg 2 for scanf
        xor     eax, eax    ; set rax to 0
        call    scanf
        mov     rdi, [x]    ; move x for fact call
        call    fact
        lea     rdi, [printf_format]; set arg 1
        mov     rsi, [x]    ; set arg 2 for printf
        mov     rdx, rax    ; set arg 3 to be x!
        xor     eax, eax    ; set rax to 0
        call    printf
        xor     eax, eax    ; set return value to 0
        leave
        ret

fact:                           ; recursive function
n       equ         8
        push    rbp
```

116

```
      mov     rbp, rsp
      sub     rsp, 16
      ; make room for n
      cmp     rdi, 1      ; compare n with 1
      jg      greater     ; if n <= 1, return 1
      mov     eax, 1      ; set return value to 1
      leave
      ret
greater:
      mov     [rsp+n], rdi; save n
      dec     rdi         ; call fact with n-1
      call    fact
      mov     rdi, [rsp+n]; restore original n
      imul    rax, rdi    ; multiply fact(n-1)*n
      leave
      ret
```

You will notice that I have set rax prior to calling scanf and printf. The value of rax is the number of floating point parameters when you make a call to a function with a variable number of parameters.

In the fact function I have used an equate for the variable n. The equ statement defines the label n to have the value 8. In the body of the function I save the value of n on the stack prior to making a recursive call. The reference [rsp+n] is equivalent to [rsp+8], but it allows more flexibility in coding while being clearer.

Exercises

1. Write an assembly program to produce a billing report for an electric company. It should read a series of customer records using scanf and print one output line per customer giving the customer details and the amount of the bill. The customer data will consist of a name (up to 64 characters not including the terminal 0) and a number of kilowatt hours per customer. The number of kilowatt hours is an integer. The cost for a customer will be $20.00 if the number of kilowatt hours is less than or equal to 1000 or $20.00 plus 1 cent per kilowatt hour over 1000 if the usage is greater than 1000. Use quotient and remainder after dividing by 100 to print the amounts as normal dollars and cents. Write and use a function to compute the bill amount (in pennies).

2. Write an assembly program to generate an array of random integers (by calling the C library function random), to sort the array using a bubble sort function and to print the array. The array should be stored in the .bss segment and does not need to be dynamically allocated. The number of elements to fill, sort and print should be stored in a memory location. Write a function to loop through the array elements filling the array with random integers. Write a function to print the array contents. If the array size is less than or equal to 20, call your print function before and after printing.

3. A Pythagorean triple is a set of three integers, a, b and c, such that $a^2 + b^2 = c^2$. Write an assembly program to print all the Pythagorean triples where $c <= 500$. Use a function to test whether a number is a Pythagorean triple.

4. Write an assembly program to keep track of 10 sets of size 1000000. Your program should read accept the following commands: "add", "union", "print" and "quit". The program should have a function to read the command string and determine which it is and return 0, 1, 2 or 3 depending on the string read. After reading "add" your program should read a set number from 0 to 9 and an element number from 0 to 999999 and insert the element into the proper set. You need to have a function to add an element to a set. After reading "union" your program should read 2 set numbers and make the first set be equal to the union of the 2 sets. You need a set union function. After reading "print" your program should print all the elements of the set. You

118

can assume that the set has only a few elements. After reading "quit" your program should exit.

5. A sequence of numbers is called bitonic if it consists of an increasing sequence followed by a decreasing sequence or if the sequence can be rotated until it consists of an increasing sequence   followed by a decreasing sequence. Write an assembly program to read a sequence of integers into an array and print out whether the sequence is bitonic or not. The maximum number of elements in the array should be 100. You need to write 2 functions: one to read the numbers into the array and a second to determine   whether the sequence is bitonic. Your bitonic test should not actually rotate the array.

6. Write an assembly program to read two 8 byte integers with scanf and compute their greatest common divisor using Euclid's algorithm, which is based on the recursive definition

$$\gcd(a,b) = \begin{cases} a & \text{if } b = 0 \\ \gcd(b, a \bmod b) & \text{otherwise} \end{cases}$$

7. Write an assembly program to read a string of left and right parentheses and determine whether the string contains a balanced set of parentheses. You can read the string with scanf using "%79s" into a character array of length 80. A set of parentheses is balanced if it is the empty string or if it consists of a left parenthesis followed by a sequence of balanced sets and a right parenthesis. Here's an example of a balanced set of parentheses: "((()())())".

Chapter 10
Arrays

An array is a contiguous collection of memory cells of a specific type. This means that an array has a start address. The start address is the lowest address in the array and is identified by the label used when defining an array in the text or bss segment.

Elements of the array are accessed by index with the smallest index being 0 as in C. Subsequent indices access higher memory addresses. The final index of an array of size n is n-1.

It would be possible to define arrays with different starting indices. In fact the default for FORTRAN is for arrays to start at index 1 and you can define the range of indices in many high level languages. However it is quite natural to use 0 as the first index for arrays. The assembly code is simpler in this way which helps with efficiency in C and C++.

10.1 Array address computation

There can be arrays of many types of data. These include the basic types: bytes, words, double words, and quad-words. We can also have arrays of structs (defined later).

Array elements are of a specific type so each array element occupies the same number of bytes of memory. This makes it simple to compute the location of any array element. Suppose that the array a with base address base uses m bytes per element, then element a[i] is located at base + i*m.

Let's illustrate the indexing of arrays using the following program:

```
    segment .bss
a   resb    100 ; array of 100 bytes
b   resd    100 ; array of 100 double words
    align   8
c   resq    100 ; array of 100 quad-words
    segment .text
```

```
    global  main
main:
    push  rbp
    mov   rbp, rsp
    sub   rsp, 16
    leave
    ret
```

The program has 3 arrays of different types. We will run gdb and print addresses of various array elements to see the effect. Unfortunately gdb is unaware of the types of variables. It knows the location of variables a, b and c by name and, without knowing the type, it assumes that each is a double word integer. However if we take the address of a variable, say &a, we can prefix it with a typecast and turn that address into a pointer of the proper type: (char *)&a. We can then use that pointer to advantage.

Here is a gdb session:

```
(gdb) p (unsigned char *)&a
$1 = (unsigned char *) 0x6010d8 ""
(gdb) p &((unsigned char *)&a)[1]
$2 = (unsigned char *) 0x6010d9 ""
(gdb) p &((unsigned char *)&a)[2]
$3 = (unsigned char *) 0x6010da ""
(gdb) p (int *)&b
$4 = (int *) 0x60113c
(gdb) p &((int *)&b)[1]
$5 = (int *) 0x601140
(gdb) p &((int *)&b)[2]
$6 = (int *) 0x601144
(gdb) p (long *)&c
$7 = (long *) 0x6012d0
(gdb) p ((long *)&c)[1]
$8 = (long *) 0x6012d8
(gdb) p ((long *)&c)[2]
$9 = (long *) 0x6012e0
```

When we use "p (unsigned char *)&a", it prints the address of a with the interpretation that the address is a pointer to an unsigned char. You can see from the first 3 results that the elements of a are at 1 byte intervals in memory. Next we see the same pattern repeated for array b which is an array of double words (int in C and gdb) and that the array elements are placed at 4 byte intervals in memory. Finally we see the results for inspecting c which is an array of quad-word integers (long in C and gdb) and that these array elements are placed at 8 byte intervals.

Fortunately it is not really necessary to see the actual first address of an array to observe the array in ebe. Instead we can use a control-right-click on the variable name a in the source code window (or we can mark the variable name and use a right click) to bring up a variable definition window and set it to print hexadecimal numbers with size 1 to add a to the data window.

After defining a properly we can now view the selected locations of the array.

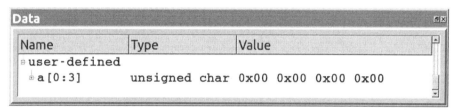

10.2 General pattern for memory references

So far we have used array references in sample code without discussing the options for memory references. A memory reference can be expressed as

[label]   the value contained at label

[label+2*ind]   the value contained at the memory address obtained by adding the label and index register times 2

[label+4*ind]   the value contained at the memory address obtained by adding the label and index register times 4

[label+8*ind]   the value contained at the memory address obtained by adding the label and index register times 8

[reg]   the value contained at the memory address in the register

[reg+k*ind]   the value contained at the memory address obtained by adding the register and index register times k

[label+reg+k*ind] the value contained at the memory address obtained by adding the label, the register and index register times k

[number+reg+k*ind]   the value contained at the memory address
   obtained by adding the number, the register and index register times
   k

This allows a lot of flexibility in array accesses. For arrays in the text
and data segments it is possible to use the label along with an index
register with a multiplier for the array element size (as long as the array
element size is 1, 2, 4 or 8). With arrays passed into functions, the address
must be placed in a register. Therefore the form using a label is not
possible. Instead we can use a base register along with an index register.
Any of the 16 general purpose registers may be used as a base register or
an index register, however it is unlikely that you would use the stack
pointer register as an index register.

Let's look at an example using a base register and an index register.
Let's suppose we wish to copy an array to another array in a function.
Then the two array addresses could be the first 2 parameters (rdi and
rsi) and the number of array elements could be the third parameter rdx.
Let's assume that the arrays are double word arrays.

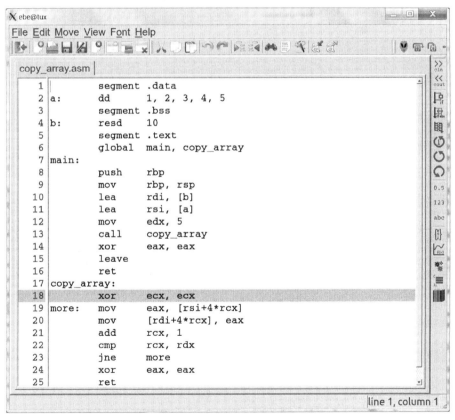

It is easy to monitor data processed in a function with ebe. You can see
that a breakpoint was placed on line 18 and the program was run. At this

point the `copy_array` function has been called and the parameters are in registers `rdi`, `rsi`, and `rdx`.

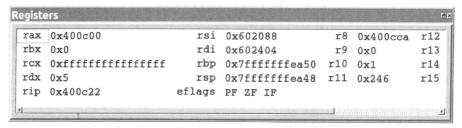

By left clicking on the value of `rdi`, 0x601040, and then right-clicking we can bring up a form to define a variable with the address in `rdi`. The form needs the name, type, format, array variable, first and last completed for a.

This was done for both the source and destination arrays allowing both arrays to be observed as the function executes. Here is a view of the arrays after 3 values have been copied.

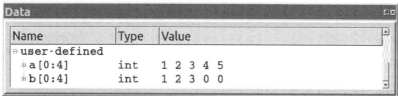

In the `copy_array` function we used the parameters as they were provided. We used `rsi` as the base address register for the source array and `rdi` as the base address register for the destination array. For both accesses we used `rcx` as the index register with a multiplier of 4 since the arrays have 4 byte elements. This allows us to compare `rcx` versus `rdx` to see if there are more elements to copy.

Note that multiplying by 2, 4 or 8 is a shift of 1, 2 or 3 bits, so there is effectively 0 cost to using the multiplier. Alternatively we could add 4 to `ecx` in each loop iteration after shifting `rdx` left 2 positions.

The last pattern would be useful for accessing an array of structs. If you had an array of structs with each struct having a character array and a pointer, then the number part of the reference could be the offset of the struct element within the struct, while the base register and index register could define the address of a particular struct in the array.

10.3 Allocating arrays

The simplest way to allocate memory in assembly is probably to use the C library malloc function. The prototype for malloc is

```
void *malloc ( long size );
```

On success malloc returns a pointer to the allocated memory, while failure results in malloc returning 0. The memory returned by malloc is bounded on 16 byte boundaries, which is useful as an address for any type of object (except for arrays needing to be on 32 byte boundaries for AVX instructions). The memory can be returned for potential reuse by calling the free function with the pointer returned by malloc

```
void free ( void *ptr );
```

Here is an assembly segment to allocate an array of 1000000000 bytes

```
extern  malloc
...
mov     rdi, 1000000000
call    malloc
mov     [pointer], rax
```

There are several advantages to using allocated arrays. The most obvious one is that you can have arrays of exactly the right size. Frequently you can compute the size of array needed in your code and allocate an array of the correct size. If you use statically defined arrays either in the data or bss segment, you have to know the size needed before running the program (or guess).

Another less obvious reason for using allocated arrays is due to size limitations imposed on the data and bss sections by either the assembler, linker or operating system. Yasm reports "FATAL: out of memory" when you try to allocate an array of much more than 2 billion bytes. It succeeds with an array of 2 billion bytes in the bss segment. It took approximately 104 seconds on a 2.4 GHz Opteron system to assemble and link a test program with a 2 GB array. In addition both the object file and the executable file exceeded 2 billion bytes in size. It is much faster (less than 1 second) to assemble and link a program using malloc and the executable size was about 10 thousand bytes.

The program using malloc was modified to allocate 20 billion bytes and still assembled and linked in less than 1 second. It executed in 3 milliseconds. There is no more practical way to use large amounts of memory than using allocated memory.

The user should be cautioned not to attempt to assemble programs with large static memory needs on a computer with less RAM than required. This will cause disk thrashing while assembling and linking, using far more than 100 seconds and nearly crippling the computer during the process. Also it can be quite painful to use arrays larger than memory even if they are allocated. Disk thrashing is not cool.

10.4 Processing arrays

Here we present an example application with several functions which process arrays. This application allocates an array using malloc, fills the array with random numbers by calling random and computes the minimum value in the array. If the array size is less than or equal to 20, it prints the values in the array.

Creating the array

The array is created using the create function shown below. This function is perhaps too short to be a separate function. It multiplies the array size by 4 to get the number of bytes in the array and then calls malloc.

```
;        array = create ( size );
create:
        push    rbp
        mov     rbp, rsp
        imul    rdi, 4
        call    malloc
        leave
        ret
```

Filling the array with random numbers

The fill function uses storage on the stack for local copies of the array pointer and its size. It also stores a local variable on the stack. These 3 variables require 24 bytes of storage, so we subtract 32 from rsp to maintain the 16 byte alignment of the stack. We store data in the array using "mov [rdi+rcx*4], rax", where rdi holds the address of the start of the array and rcx contains the index of the current array element.

Here we use several local labels. A local label is a label beginning with a dot. Their scope is between normal labels. So in the fill function, labels .array, .size, .i and .more are local. This allows reusing these same labels in other functions, which simplifies the coding of this application.

```
;        fill ( array, size );
fill:
.array  equ     0
.size   equ     8
.i      equ     16
        push    rbp
        mov     rbp, rsp
```

```
        sub     rsp, 32
        mov     [rsp+.array], rdi
        mov     [rsp+.size], rsi
        xor     ecx, ecx
.more   mov     [rsp+.i], rcx
        call    random
        mov     rcx, [rsp+.i]
        mov     rdi, [rsp+.array]
        mov     [rdi+rcx*4], eax
        inc     rcx
        cmp     rcx, [rsp+.size]
        jl      .more
        leave
        ret
```

Printing the array

Printing the array is done with printf. The print function, just like fill, needs to save 3 values on the stack since it calls another function. The code is somewhat similar to fill, except that array values are loaded into a register rather than values being stored in the array. You will notice that the data segment is used to store the printf format in a spot near the printf call. You will also notice that I have reused several local labels.

```
;       print ( array, size );
print:
.array  equ     0
.size   equ     8
.i      equ     16
        push    rbp
        mov     rbp, rsp
        sub     rsp, 32
        mov     [rsp+.array], rdi
        mov     [rsp+.size], rsi
        xor     ecx, ecx
        mov     [rsp+.i], rcx
        segment .data
.format:
        db      "%10d",0x0a,0
        segment .text
.more   lea     rdi, [.format]
        mov     rdx, [rsp+.array]
        mov     rcx, [rsp+.i]
        mov     esi, [rdx+rcx*4]
        mov     [rsp+.i], rcx
        call    printf
        mov     rcx, [rsp+.i]
        inc     rcx
        mov     [rsp+.i], rcx
        cmp     rcx, [rsp+.size]
        jl      .more
        leave
        ret
```

Finding the minimum value

The min function is a leaf function (does not call any other functions), so there is no real need for a stack frame and no need to align the stack at a 16 byte boundary. A conditional move instruction is used to avoid interrupting the instruction pipeline.

```
;       x = min ( array, size );
min:
        mov     eax, [rdi]
        mov     rcx, 1
.more   mov     r8d, [rdi+rcx*4]
        cmp     r8d, eax
        cmovl   eax, r8d
        inc     rcx
        cmp     rcx, rsi
        jl      .more
        ret
```

Main program for the array minimum

The main program is shown below. It uses stack space for the local variables .array and .size. It uses a command line parameter for the array size, which is discussed in the next section. Comments in the code outline the behavior.

```
main:
.array equ     0
.size  equ     8
        push    rbp
        mov     rbp, rsp
        sub     rsp, 16

        mov     ecx, 10         ; set default size
        mov     [rsp+.size], rcx

;       check for argv[1] providing a size
        cmp     edi, 2
        jl      .nosize
        mov     rdi, [rsi+8]
        call    atoi
        mov     [rsp+.size], rax

.nosize:
;       create the array
        mov     rdi, [rsp+.size]
        call    create

        mov     [rsp+.array], rax
;       fill the array with random numbers
        mov     rdi, rax
        mov     rsi, [rsp+.size]
        call    fill

;       if size <= 20 print the array
        mov     rsi, [rsp+.size]
```

```
        cmp     rsi, 20
        jg      .toobig
        mov     rdi, [rsp+.array]
        call    print

.toobig:
;       print the minimum
        segment .data
.format:
        db      "min: %ld",0xa,0
        segment .text
        mov     rdi, [rsp+.array]
        mov     rsi, [rsp+.size]
        call    min
        lea     rdi, [.format]
        mov     rsi, rax
        call    printf
        leave
        ret
```

10.5 Command line parameter array

The command line parameters are available to a C program as parameters
to main. The number of command line parameters is the first argument to
main and an array of character pointers is the second argument to main.
The first parameter is always the name of the executable file being run.
The remaining parameters are the expansion by the user's shell of the rest
of the command line. This expansion makes it convenient to use patterns
like "*.dat" on the command line. The shell replaces that part of the
command line with all the matching file names.

Here is a simple C program to print the command line parameters:

```
#include <stdio.h>

int main ( int argc, char *argv[] )
{
    int i;
    for ( i = 0; i < argc; i++ ) {
        printf("%sn", argv[i]);
    }
    return 0;
}
```

When executed as "./args hello world", it prints

```
./args
hello
world
```

The argv array is passed like all C arrays by placing the address of the
first element of the array in a register or on the stack. In the case of argv
its address is in register rsi. Below is a translation of the program to

129

assembly, though the assembly code takes advantage of the fact that there is a `NULL` pointer at the end of the `argv` array.

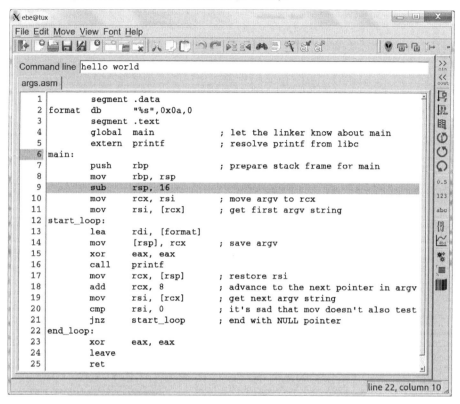

You will notice that "hello world" has been entered in the "Command line" text box. When this program executes it will print the program name followed by "hello" and "world" on separate lines in the ebe terminal window. This terminal window will also be used by ebe for all reads from standard input.

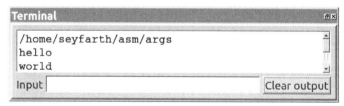

Exercises

1. Write 2 test programs: one to sort an array of random 4 byte integers using bubble sort and a second program to sort an array of random 4 bytes integers using the qsort function from the C library. Your program should use the C library function atol to convert a number supplied on the command line from ASCII to long. This number is the size of the array (number of 4 byte integers). Then your program can allocate the array using malloc and fill the array using random. You call qsort like this

    ```
    qsort ( array, n, 4, compare );
    ```

    The second parameter is the number of array elements to sort and the third is the size in bytes of each element. The fourth parameter is the address of a comparison function. Your comparison function will accept two parameters. Each will be a pointer to a 4 byte integer. The comparison function should return a negative, 0 or positive value based on the ordering of the 2 integers. All you have to do is subtract the second integer from the first.

2. Write a program to use qsort to sort an array of random integers and use a binary search function to search for numbers in the array. The size of the array should be given as a command line parameter. Your program should use random()%1000 for values in the array. This will make it simpler to enter values to search for. After building the array and sorting it, your program should enter a loop reading numbers with scanf until scanf fails to return a 1. For each number read, your program should call your binary search function and either report that the number was found at a particular index or that the number was not found.

3. Write an assembly program to compute the Adler-32 checksum value for the sequence of bytes read using fgets to read 1 line at a time until end of file. The prototype for fgets is

    ```
    char *fgets( char *s, int size, FILE *fp);
    ```

    The parameter s is a character array which should be in the bss segment. The parameter size is the number of bytes in the array s. The parameter fp is a pointer and you need stdin. Place the following line in your code to tell the linker about stdin

```
extern stdin
```

fgets will return the parameter s when it succeeds and will return 0 when it fails. You are to read until it fails. The Adler-32 checksum is computed by

```
long adler32(char *data, int len)
{
    long a = 1, b = 0;
    int i;
        for ( i = 0; i < len; i++ ) {
            a = (a + data[i]) % 65521;
            b = (b + a) % 65521;
        }
    return (b << 16) | a;
}
```

Your code should compute 1 checksum for the entire file. If you use the function shown for 1 line, it works for that line, but calling it again restarts.

4. Write a test program to evaluate how well the hashing function below works.

```
int multipliers[] = {
    123456789,
    234567891,
    345678912,
    456789123,
    567891234,
    678912345,
    789123456,
    891234567
};

int hash ( unsigned char *s )
{
    unsigned long h = 0;
    int i = 0;

    while ( s[i] ) {
        h = h + s[i] * multipliers[i%8];
        i++;
    }
    return h % 99991;
}
```

Your test program should read a collection of strings using scanf with the format string "%79s" where you are reading into a character array of 80 bytes. Your program should read until scanf fails to return 1. As it reads each string it should call hash (written in assembly) to get a number h from 0 to 99990. It should increment location h of an array of integers of size 99991. After entering all the data, this array contains a count of how many words mapped to each location in the array. What we want to know is how many of these array entries have 0 entries, how many have 1 entry, how many have 2 entries, etc. When

132

multiple words map to the same location, it is called a "collision". So the next step is to go through the array collision counts and increment another array by the index there. There should be no more than 1000 collisions, so this could be done using

```
for ( i = 0; i < 99991; i++ ) {
    k = collisions[i];
    if ( k > 999 ) k = 999;
    count[k]++;
}
```

After the previous loop the count array has interesting data. Use a loop to step through this array and print the index and the value for all non-zero locations. An interesting file to test is "/usr/share/dict/words". Write an assembly program to read a sequence of integers using scanf and determine if the first number entered can be formed as a sum of some of the other numbers and print a solution if it exists. You can assume that there will be no more than 20 numbers. Suppose the numbers are 20, 12, 6, 3, and 5. Then $20 = 12 + 3 + 5$. Suppose the numbers are 25, 11, 17 and 3. In this case there are no solutions.

Chapter 11
Floating point instructions

The 8086 CPU used a floating point coprocessor called the 8087 to perform floating point arithmetic. Many early personal computers lacked the 8087 chip and performed floating point operations in software. This arrangement continued until the 486 which contained a coprocessor internally. The 8087 used instructions which manipulated a stack of 80 bit floating point values. These instructions are still part of modern CPUs, though there is a completely separate floating point facility available which has sixteen 128 bit registers (256 bits for the Intel Core i series) in 64 bit mode. We will study the newer instructions.

If you study the Intel 64 and IA-32 Architectures Software Developer's Manual, you will find many instructions such as fadd which work with registers named ST0, ST1, ... These instructions are for the math coprocessor. There are newer instructions such as addsd which work with Streaming SIMD Extensions (SSE) registers xmm0, xmm1, ..., xmm15. SIMD is an acronym for "Single Instruction - Multiple Data". These instructions are the focus of this chapter.

11.1 Floating point registers

There are 16 floating point registers which serve multiple purposes holding either 1 value or multiple values. The names for these registers are xmm0, xmm1, ..., xmm15. These registers can be used with instructions operating on a single value in each register or on a vector of values. When used as a vector an XMM register can be used as either 4 floats or 2 doubles. The registers can also be used for collections of integers of various sizes, though the SSE integer instructions are basically ignored in this book.

The Core i series of computers introduced the Advanced Vector Extensions (AVX) which doubled the size of the floating point registers and added some new instructions.AVX To use the full 256 bits (8 floats or 4 doubles) you need to use a register name from ymm0, ymm1, ... ymm15. Each XMM register occupies the first 128 bits of the corresponding YMM register.

For most of this chapter the discussion refers only to XMM registers. In all cases the same instruction (prefixed by the letter "v") can be used with YMM registers to operate on twice as many data values. Stating this repeatedly would probably be more confusing than accepting it as a rule.

Ebe makes it easy to view the contents of floating point registers. The lower section of the registers window displays the floating point registers in a variety of different formats. Consider this simple program which loads 2 float values and adds them:

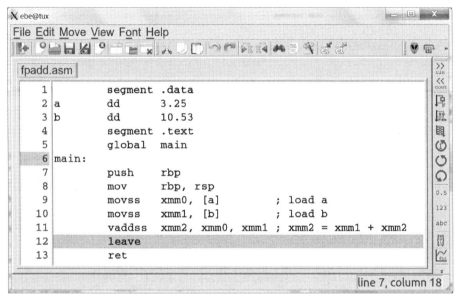

Below are the floating point registers after executing the vaddss instruction at line 11.

Floating Point Registers			
xmm0	3.25	xmm8	0
xmm1	10.53	xmm9	0
xmm2	13.78	xmm10	0
xmm3	0	xmm11	0
xmm4	2.34181e-38	xmm12	0
xmm5	0	xmm13	0
xmm6	0	xmm14	0
xmm7	0	xmm15	0

135

11.2 Moving floating point data

The SSE registers are 128 bits on most x86-64 CPUs (256 bits for the AVX registers). These registers can be used to do 1 operation at a time or multiple operations at a time. There are instructions for moving 1 data value and instructions from moving multiple data items, referred to as "packed" data.

Moving scalars

There are two instructions for moving scalar (1 value) floating point values to/from SSE registers: movss which moves 32 bit floating point values (floats) and movsd which moves 64 bit floating point values (doubles). These two instructions move a floating value from memory to/from the lower part of a XMM register or from one XMM register to another. There is no implicit data conversion - after movss a 32 bit value exists in the destination. Here is a sample:

```
movss    xmm0, [x]    ; xmm0 = value at x
movsd    [y], xmm1    ; move xmm1 to y
movss    xmm2, xmm0   ; xmm2 = xmm0
```

Moving packed data

There are instructions for loading integer packed data and floating point packed data. We will concentrate here on packed floating point data. You can move packed floats or packed doubles. There are instructions for moving aligned or unaligned packed data. The aligned instructions are movaps for moving four floats and movapd for moving two doubles using XMM registers. The unaligned versions are movups and movupd. Moving packed data to/from YMM registers moves twice as many values.

Aligned data means that it is on a 16 byte boundary in memory. This can be arranged by using align 16 for an array in the data section. The alignb pseudo-op for an array in the bss section does not do the job properly. Arrays allocated by malloc will be on 16 byte boundaries. Your program will fail with a segmentation fault if you attempt to use an aligned move to an unaligned address. Fortunately on the Core i series of CPUs the unaligned moves are just as fast as the aligned moves when the data is aligned. Note that the instructions using AVX registers begin with "v". Here is a sample.

```
movups    xmm0, [x]    ; move 4 floats to xmm0
vmovups   ymm0, [x]    ; move 8 floats to ymm0
vmovupd   ymm1, [x]    ; move 4 doubles to ymm1
movupd    [a], xmm15   ; move 2 doubles to a
```

11.3 Addition

The instructions for adding floating point data come in scalar and packed varieties. The scalar add instructions are addss to add two floats and addsd to add two doubles. Both these operate on a source operand and destination operand. The source can be in memory or in an XMM register while the destination must be in an XMM register. Unlike the integer add instruction the floating point add instructions do not set any flags, so testing must be done using a compare instruction.

The packed add instructions are addps which adds 4 floats from the source to 4 floats in the destination and addpd which adds 2 doubles from the source to 2 doubles in the destination using XMM registers. Like the scalar adds the source can be either memory or an XMM register, while the destination must be an XMM register. Using packed adds vaddps or vaddpd with YMM registers adds either 8 pairs of floats or 4 pairs of doubles.

```
movss    xmm0, [a]    ; load a
addss    xmm0, [b]    ; add b to a
movss    [c], xmm0    ; store sum in c
movapd   xmm0, [a]    ; load 2 doubles from a
addpd    xmm0, [b]    ; a[0]+b[0], a[1]+b[1]
movapd   [c], xmm0    ; store 2 sums in c
vmovupd  ymm0, [a]    ; load 4 doubles from a
vaddpd   ymm0, [b]    ; add 4 pairs of doubles
movupd   [c], ymm0    ; store 4 sums in c
```

11.4 Subtraction

Subtraction operates like addition on either scalar floats or doubles or packed floats or doubles. The scalar subtract instructions are subss which subtracts the source float from the destination float and subsd which subtracts the source double from the destination double. The source can be either in memory or in an XMM register, while the destination must be an XMM register. No flags are affected by the floating point subtraction instructions.

The packed subtract instructions are subps which subtracts 4 source floats from 4 floats in the destination and the subpd which subtracts 2 source doubles from 2 doubles in the destination using XMM registers. Again the source can be in memory or in an XMM register, while the destination must be an XMM register. Using packed subtracts (vsubps or vsubpd) with YMM registers subtracts either 8 pairs of floats or 4 pairs of doubles.

```
movss   xmm0, [a] ; load a
subss   xmm0, [b] ; subtract b from a
movss   [c], xmm0 ; store a-b in c
movapd  xmm0, [a] ; load 2 doubles from a
subpd   xmm0, [b] ; a[0]-b[0], a[1]-b[1]
movapd  [c], xmm0 ; store 2 results in c
vmovapd ymm0, [a] ; load 4 doubles from a
vmovapd [c], ymm0 ; store 4 results in c
```

11.5 Multiplication and division

Multiplication and division follow the same pattern as addition and subtraction in that they operate on memory or register operands. They support floats and doubles and they support scalar and packed data. The basic mathematical instructions for floating point data are

instruction	effect
addsd	add scalar double
addss	add scalar float
addpd	add packed double
addps	add packed float
subsd	subtract scalar double
subss	subtract scalar float
subpd	subtract packed double
subps	subtract packed float
mulsd	multiple scalar double
mulss	multiply scalar float
mulpd	multiple packed double
mulps	multiple packed float
divsd	divide scalar double
divss	divide scalar float
divpd	divide packed double
divps	subtract packed float

11.6 Conversion

It is relatively common to need to convert numbers from one length integer to another, from one length floating point to another, from integer to floating point or from floating point to integer. Converting from one length integer to another is accomplished using the various move instructions presented so far. The other operations take special instructions.

Converting to a different length floating point

There are 2 instructions to convert floats to doubles: cvtss2sd which converts one float to a double and cvtps2pd which converts 2 packed floats to 2 packed doubles. The source can be a memory location or an XMM register while the destination must be an XMM register.

Similarly 2 instructions convert doubles to floats: cvtsd2ss which converts a double to a float and cvtpd2ps which converts 2 packed doubles to 2 packed floats. It has the same restriction that the destination must be an XMM register.

```
cvtss2sd xmm0, [a]     ; convert a to double in xmm0
addsd    xmm0, [b]     ; add a double to a
cvtsd2ss xmm0, xmm0    ; convert to float
movss    [c], xmm0     ; move float sum to c
```

Converting floating point to/from integer

There are 2 instructions which convert floating point to integers by rounding: cvtss2si which converts a float to a double or quad word integer and cvtsd2si which converts a double to a double or quad word integer. The source can be an XMM register or a memory location, while the destination must be a general purpose register. There are 2 instructions which convert by truncating: cvttss2si and cvttsd2si.

There are 2 instructions which convert integers to floating point: cvtsi2ss which converts a double or quad word integer to a float and cvtsi2sd which converts a double or quad word integer to a double. The source can be a general purpose register or a memory location, while the destination must be an XMM register. When using a register for the source the size is implicit in the register name. When using a memory location you need to add "dword" or "qword" to the instruction to specify the size.

```
cvtss2si eax, xmm0        ; convert to int
cvtsi2sd xmm0, rax        ; long to double
cvtsi2sd xmm0, dword [x]  ; dword to double
```

11.7 Floating point comparison

The IEEE 754 specification for floating point arithmetic includes 2 types of "Not a Number" or NaN. These 2 types are quiet NaNs and signaling NaNs. A quiet NaN (QNaN) is a value which can be safely propagated through code without raising an exception. A signaling NaN (SNaN) always raises an exception when it is generated. Perhaps you have witnessed a program failing with a divide by 0 error which is caused by a signal.

Floating point comparisons are considered to be either "ordered" or "unordered". An ordered comparison causes a floating point exception if either operand is a QNaN or SNaN. An unordered comparison causes an exception for only an SNaN. The gcc compiler uses unordered comparisons, so I will do the same.

The unordered floating point comparison instructions are `ucomiss` for comparing `floats` and `ucomisd` for comparing `doubles`. The first operand must be an XMM register, while the second operand can be memory or an XMM register. They set the zero flag, parity flag and carry flag to indicate the type of result: unordered (at least 1 operand is NaN), less than, equal or greater than. A conditional jump seems like a natural choice after a comparison, but we need some different instructions for floating point conditional jumps. It will look good to use an instruction like `jge` (jump if greater than or equal), but the effect is different from `jae` (jump if above or equal).

instruction	meaning	aliases	flags
jb	jump if $<$	jc jnae	CF=1
jbe	jump if $\leq$	jna	CF=1 or ZF=1
ja	jump if $>$	jnbe	ZF=0 and CF=0
jae	jump if $\geq$	jnc jnb	CF=0

Here is an example

```
movss    xmm0, [a]
mulss    xmm0, [b]
ucomiss  xmm0, [c]
jbe      less_eq      ; jmp if a*b <= c
```

11.8 Mathematical functions

The 8087 coprocessor implemented a useful collection of transcendental functions like sine, cosine and arctangent. These instructions still exist in the modern CPUs, but they use the floating point register stack and are no longer recommended. Instead efficient library functions exist for these functions.

The SSE instructions include floating point functions to compute minimum and maximum, perform rounding, and compute square roots and reciprocals of square roots.

Minimum and maximum

The minimum and maximum scalar instructions are `minss` and `maxss` to compute minimums and maximums for `float`s and `minsd` and `maxsd` to do the same for `double`s. The first operand (destination) must be an XMM register, while the second operand (source) can be either an XMM register or a memory location. The result is placed in the destination register.

There are packed versions of the minimum and maximum instructions: `minps`, `maxps`, `minpd` and `maxpd` which operate on either 4 `float`s (the ps versions) or 2 `double`s (the pd versions). The packed instructions require an XMM register for the first operand and either an XMM register or memory for the second. The `float` versions compute 4 results while the `double` versions compute 2 results.

```
movss  xmm0, [x]  ; move x into xmm0
maxss  xmm0, [y]  ; xmm0 has max(x,y)
movapd xmm0, [a]  ; move a[0], a[1] to xmm0
minpd  xmm0, [b]  ; xmm0[0] = min(a[0],b[0])
                  ; xmm0[1] = min(a[1],b[1])
```

Rounding

The SSE instructions include 4 instructions for rounding floating point numbers to whole numbers: `roundss` which rounds 1 `float`, `roundps` which rounds 4 `float`s, `roundsd` which rounds 1 `double` and `roundpd` which rounds 2 `double`s. The first operand must be an XMM register, while the second operand can be either an XMM register or a memory location. There is a third operand which selects a rounding mode. A simplified view of the possible rounding modes is in the table below:

mode	meaning
0	round, giving ties to even numbers
1	round up
2	round toward 0 (truncate)

Square roots

The SSE instructions include 4 square root instructions: `sqrtss` which computes 1 `float` square root, `sqrtps` which computes 4 `float` square roots, `sqrtsd` which computes 1 `double` square root and `sqrtpd` which computes 2 `double` square roots. As normal the first operand (destination) must be an XMM register, and the second operand can be either an XMM register or a memory location. Bounding to 16 byte boundaries is required for a packed instruction with a memory reference.

141

11.9 Sample code

Here we illustrate some of the instructions we have covered in some fairly practical functions.

Distance in 3D

We can compute distance in 3D using a function which accepts 2 float arrays with x, y and z coordinates. The 3D distance formula is

$$d = \sqrt{(x_1 - x_2)^2 + (y_1 - y_2)^2 + (z_1 - z_2)^2}$$

Here is assembly code for 3D distance:

```
distance3d:
        movss   xmm0, [rdi]     ; x of first point
        subss   xmm0, [rsi]     ; - x of second point
        mulss   xmm0, xmm0      ; (x1-x2)^2
        movss   xmm1, [rdi+4]   ; y of first point
        subss   xmm1, [rsi+4]   ; - y of second point
        mulss   xmm1, xmm1      ; (y1-y2)^2
        movss   xmm2, [rdi+8]   ; z of first point
        subss   xmm2, [rsi+8]   ; - z of second point
        mulss   xmm2, xmm2      ; (z1-z2)^2
        addss   xmm0, xmm1      ; add x and y parts
        addss   xmm0, xmm2      ; add z part
        sqrtss  xmm0, xmm0
        ret
```

Dot product of 3D vectors

The dot product of two 3D vectors is used frequently in graphics and is computed by

$$x_1 x_2 + y_1 y_2 + z_1 z_2$$

Here is a function computing the dot product of 2 float vectors passed as 2 arrays

```
dot_product:
        movss   xmm0, [rdi]     ; get x1
        mulss   xmm0, [rsi]     ; times x2
        movss   xmm1, [rdi+4]   ; get y1
        mulss   xmm1, [rsi+4]   ; times y2
        addss   xmm0, xmm1      ; x1*x2+y1*y2
        movss   xmm2, [rdi+8]   ; get z1
        mulss   xmm2, [rsi+8]   ; times z2
        addss   xmm0, xmm2      ; dot product
        ret
```

Polynomial evaluation

The evaluation of a polynomial of 1 variable could be done at least 2 ways. First is the obvious definition:

$$P(x) = p_0 + p_1 x + p_2 x^2 + \cdots + p_n x^n$$

A more efficient way to compute the value is using Horner's Rule:

$$
\begin{aligned}
b_n &= p_n \\
b_{n-1} &= p_{n-1} + b_n x \\
b_{n-2} &= p_{n-2} + b_{n-1} x \\
&\cdots \quad \cdots \\
b_0 &= p_0 + b_1 x
\end{aligned}
$$

Then $P(x) = b_0$.

Written as a function with an array of double coefficients as the first parameter (rdi), a value for x as the second parameter (xmm0) and the degree of the polynomial as the third parameter (rsi) we have:

```
horner:
        movsd   xmm1, xmm0          ; use xmm1 as x
        movsd   xmm0, [rdi+rsi*8]   ; xmm0 = b_k
        cmp     esi, 0              ; is the degree 0
        jz      done
more:
        sub     esi, 1
        mulsd   xmm0, xmm1          ; b_k * x
        addsd   xmm0, [rdi+rsi*8]   ; add p_k
        jnz     more
done:
        ret
```

143

Exercises

1. Write a program testing a function to compute $\sin x$. The formula for $\sin x$ is given as the Taylor's series:

$$\sin x = x - \frac{x^3}{3!} + \frac{x^5}{5!} - \frac{x^7}{7!} \cdots$$

Your function should work with doubles. Your program should read 2 numbers at a time using scanf. The first number is x and the second number is the number of terms of the expansion to compute. Your program should call your sine function and print the value it computes using scanf. The reading and computing should continue until scanf fails to return 2.

2. Write a program to compute the area of a polygon. You can use this formula for the area

$$A = \frac{1}{2} \sum_{i=0}^{n-1} (x_i y_{i+1} - x_{i+1} y_i)$$

Your area function should have 3 parameters. The first parameter is an array of doubles holding x values. The second is an array of doubles holding y values. The third is the value n. Your arrays should be size $n + 1$ and location n of both arrays should be repeats of location 0. The number of vertices will be read using scanf. Then your program should allocate arrays of size $n + 1$ and read the coordinates using scanf. Lastly your program should compute and print the area.

3. Write a program to approximate the definite integral of a polynomial function of degree 5 using the trapezoidal rule. A polynomial of degree 5 is defined by 6 coefficients $p_0, p_1, \cdots, p_5$, where

$$p(x) = p_0 + p_1 x + p_2 x^2 + p_3 x^3 + p_4 x^4 + p_5 x^5$$

The trapezoidal rule states that the integral from c to d of a function $f(x)$ can be approximated as

$$(d - c) \frac{f(c) + f(d)}{2}$$

To use this to get a good approximation you divide the interval from a to b into a collection of sub-intervals and use the trapezoidal rule on each sub-interval. Your program should read the values of a

and b. Then it should read the number of sub-intervals n. Last it should read the coefficients of the polynomial in the order p_0, p_1, $\cdots$ p_5. Then it should perform the computation and print the approximate integral.

4. Write a program to perform integration and differentiation of polynomials. The program should prompt for and read the degree of the polynomial. Then it should allocate arrays of the correct size for a polynomial, its derivative and its integral. Then the program should prompt for and read the coefficients of the polynomial. The last input will be two values from the domain, a and b. The program should evaluate and print the polynomial and its derivative at a and b. Last it should print the integral from a to b.

Chapter 12
System calls

A system call is essentially a function call which changes the CPU into kernel mode and executes a function which is part of the kernel. When you run a process on Linux it runs in user mode which means that it is limited to executing only "safe" instructions. It can move data within the program, do arithmetic, do branching, call functions, ... , but there are instructions which your program can't do directly. For example it would be unsafe to allow any program to read or write directly to the disk device, so this is avoided by preventing user programs from executing input or output instructions. Another prohibited action is directly setting page mapping registers.

When a user program needs to do something like open a disk file, it makes a system call. This changes the CPU's operating mode to kernel mode where the CPU can execute input and output instructions. The kernel open call will verify that the user program has permission to open the file and then open it, performing any input or output instructions required on behalf of the program

The Linux system call interface is different for 32 bit mode and 64 bit mode. Under 64 bit Linux the 32 bit interface is still available to support 32 bit applications and this will work to some extent for 64 bit programs.

12.1 32 bit Linux system calls

Each system call is defined in "/usr/include/asm/unistd_32.h". To execute the system call you must place the system call number in register eax and use the software interrupt instruction to effect the call: int 0x80. System calls have parameters which are placed in registers ebx, ecx, edx, esi, edi, and ebp. Return values are placed in eax.

Here is a system call to write to stdout:

```
    segment .data
hello:
```

```
        db        "Hello world!",0x0a
        segment .text
        ...
        mov       eax, 4       ; syscall 4 is write (Linux)
        mov       ebx, 1       ; file descriptor
        lea       ecx, [hello] ; array to write
        mov       rdx, 13      ; write 13 bytes
        int       0x80
```

OS X also supports 32 bit system calls and uses int 0x80 like Linux with the system call number in eax. However the parameters are passed on the stack rather than in registers. The system calls are different numbers than for Linux.

12.2 64 bit Linux system calls

The system calls for 64 bit Linux are different integers than for 32 bit Linux and are defined in "/usr/include/asm/unistd_64.h". Again the system calls use registers for parameters, though the registers are different. The system call number is placed in rax and the parameters are placed in rdi, rsi, rdx, r10, r8 and r9. Return values are placed in rax. The registers are the same as in C function calls except that r10 has replaced rcx for parameter 4.

Instead of using the software interrupt instruction, x86-64 Linux uses the syscall instruction to execute a system call. Here is the 64 bit version of "Hello world":

```
        segment .data
  hello:
        db        "Hello world!",0x0a
        segment .text
        global _start
_start:
        mov       eax, 1       ; syscall 1 is write
        mov       edi, 1       ; file descriptor
        lea       rsi, [hello] ; array to write
        mov       edx, 13      ; write 13 bytes
        syscall
        mov       eax, 60      ; syscall 60 is exit
        xor       edi, edi     ; exit(0)
        syscall
```

12.3 64 bit OS X system calls

OS X uses the same 64 bit system call ABI as Linux. There is a difference in the way OS X handles system call numbers. The Linux system call numbers are small numbers, while OS X adds 0x2000000 to the common

147

system calls. The reason is that OS X has 4 different classes of system calls, each identified by bits 23-25 of rax. Here are the different classes.

offset	class
0x1000000	Mach
0x2000000	UNIX/BSD
0x3000000	Machine dependent
0x4000000	Diagnostic

The OS X system calls are identified in /usr/include/sys/syscall.h, though without the 0x2000000 offset.

12.4 C wrapper functions

The *lingua franca* of UNIX is C, so every system call is usable via a C wrapper function. For example there is a write function in the C library which does very little other than use the syscall instruction to perform the write request. Using these functions rather than the explicit syscall instruction is the preferred way to use the system calls. You won't have to worry about finding the numbers and you won't have to cope with the slightly different register usage.

The Linux and OS X system calls are documented in section 2 of the on-line manual, so you can use

```
man 2 write
```

to learn how to use the write system call wrapper. I tend to call this the write system call for simplicity.

The previous "Hello world" program can be rewritten using write and exit as

```
        segment .data
msg:    db      "Hello World!",0x0a
len:    equ     $-msg          ; Length of the string
        segment .text
        global  main
        extern  write, exit
main:
        mov     edx, len       ; Arg 3 is the length
        mov     rsi, msg       ; Arg 2 is the array
        mov edi, 1             ; Arg 1 is the fd
        call    write
        xor edi, edi           ; 0 return = success
        call    exit
```

Here you will notice that I have used a yasm equate to define len to be the current assembly point, $, minus the address of msg. equ is a pseudo-op which defines a symbolic name for an expression. This saves the

148

trouble of counting characters and insulates the program from slight changes.

You might also have noticed the use of `extern` to tell the linker that `write` and `exit` are to be defined in some other place, in this case from the C library.

open system call

In order to read and write a file, it must be opened. For ordinary files this is done using the `open` system call:

```
int open ( char *pathname, int flags [, int mode ] );
```

The `pathname` is a C string (character array terminated with a 0 byte). The `flags` are a set of bit patterns which are or'ed together to define how the file is to be opened: read-only mode, write mode or read-write mode and other characteristics like whether the file is to be created. If the file is to be created the `mode` parameter defines the permissions to assign to the new file.

The `flags` are defined in the table below:

bits	meaning
0	read-only
1	write-only
2	read and write
0x40	create if needed
0x200	truncate the file
0x400	append

The basic permissions are read, write and execute. A process must have read permission to read an object, write permission to write it, and execute permission to execute it. Execute permission for a file means that the file (either a program or a script) can be executed. Execute permission for a directory allows traversal of the directory.

These three permissions are granted or denied for 3 categories of accounts: user, group and other. When a user logs in to a Linux system the user's shell is assigned the user's user-id which is an integer identifying the user. In addition the user has a group-id (also an integer) which identifies the user as being in a particular group of users. A user can belong to multiple groups though only one is the active group. You can use the "id" command in the shell to print your user-id, group-id and the list of groups you belong to.

The basic permissions are 3 permissions for 3 groups. The permissions are 1 bit each for read, write and execute. This makes an ideal situation for using octal numbers. One octal "digit" represents 3 bits. Using 9 bits you can specify the basic permissions for user, group and others. Using yasm an octal number can be represented by a sequence of digits ending in either "o" or "q". Thus you could specify permissions for read and write for the user as 6, read for the group as 4 and no permissions for others as 0. Putting all these together we get 640o.

The return value from open is a file descriptor if the value is greater than or equal to 0. An error is indicated by a negative return. A file descriptor is an integer identifying the connection made by open. File descriptors start at 0 and increase for each opened file. Here is some code to open a file:

```
        segment .data
fd:     dd       0
name:   db       "sample",0
        segment .text
        extern  open
        lea     rdi, [name] ; pathname
        mov     esi, 0x42   ; read-write|create
        mov     rdx, 600o   ; read-write for me
        call    open
        cmp     eax, 0
        jl      error       ; failed to open
        mov     [fd], eax
```

read and write system calls

The system calls to read and write data to files are read and write. Their prototypes are quite similar:

```
int read(int fd, void *data, long count);
int write(int fd, void *data, long count);
```

The data array can be any type of data. Whatever the type is, the count is the number of bytes to read or write. Both functions return the number of bytes read or written. An error is indicated by returning -1 and setting the extern variable errno to an integer indicating the type of error. You can use the perror function call to print a text version of the error.

lseek system call

When reading or writing files, it is sometimes necessary to position to a specific spot in the file before reading or writing. An example would be writing record number 1000 from a file with records which are 512 bytes each. Assuming that record numbers begin with 0, then record 1000 would start at byte position $1000 * 512 = 512000$. It can be very quick to position to 512000 and write 512 bytes. This is also easier than reading and writing the whole file.

150

The lseek system call allows you to set the current position for reading or writing in a file. Its prototype is

```
long lseek(int fd, long offset, int whence);
```

The offset parameter is frequently simply the byte position in the file, but the meaning of offset depends on the value of whence. If whence is 0, then offset is the byte position. If whence is 1, then offset is relative to the current position. If whence is 2, then offset is relative to the end of file. The return value from lseek is the position of the next read or write for the file.

Using lseek with offset 0 and whence equal to 2, lseek will return a byte position 1 greater than the last byte of the file. This is an easy way to determine the file size. Knowing the size, you could allocate an array and read the entire file (as long as you have enough RAM).

```
mov     rdi, [fd]
xor     esi, esi      ; set offset to 0
mov     edx, 2        ; set whence to 2
call    lseek         ; determine file size
mov     [size], rax
mov     rdi, rax
call    malloc        ; allocate an array
mov     [data], rax
mov     rdi, [fd]
xor     esi, esi      ; set offset to 0
xor     edx, edx      ; set whence to 0
call    lseek         ; seek to start of file
mov     rdi, [fd]
mov     rsi, [data]
mov     rdx, [size]
call    read          ; read the entire file
```

With both 64 bit Linux and OS X, lseek uses a 64 bit integer for the offset parameter and this makes it possible to seek to positions greater than 2^{32}. Doing the same with 32 bit Linux would require using lseek64.

close system call

When you are done reading or writing a file you should close it. The only parameter for the close system call is the file descriptor for the file to close. If you exit a program without closing a file, it will be closed by the operating system. Data read or written using file descriptors is not buffered in the user program, so there will not be any unwritten data which might be lost. This is not true for using FILE pointers which can result in lost data if there is no close. The biggest advantages to closing files are that it reduces overhead in the kernel and avoids running into the per-process limit on the number of open files.

```
mov     edi, [fd]
call    close
```

Exercises

1. Write a copy program using syscall and a second copy program using the equivalent library wrapper functions. Your copy program should accept 2 file names and an integer on the command line. The first name is the name of the input file and the second is the name of the output file. The number on the command line is the number of bytes to allocate for an array for input and output. Making the size a multiple of 4096 bytes will make a very slight performance improvement. You might experiment to discover which size works more rapidly for your tests. The challenge is that for many files, both input and output files will fit in buffer cache and there will be no actual disk I/O required to read the file and the writing will be delayed. Can you measure the difference in time between the syscall version and the library version?

2. Write a program which processes a collection of files named on the command line. For each file the program should print the number of bytes, words and lines much like the wc program does.

3. Write a program which expects 2 strings on the command line. The first string is a string to find and the second is the name of a file to search through for the string. The program should print all matching lines. This is a greatly simplified version of grep.

Chapter 13
Structs

It is fairly simple to use structs compatible with C by defining a struct in yasm. A struct is a compound object which can have data items of different types. Let's consider the C struct Customer:

```
struct Customer {
    int  id;
    char name[64];
    char address[64];
    int  balance;
};
```

We could access the customer data using assembly code assuming that we know the offsets for each item of the struct.

```
mov   rdi, 136      ; size of a Customer
call  malloc
mov   [c], rax      ; save the address
mov   [rax], dword 7; set the id
lea   rdi, [rax+4]  ; name field
lea   rsi, [name]   ; name to copy to struc
call  strcpy
mov   rax, [c]
lea   rdi, [rax+68] ; address field
lea   rsi, [address]; address to copy
call  strcpy
mov   rax, [c]
mov   edx, [balance]
mov   [rax+132], edx
```

13.1 Symbolic names for offsets

Well that was certainly effective but using specific numbers for offsets within a struct is not really ideal. Any changes to the structure will require code modification and errors might be made adding up the offsets. It is better to have yasm assist you with structure definition. The yasm keyword for starting a struct is "struc". Struct components are defined between "struc" and "endstruc". Here is the definition of Customer:

```
        struc   Customer
id      resd    1
name    resb    64
address resb    64
balance resd    1
        endstruc
```

Using this definition gives us the same effect as using equ to set symbolic names for the offsets. These names are globally available, so you would not be permitted to have id in multiple structs. Instead you can prefix each of these names with a period like this:

```
         struc    Customer
.id      resd     1
.name    resb     64
.address resb     64
.balance resd     1
         endstruc
```

Now you must use "Customer.id" to refer to the offset of the id field. A good compromise is to prefix the field names with a short abbreviation of the struct name. In addition to giving symbolic names to the offsets, yasm will also define Customer_size to be the number of bytes in the struct. This makes it easy to allocate memory for the struct. Below is a program to initialize a struct from separate variables.

```
          segment .data
name      db      "Calvin", 0
address   db      "12 Mockingbird Lane",0
balance   dd      12500
          struc   Customer
c_id      resd    1
c_name    resb    64
c_address resb    64
c_balance resd    1
          endstruc
c         dq      0
          segment .text
          global  main
          extern  malloc, strcpy
main:
          push    rbp
          mov     rbp, rsp
          sub     rsp, 32
          mov     rdi, Customer_size
          call    malloc
          mov     [c], rax        ; save the pointer
          mov     [rax+c_id], dword 7
          lea     rdi, [rax+c_name]
          lea     rsi, [name]
          call    strcpy
          mov     rax, [c]        ; restore the pointer
          lea     rdi, [rax+c_address]
          lea     rsi, [address]
          call    strcpy
```

```
        mov     rax, [c]        ; restore the pointer
        mov     edx, [balance]
        mov     [rax+c_balance], edx
        xor     eax, eax
        leave
        ret
```

Now this is all great but there is a possible alignment problem versus
C if we make the address field 1 byte larger. In C this makes the offset of
balance increase from 132 to 136. In yasm it increases from 132 to 133. It
still works but the struct definition does not match the alignment of C. To
do so we must place align 4 before the definition of c_balance.

Another possibility is to have a static variable of type Customer. To do
this with default data, simply use this:

```
c       istruc  Customer
        iend
```

If you wish to define the fields, define them all in order.

```
c       istruc  Customer
        at c_id, dd 7
        at c_name, db "Calvin", 0
        at c_address, db "12 Mockingbird Lane", 0
        at c_balance, dd 12500
        iend
```

13.2 Allocating and using an array of structs

If you wish to allocate an array of structs, then you need to multiply the
size of the struct times the number of elements to allocate enough space.
But the size given by Customer_size might not match the value from
sizeof(struct Customer) in C. C will align each data item on
appropriate boundaries and will report a size which will result in each
element of an array having aligned fields. You can assist yasm by adding
a terminal align x where x represents the size of the largest data item in
the struct. If the struct has any quad word fields then you need align 8
to force the _size value to be a multiple of 8. If the struct has no quad
word byte fields but has some double word fields you need align 4.
Similarly you might need align 2 if there are any word fields.

So our code to declare a struct (slightly changed) and allocate an array
would look like this

```
                segment .data
                struc   Customer
c_id            resd    1       ; 4 bytes
c_name          resb    65      ; 69 bytes
c_address       resb    65      ; 134 bytes
                align   4       ; aligns to 136
c_balance       resd    1       ; 140 bytes
c_rank          resb    1       ; 141 bytes
```

```
          align   4      ; aligns to 144
          endstruc
customers dq      0
          segment .text
          mov   edi, 100 ; for 100 structs
          mul   edi, Customer_size
          call  malloc
          mov   [customers], rax
```

Now to work with each array element we can start with a register holding the value of customers and add Customer_size to the register after we process each customer.

```
          segment .data
format    db     "%s %s %d",0x0a,0
          segment .text
          push  r15
          push  r14

;         We're using r14 and r15 since
;         they are preserved through calls

          mov   r15, 100        ; loop counter
          mov   r14, [customers]
more      lea   edi, [format]
          lea   esi, [r14+c_name]
          lea   rdx, [r14+c_address]
          mov   rcx. [r14+c_balance]
          call  printf
          add   r14, Customer_size
          sub   r15, 1
          jnz   more

;         r14 and r15 must be restored
;         for the calling function

          pop   r14
          pop   r15
          ret
```

Exercises

1. Design a struct to represent a set. The struct will hold the maximum set size and a pointer to an array holding 1 bit per possible element of the set. Members of the set will be integers from 0 to the set size minus 1. Write a test program to read commands which operate on the set. The commands will be "add", "remove", and "test". Each command will have an integer parameter entered with it. Your program will then be able to add elements to the set, remove elements to the set and test numbers for membership.

2. Using the design for sets from exercise 1, write a program to manipulate multiple sets. Implement commands "add", "union", "print" and "intersect". Create 10 sets with size equal to 10000. "add s k" will add k to set s. "union s t" will replace set s with $s \cup t$. "intersect s t" will replace set s with $x \cap t$. "print s" will print the elements of s.

3. Design a struct to represent large integers. For simplicity use quad word arrays as the data for the large integers. Each quad word will represent 18 digits of the number. So 1 quad word can store a number up to 999,999,999,999,999,999. 2 quad words can store a number up to 999,999,999,999,999,999,999,999,999,999,999,999. Implement only positive numbers. Implement addition and multiplication (based on addition). Compute 50!. You are permitted to write a main routine and the factorial function in C or C++ using assembly code to perform all long arithmetic.

157

Chapter 14
Using the C stream I/O functions

The functions callable from C include a wide variety of functions in many areas including process management, file handling, network communications, string processing and graphics programming. Studying much of these capabilities would lead us too far afield from the study of assembly language. The stream input and output facilities provide an example of a higher level library which is also quite useful in many programs.

In the chapter on system calls we focused on open, read, write and close which are merely wrapper functions for system calls. In this chapter we will focus on a similar collection of functions which perform buffered I/O. Buffered I/O means that the application maintains a data buffer for each open file.

Reading using a buffered I/O system can be more efficient. Let's suppose you ask the buffered I/O system to read 1 byte. It will attempt to read 1 byte from the buffer of already read data. If it must read, then it reads enough bytes to fill its buffer - typically 8192 bytes. This means that 8192 reads of 1 byte can be satisfied by 1 actual system call. Reading a byte from the buffer is very fast. In fact reading a large file is over 20 times as fast reading 1 byte at a time using the C stream getchar function compared to reading one byte at a time using read.

You should be aware that the operating system also uses buffers for open files. When you call read to read 1 byte, the operating system is forced by the disk drive to read complete sectors, so it must read at least 1 sector (probably 512 bytes). Most likely the operating system reads 4096 bytes and saves the data which has been read in order to make use of the data in subsequent reads. If the operating system did not use buffers, reading 1 byte at a time would require interacting with the disk for each byte which would be perhaps 10 to 20 times slower than using the buffer.

The net result from this discussion is that if your program needs to read or write small quantities of data, it will be faster to use the stream I/O facilities rather than using the system calls. It is generally possible to use the system calls and do your own buffering which is tailored for your needs thereby saving time. You will of course pay for this improved efficiency by working harder. You must weigh the importance of improved performance versus increased labor.

14.1 Opening a file

The function to open a file using the stream I/O functions is fopen. It, like the other stream I/O functions, begins with the letter "f" to make the name distinct from the system call wrapper function it resembles. The prototype for fopen is

```
FILE *fopen ( char *pathname, char *mode );
```

The file to be opened is named in the first parameter and the mode is named in the second parameter. The mode can be any of the values from the table below

mode	meaning
r	read-only
r+	read and write, truncates or creates
w	write-only, truncates or creates
w+	read and write, truncates or creates
a	write only, appends or creates
a+	read and write, appends or creates

The return value is a pointer to a FILE object. This is an opaque pointer in the sense than you never need to know the components of the FILE object. Most likely a FILE object is a struct which contains a pointer to the buffer for the file and various "house-keeping" data items about the file. This pointer is used in the other stream I/O functions. In assembly language it is sufficient to simply store the pointer in a quad-word and use that quad-word as needed for function calls. Here is some code to open a file:

```
        segment .data
name    db      "customers.dat",0
mode    db      "w+",0
fp      dq      0
        segment .text
        global  fopen
        lea     rdi, [name]
        lea     rsi, [mode]
```

159

```
call    fopen
mov     [fp], rax
```

14.2 fscanf and fprintf

You have encountered scanf and printf in previous code. scanf is a
function which calls fscanf with a FILE pointer named stdin as its first
parameter, while printf is a function which calls fprintf with FILE
pointer stdout as its first parameter. The only difference between these
pairs of functions is that fscanf and fprintf can work with any FILE
pointer. Their prototypes are

```
int fscanf( FILE *fp, char *format, ... );
int fprintf( FILE *fp, char *format, ... );
```

For simple use consult Appendix B which discusses scanf and printf.
For more information use "man fscanf" or "man fprintf" or consult a C
book.

14.3 fgetc and fputc

If you need to process data character by character, it can be convenient to
use fgetc to read characters and fputc to write characters. Their
prototypes are

```
int fgetc ( FILE *fp );
int fputc ( int c, FILE *fp );
```

The return value of fgetc is the character which has been read, except
for end of file or errors when it returns the symbolic value EOF which is -
1. The function fputc writes the character provided in c to the file. It
returns the same character it has written unless there is an error when it
returns EOF.

Fairly often it is convenient to get a character and do something which
depends on the character read. For some characters you may need to give
control over to another function. This can be simplified by giving the
character back to the file stream using ungetc. You are guaranteed only
1 pushed back character, but having 1 character of look-ahead can be
quite useful. The prototype for ungetc is

```
int ungetc ( int c, FILE *fp );
```

Below is a loop copying a file from one stream to another using fgetc
and fputc.

```
more:   mov     rdi, [ifp]   ; input file pointer
        call    fgetc
        cmp     eax, -1
        je      done
        mov     rdi, rax
        mov     rsi, [ofp]   ; output file pointer
        call    fputc
        jmp     more
done:
```

14.4 fgets and fputs

Another common need is to read lines of input and process them line by line. The function fgets reads 1 line of text (or less if the array is too small) and fputs writes 1 line of text. Their prototypes are

```
char *fgets(char *s, int size, FILE *fp);
int fputs(char *s, FILE *fp);
```

The first parameter to fgets is an array of characters to receive the line of data and the second parameter is the size of the array. The size is passed into the function to prevent buffer overflow. fgets will read up to size - 1 characters into the array. It stops reading when it hits a new-line character or end of file. If it reads a new-line it stores the new-line in the buffer. Whether it reads a complete line or not, fgets always places a 0 byte at the end of the data it has read. It returns s on success and a NULL pointer on error or end of file.

fputs writes the string in s without the 0 byte at the end of the string. It is your responsibility to place any required new-lines in the array and add the 0 byte at the end. It returns a non-negative number on success or EOF on error.

It can be quite useful following fgets to use sscanf to read data from the array. sscanf is like scanf except that the first parameter is an array of characters which it will attempt to convert in the same fashion as scanf. Using this pattern gives you an opportunity to read the data with sscanf, determine that the data was not what you expected and read it again with sscanf with a different format string.

Here is some code which copies lines of text from one stream to another, skipping lines which start with a ";"

```
more:   lea     rdi, [s]
        mov     esi, 200
        mov     rdx, [ifp]
        call    fgets
        cmp     rax, 0
        je      done
        mov     al, [s]
        cmp     al, ';'
        je      more
```

```
        lea     rdi, [s]
        mov     rsi, [ofp]
        call    fputs
        jmp     more
done:
```

14.5 fread and fwrite

The fread and fwrite functions are designed to read and write arrays of data. Their prototypes are

```
int fread(void *p, int size, int nelts, FILE *fp);
int fwrite(void *p, int size, int nelts, FILE *fp);
```

The first parameter to these functions is an array of any type. The next parameter is the size of each element of the array, while the third is the number of array elements to read or write. They return the number of array elements read or written. In the event of an error or end of file, the return value might be less than nelts or 0.

Here is some code to write all 100 elements of the customers array to a disk file

```
        mov     rdi, [customers] ; allocated array
        mov     esi, Customer_size
        mov     edx, 100
        mov     rcx, [fp]
        call    fwrite
```

14.5 fseek and ftell

Positioning a stream is done using the fseek function, while ftell is used to determine the current position. The prototype for these functions are

```
int fseek ( FILE *fp, long offset, int whence );
long ftell ( FILE *fp );
```

The second parameter, offset, of fseek is a byte position value which is dependent on the third parameter, whence, to define its meaning. The meaning of whence is exactly like in lseek. If whence is 0, then offset is the byte position. If whence is 1, then offset is relative to the current position. If whence is 2, then offset is relative to the end of file.

The return value of fseek is 0 for success and -1 for errors. If there is an error the variable errno is set appropriately. The return value of ftell is the current byte position in the file unless there is an error. On error it returns -1.

Here is a function to write a Customer record to a file.

```
;       void write_customer(FILE *fp, struct Customer *c,
;                           int record_number );
        segment .text
        global  write_customer write_customer:
```

```
.fp    equ    0
.c     equ    8
.rec   equ    16
       push   rbp
       mov    rbp, rsp
       sub    rsp, 32          ; space for parameters
       mov    [rsp+.fp], rdi   ; save parameters
       mov    [rsp+.c], rsi
       mov    [rsp+.rec], rdx
       mul    rdx, Customer_size
       mov    rsi, rdx         ; offset for ftell
       mov    rdx, 0           ; whence
       call   ftell            ; position file
       mov    rdi, [rsp+.c]
       mov    rsi, Customer_size
       mov    rdx, 1
       mov    rcx, [rsp+.fp]
       call   fwrite           ; write the record
       leave
       ret
```

14.6 fclose

fclose is used to close a stream. This is important since a stream may have data in its buffer which needs to be written. This data will be written when you call fclose and will be forgotten if you fail to call it. A FILE pointer is the only parameter to fclose.

Exercises

1. Write an assembly program which will create a new Customer using the struct definition from this chapter. Your program should prompt for and read the file name, the customer name, address, balance and rank fields. Then your code should scan the data in the file looking for an empty position. An empty position is a record with 0 in the id field. In general the id value will be 1 greater than the record number for a record. If there is no empty record, then add a new record at the end of the file. Report the customer's id.

2. Write an assembly program to update the balance for a customer. The program should accept from the command line the name of a data file, a customer id and an amount to add to the balance for that customer. The customer's id is 1 greater than the record number. Report an error if the customer record is unused (id = 0).

3. Write an assembly program to read the customer data in a file, sort it by balance and print the data in increasing balance order. You should open the file and use fseek to seek to the end and use ftell to determine the number of records in the file. It should allocate an array large enough to hold the entire file, read the records one at a time, skipping past the unused records (id = 0). Then it should sort using qsort. You can call qsort using

   ```
   qsort(struct Customer *c, int count, int size, compare);
   ```

   The count parameter is the number of structs to sort and size is the size of each in bytes. The compare parameter is the address of a function which will accept 2 parameters, each a pointer to a struct Customer. This function will compare the balance fields of the 2 structs and return a negative, 0, or positive value based on the order of the 2 balances.

Chapter 15
Data structures

Data structures are widely used in application programming. They are frequently used for algorithmic purposes to implement structures like stacks, queues and heaps. They are also used to implement data storage based on a key, referred to as a "dictionary". In this chapter we discuss implementing linked lists, hash tables, doubly-linked lists and binary trees in assembly.

One common feature of all these data structures is the use of a structure called a "node" which contains data and one or more pointers to other nodes. The memory for these nodes will be allocated using malloc.

15.1 Linked lists

A linked list is a structure composed of a chain of nodes. Below is an illustration of a linked list:

You can see that the list has 4 nodes. Each node has a data value and a pointer to another node. The last node of the list has a NULL pointer (value 0), which is illustrated as a filled circle. The list itself is represented as a pointer. We can illustrate the list more completely by placing the list's first pointer in a box and giving it a name:

list

This list has no obvious order to the data values in the nodes. It is either unordered or possibly ordered by time of insertion. It is very easy to insert a new node at the start of a list, so the list could be in decreasing time of insertion order.

The list is referenced using the pointer stored at the memory location labeled list. The nodes on the list are not identified with specific labels in the code which maintains and uses the list. The only way to access these nodes is by using the pointers in the list.

List node structure

Our list node will have 2 fields: a data value and a pointer to the next node. The yasm structure definition is

```
        struc   node
n_value resq    1
n_next  resq    1
        align   8
        endstruc
```

The alignment instruction is not needed with 2 quad-words in the structure, but it may protect us from confusion later.

Creating an empty list

The first decision in designing a container structure is how to represent an empty container. In this linked list design we will take the simplest choice of using a NULL pointer as an empty list. Despite this simplicity it may be advantageous to have a function to create an empty list.

```
newlist:
        xor     eax, eax
        ret
```

Inserting a number into a list

The decision to implement an empty list as a NULL pointer leaves a small issue for insertion. Each insertion will be at the start of the list which means that there will be a new pointer stored in the list start pointer for each insertion. There are 2 possible ways to cope with this. One way is to pass the address of the pointer into the insertion function. A second way is to have the insertion pointer return the new pointer and leave it to the insertion code to assign the new pointer upon return. It is less confusing to dodge the address of a pointer problem. Here is the insertion code:

```
;   list = insert ( list, k );
insert:
.list equ     0
.k    equ     8
      push rbp
      mov  rbp, rsp
      sub  rsp, 16
      mov  [rsp+.list], rdi  ; save list pointer
```

```
        mov   [rsp+.k], rsi       ; and k on stack
        mov   edi, node_size
        call  malloc              ; rax = node pointer
        mov   r8, [rsp+.list]     ; get list pointer
        mov   [rax+n_next], r8    ; save list pointer in new node
        mov   r9, [rsp+.k]        ; get k
        mov   [rax+n_value], r9   ; save k in node
        leave
        ret
```

Traversing the list

Traversing the list requires using an instruction like

```
        mov       rbx, [rbx+n_next]
```

to advance from a pointer to one node to a pointer to the next node. We start by inspecting the pointer to see if it is NULL. If it is not then we enter the loop. After processing a node we advance the pointer and repeat the loop if the pointer is not NULL. The print function below traverses the list and prints each data item. The code shows a good reason why it is nice to have a few registers protected in calls. We depend on rbx being preserved by printf.

```
print:
        segment .data
.print_fmt:
        db    "%ld ",0
.newline:
        db    0x0a,0
        segment .text
.rbx    equ     0
        push  rbp
        mov   rbp, rsp
        sub   rsp, 16
        mov   [rsp+.rbx], rbx     ; save old rbx
        cmp   rdi, 0              ; skip the loop if
        je    .done              ; list pointer == 0
        mov   rbx, rdi           ; get first node
.more:
        lea   rdi, [.print_fmt]
        mov   rsi, [rbx+n_value]
        xor   eax, eax
        call  printf             ; print node value
        mov   rbx, [rbx+n_next]   ; p = p->next
        cmp   rbx, 0             ; end the loop if
        jne   .more             ; node pointer == 0
.done:
        lea   rdi, [.newline]
        xor   eax, eax
        call  printf             ; print a new-line
        mov   rbx, [rsp+.rbx]     ; restore rbx
        leave
        ret
```

167

Last we have a main function which creates a list, reads values using scanf, inserts the values into the list and prints the list after each insertion.

```
main:
.list   equ     0
.k      equ     8
        segment .data
.scanf_fmt:
        db      "%ld",0
        segment .text
        push    rbp
        mov     rbp, rsp
        sub     rsp, 16
        call    newlist         ; create a list
        mov     [rsp+.list], rax
.more   lea     rdi, [.scanf_fmt]
        lea     rsi, [rsp+.k]
        xor     eax, eax
        call    scanf           ; read k
        cmp     rax, 1          ; if the read fails return
        jne     .done
        mov     rdi, [rsp+.list]
        mov     rsi, [rsp+.k]
        call    insert          ; insert k
        mov     [rsp+.list], rax
        mov     rdi, rax
        call    print           ; print the list
        jmp     .more
.done   leave
        ret
```

Here is a sample session using the program, entering the numbers 1 through 5 (input in boldface):

1
1

2
2 1

3
3 2 1

4
4 3 2 1

5
5 4 3 2 1

You can see the most recently printed number is at the first of the list. By adding a function to get and remove (pop) the first element of the list, we could turn this into a stack. This is one of the exercises for this chapter.

15.2 Doubly-linked lists

A doubly-linked list has 2 pointers for each node: one points to the next node and one points to the previous node. It becomes quite simple to manage a doubly-linked list if you make the list circular and if you retain an unused cell at the start of the list. Here is an example list with 4 data nodes:

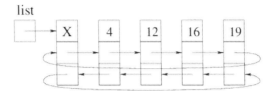

We see that the variable list points to the first node of the list, called the "head node". The head node has a value, but we never use the value. The top pointer in each node points to the next node in the list and the bottom pointer points to the previous node in the list. The previous pointer of the head node is the last node in the list. This makes this list capable of implementing a stack (last-in first-out), a queue (first-in first-out) or a double-ended queue (deque). The primary advantage of this design is that the list is never really empty - it can be logically empty but the head node remains. Furthermore, once a list is created, the pointer to the head node never changes.

Doubly-linked list node structure

Our list node will have 3 fields: a data value, a pointer to the next node and a pointer to the previous node. The yasm structure definition is

```
        struc   node
n_value resq    1
n_next  resq    1
n_prev  resq    1
        align   8
        endstruc
```

Creating a new list

The code for creating a new doubly-linked list allocates a new node and sets its next and previous pointers to itself. The calling function receives a pointer which does not change during the execution of the program. Here is the creation code:

```
;       list = newlist();
newlist:
        push    rbp
```

169

```
        mov     rbp, rsp
        mov     edi, node_size
        call    malloc
        mov     [rax+n_next], rax   ; head points forward
        mov     [rax+n_prev], rax   ; and back to itself
        leave
        ret
```

When it returns the empty list looks like the diagram below:

Inserting at the front of the list

To insert a new node at the front of the list you need to place the head node's next pointer in the new node's next slot and place the head pointer into the new node's previous slot. After doing that you can make the head node point forward to the new node and make the head's former next point backwards to the new node. These steps are illustrated in the diagram below. The old links are in dashed lines and the new links are numbered, with bold lines.

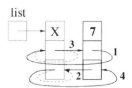

One of the elegant features of the doubly-linked circular list is the elimination of special cases. Inserting the first node is done with exactly the same code as inserting any other node.

The code for insertion is

```
;    insert ( list, k );
insert:
.list equ   0
.k      equ   8
        push  rbp
        mov   rbp, rsp
        sub   rsp, 16
        mov   [rsp+.list], rdi   ; save list pointer
        mov   [rsp+.k], rsi      ; and k on stack
        mov   edi, node_size
        call  malloc             ; rax = new node
        mov   r8, [rsp+.list]    ; get list pointer
        mov   r9, [r8+n_next]    ; get head's next
        mov   [rax+n_next], r9   ; p->next = h->next
        mov   [rax+n_prev], r8   ; p->prev = h
        mov   [r8+n_next], rax   ; h->next = p
        mov   [r9+n_prev], rax   ; p->next->prev = p
```

```
        mov    r9, [rsp+.k]        ; get k
        mov    [rax+n_value], r9 ; save k in node
        leave
        ret
```

List traversal

List traversal of a doubly-linked list is somewhat similar to traversal of a
singly-linked list. We do need to skip past the head node and we need to
test the current pointer against the pointer to the head node to detect the
end of the list. Here is the code for printing the list:

```
;    print ( list );
print:
        segment .data
.print_fmt:
        db     "%ld ",0
.newline:
        db     0x0a,0
        segment .text
.list equ   0
.rbx  equ   8
        push   rbp
        mov    rbp, rsp
        sub    rsp, 16
        mov    [rsp+.rbx], rbx   ; save rbx
        mov    [rsp+.list], rdi ; keep head pointer
        mov    rbx, [rdi+n_next]; get first node
        cmp    rbx, [rsp+.list] ; if it's head node
        je     .done            ; the list is empty
.more:
        lea    rdi, [.print_fmt]
        mov    rsi, [rbx+n_value]
        call   printf           ; print node value
        mov    rbx, [rbx+n_next]; get next node
        cmp    rbx, [rsp+.list] ; if it's head node
        jne    .more            ; end the loop
.done:
        lea    rdi, [.newline]
        call   printf           ; print a newline
        mov    rbx, [rsp+.rbx]  ; restore rbx
        leave
        ret
```

15.3 Hash tables

A hash table is an efficient way to implement a dictionary. The basic idea
is that you compute a hash value for the key for each item in the
dictionary. The purpose of the hash value is to spread the keys throughout
an array. A perfect hash function would map each key to a unique location
in the array used for hashing, but this is difficult to achieve. Instead we
must cope with keys which "collide".

The simplest way to cope with collisions is to use a linked list for each location in the hash array. Consider the illustration below:

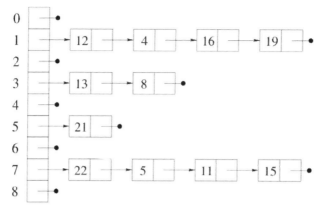

In this hash table, keys 12, 4, 16 and 9 all have hash values of 1 and are placed on the list in location 1 of the hash array. Keys 13 and 8 both have hash values 3 and are placed on the list in location 3 of the array. The remaining keys are mapped to 5 and 7.

One of the critical issues with hashing is to develop a good hashing function. A hashing function should appear almost random. It must compute the same value for a particular key each time it is called for the key, but the hash values aren't really important - it's the distribution of keys onto lists which matters. We want a lot of short lists. This means that the array size should be at least as large as the number of keys expected. Then, with a good hash function, the chains will generally be quite short.

A good hash function for integers

It is generally recommended that a hash table size be a prime number. However this is not very important if there is no underlying pattern to the numbers used as keys. In that case you can simply use n mod t where n is the key and t is the array size. If there is a pattern like many multiples of the same number, then using a prime number for t makes sense.

Here is the hash function for the example code:

```
;           i = hash ( n );
  hash      mov
            rax, rdi
            and      rax, 0xff
            ret
```

The table size is 256 in the example, so using and gives n mod 256.

A good hash function for strings

A good hash function for strings is to treat the string as containing polynomial coefficients and evaluate $p(n)$ for some prime number n. In the code below we use the prime number 191 in the evaluation. After evaluating the polynomial value, you can perform a modulus operation using the table size (100000 in the sample code).

```
int hash ( unsigned char *s )
{
    unsigned long h = 0;
    int i = 0;
    while ( s[i] ) {
        h = h*191 + s[i];
        i++;
    }
    return h % 100000;
}
```

Hash table node structure and array

In the sample hash table the table size is 256, so we need an array of 256 NULL pointers when the program starts. Since this is quite small, it is implemented in the data segment. For a more realistic program, we would need a hash table creation function to allocate an array and fill it with 0's. Below is the declaration of the array and the structure definition for the linked lists at each array location.

```
        Segment .data
table   times 256 dq    0
        struc   node
n_value resq    1
n_next  resq    1
        align   8
        endstruc
```

Function to find a value in the hash table

The basic purpose of a hash table is to store some data associated with a key. In the sample hash table we are simply storing the key. The find function below searches through the hash table looking for a key. If it is found, the function returns a pointer to the node with the key. If it is not found, it returns 0. A more realistic program would probably return a pointer to the data associated with the key.

The find function operates by calling hash to compute the index in the hash array for the linked list which might hold the key being sought. Then the function loops through the nodes on the list looking for the key.

```
;       p = find ( n );
;       p = 0 if not found
```

173

```
find:
.n      equ   0
        push  rbp
        mov   rbp, rsp
        sub   rsp, 16
        mov   [rsp+.n], rdi     ; save n
        call  hash              ; h = hash(n)
        mov   rax, [table+rax*8]; p = table[h]
        mov   rdi, [rsp+.n]     ; restore n
        cmp   rax, 0            ; if node pointer
        je    .done             ; is 0 quit
.more:
        cmp   rdi, [rax+n_value]; if p->value = n
        je    .done             ; return p
        mov   rax, [rax+n_next] ; p = p->next
        cmp   rax, 0            ; if node pointer
        jne   .more             ; is 0 quit
.done:
        leave
        ret
```

Insertion code

The code to insert a key into the hash table begins by calling find to avoid inserting the key more than once. If the key is found it skips the insertion code. If the key is not found, the function calls hash to determine the index for the linked list to add the key to. It allocates memory for a new node and inserts it at the start of the list.

```
;       insert ( n );
insert:
.n      equ   0
.h      equ   8
        push  rbp
        mov   rbp, rsp
        sub   rsp, 16
        mov   [rsp+.n], rdi     ; save n
        call  find              ; look for n
        cmp   rax, 0            ; if n id found
        jne   .found            ; skip insertion
        mov   rdi, [rsp+.n]     ; restore n
        call  hash              ; compute h=hash(n)
        mov   [rsp+.h], rax     ; save h
        mov   rdi, node_size
        call  malloc            ; allocate node
        mov   r9, [rsp+.h]      ; restore h
        mov   r8, [table+r9*8]  ; get first node f from
table[h]
        mov   [rax+n_next], r8  ; set next pointer of node to f
        mov   r8, [rsp+.n]      ; set value of new
        mov   [rax+n_value], r8 ; node to n
        mov   [table+r9*8], rax ; make node first on table[h]
.found:
        leave
        ret
```

Printing the hash table

The print function iterates through the indices from 0 through 255, printing the index number and the keys on each non-empty list. It uses registers r12 and r13 for safe storage of a loop counter to iterate through the locations of the hash table array and for a pointer to loop through the nodes on each linked list. This is more convenient than using registers which require saving and restoring around each printf call. It does require pushing and popping these 2 registers at the start and end of the function to preserve them for calling functions. Note that pushing and popping 16 bytes is necessary to preserve the proper stack alignment.

You will notice that the code switches back and forth between the data and text segments so that printf format strings will be placed close to their point of use in the code.

```
print:
        push    rbp
        mov     rbp, rsp
        push    r12             ; i: integer counter for table
        push    r13             ; p: pointer for list at table[i]

;       for ( i = 0; i < 256; i++ ) {
        xor     r12, r12

.more_table:
;               p = table[i];
                mov     r13, [table+r12*8]

;               if ( p != 0 ) {
                cmp     r13, 0
                je      .empty

;                       print the list header
                        segment .data
.print1:
                        db      "list %3d: ",0
                        segment .text
                        lea     rdi, [.print1]
                        mov     rsi, r12
                        call    printf

;                       do {
.more_list:
;                               print the node's value
                                segment .data
.print2                         db      "%ld ",0
                                segment .text
                                lea     rdi, [.print2]
                                mov     rsi, [r13+n_value]
                                call    printf

;                               advance to the next node
                                mov     r13, [r13+n_next]

;                       } while ( the node != 0 )
                        cmp     r13, 0
```

175

```
            jne     .more_list
;           print new line
            segment .data
 .print3: db          0x0a,0
            segment .text
            lea     rdi, [.print3]
            call    printf
 .empty:

;           i++
            inc     r12
            cmp     r12, 256
            jl      .more_table
;       } end of for loop
        pop     r13
        pop     r12
        leave
        ret
```

Testing the hash table

The main function for the hash table reads numbers with scanf, inserts
them into the hash table and prints the hash table contents after each
insertion:

```
main:
 .k       equ    0
          segment .data
 .scanf_fmt:
          db     "%ld",0
          segment .text
          push   rbp
          mov    rbp, rsp
          sub    rsp, 16
 .more:
          lea    rdi, [.scanf_fmt]
          lea    rsi, [rsp+.k]
          call   scanf          ; read k
          cmp    rax, 1         ; if the read fails
          jne    .done          ; end it all
          mov    rdi, [rsp+.k]
          call   insert         ; insert(k);
          call   print          ; print hash table
          jmp    .more
 .done:
          leave
          ret
```

Below is the printing of the hash table contents after inserting 1, 2, 3,
4, 5, 256, 257, 258, 260, 513, 1025 and 1028.

```
list    0: 256
list    1: 1025 513 257 1
list    2: 258 2
list    3: 3
```

176

```
list  4: 1028 260 4
list  5: 5
```

15.4 Binary trees

A binary tree is a structure with possibly many nodes. There is a single
root node which can have left or right child nodes (or both). Each node in
the tree can have left or right child nodes (or both).

Generally binary trees are built with an ordering applied to keys in the
nodes. For example you could have a binary tree where every node divides
keys into those less than the node's key (in the left sub-tree) and those
greater than the node's key (in the right sub-tree). Having an ordered
binary tree, often called a binary search tree, makes it possible to do fast
searches for a key while maintaining the ability to traverse the nodes in
increasing or decreasing order.

Here we will present a binary tree with integer keys with the ordering
being lower keys on the left and greater keys on the right. First are the
structures used for the tree.

Binary tree node and tree structures

The nodes in the binary tree have an integer value and two pointers. The
structure definition below uses a prefix convention in naming the value
field as n_value and the left and right pointers as n_left and n_right.

```
        struc   node
n_value resq    1
n_left  resq    1
n_right resq    1
        align   8
        endstruc
```

It would be possible to simply use a pointer to the root node to
represent the tree. However we could add features to the tree, like node
deletion or balancing, which could change the root of the tree. It seems
logical to store the root in a structure insulating us from future root
changes in a tree. We have also included in the tree structure a count of
the number of nodes in the tree.

```
        struc   tree
t_count resq    1
t_root  resq    1
        align   8
        endstruc
```

Creating an empty tree

The new_tree function allocates memory for a tree structure and sets the count and the root of the new tree to 0. By having the root of the tree in a structure the code using the binary tree always refers to a particular tree using the pointer returned by new_tree. A more robust function should check the value returned by malloc.

```
new_tree:
        push    rbp
        mov     rbp, rsp
        mov     rdi, tree_size
        call    malloc
        xor     edi, edi
        mov     [rax+t_root], rdi
        mov     [rax+t_count], rdi
        leave
        ret
```

Finding a key in a tree

To find a key in a binary search tree you start with a pointer to the root node and compare the node's key with the key being sought. If it's a match you're done. If the target key is less than the node's key you change your pointer to the node's left child. If the target key is greater than the node's key you change the pointer to the node's right child. You then repeat these comparisons with the new node. If you ever reach a NULL pointer, the key is not in the tree. Below is the code for finding a key in a binary tree. It returns a pointer to the correct tree node or NULL if not found.

```
;          p = find ( t, n );
;          p = 0 if not found
find:
        push    rbp
        mov     rbp, rsp
        mov     rdi, [rdi+t_root]
        xor     eax, eax
.more   cmp     rdi, 0
        je      .done
        cmp     rsi, [rdi+n_value]
        jl      .goleft
        jg      .goright
        mov     rax, rsi
        jmp     .done
.goleft:
        mov     rdi, [rdi+n_left]
        jmp     .more
.goright:
        mov     rdi, [rdi+n_right]
        jmp     .more
.done   leave
        ret
```

Inserting a key into the tree

The first step in inserting a key is to use the find function to see if the key is already there. If it is, then there is no insertion. If not, then a new tree node is allocated, its value is set to the new key value and its left and right child pointers are set to NULL. Then it's time to find where to place this in the tree.

There is a special case for inserting the first node in the tree. If the count of nodes in the tree is 0, then the count is incremented and the tree's root pointer is set to the new node.

If the tree is non-empty then you start by setting a current pointer to point to the root node. If the new key is less than the current node's key, then the new node belongs in the left sub-tree. To handle this you inspect the left child pointer of the current node. If it is null, you have found the insertion point, so set the left pointer to the pointer of the new node. Otherwise update your current node pointer to be the left pointer and start comparisons with this node. If the key is not less than the current node's key, it must be greater than. In that case you inspect the current node's right child pointer and either set it the new node's pointer or advance your current pointer to the right child and repeat the comparison process.

```
;       insert ( t, n );
insert:
.n      equ   0
.t      equ   8
        push  rbp
        mov   rbp, rsp
        sub   rsp, 16
        mov   [rsp+.t], rdi
        mov   [rsp+.n], rsi
        call  find               ; look for n
        cmp   rax, 0             ; if in the tree
        jne   .done             ; don't insert it
        mov   rdi, node_size
        call  malloc            ; p = new node
        mov   rsi, [rsp+.n]
        mov   [rax+n_value], rsi ; p->value = n
        xor   edi, edi
        mov   [rax+n_left], rdi  ; p->left = NULL
        mov   [rax+n_right], rdi ; p->right = NULL
        mov   rdx, [rsp+.t]
        mov   rdi, [rdx+t_count]  ; get tree size
        cmp   rdi, 0            ; count == 0 ?
        jne   .findparent
        inc   qword [rdx+t_count] ; count = 1
        mov   [rdx+t_root], rax   ; root = new node
        jmp   .done
.findparent:
        inc   qword [rdx+t_count] ; count++
        mov   rdx, [rdx+t_root]   ; p = root
.repeatfind:
        cmp   rsi, [rdx+n_value]  ; p=>value < n ?
```

179

```
        jl      .goleft
        mov     r8, rdx                 ; t = p
        mov     rdx, [r8+n_right]       ; p = p->right
        cmp     rdx, 0                  ; is p NULL ?
        jne     .repeatfind
        mov     [r8+n_right], rax       ; if so, add node
        jmp     .done                   ; and return
.goleft:
        mov     r8, rdx                 ; t = p
        mov     rdx, [r8+n_left]        ; p = p->left
        cmp     rdx, 0                  ; id p NULL ?
        jne     .repeatfind
        mov     [r8+n_left], rax        ; if so, add node
.done:                                  ; and return
        leave
        ret
```

Printing the keys in order

Printing the keys of a binary tree in order is easily performed by using recursion. The basic idea is to print the keys in the left sub-tree, print the key of the root node and print the keys of the right sub-tree. The use of a special tree structure means that there needs to be a different function to recursively print sub-trees starting with the pointer to the root. The main print function is named print and the recursive function is called rec_print.

```
rec_print:
.t      equ     0
        push    rbp
        mov     rbp, rsp
        sub     rsp, 16
        cmp     rdi, 0
        je      .done
        mov     [rsp+.t], rdi
        mov     rdi, [rdi+n_left]
        call    rec_print
        mov     rdi, [rsp+.t]
        mov     rsi, [rdi+n_value]
        segment .data
.print  db      "%ld ",0
        segment .text
        lea     rdi, [.print]
        call    printf
        mov     rdi, [rsp+.t]
        mov     rdi, [rdi+n_right]
        call    rec_print
.done   leave
        ret

;       print(t);
 print:
        push    rbp
        mov     rbp, rsp
        mov     rdi, [rdi+t_root]
        call    rec_print
        segment .data
```

```
.print db        0x0a, 0
       segment .text
       lea     rdi, [.print]
       call    printf
       leave
       ret
```

Exercises

1. Modify the singly-linked list code to implement a stack of strings. You can use the C `strdup` function to make duplicates of strings that you insert. Write a main routine which creates a stack and enters a loop reading strings. If the string entered equals "pop", then pop the top of the stack and print that value. If the string entered equals "`print`", then print the contents of the stack. Otherwise push the string onto the stack. Your code should exit when either `scanf` or `fgets` fails to read a string.

2. Modify the doubly-linked list code to implement a queue of strings. Your main routine should read strings until no more are available. If the string entered equals "dequeue", then dequeue the oldest string from the queue and print it. If the string entered equals "`print`", then print the contents of the queue. Otherwise add the string onto the end of the queue. Your code should exit when either `scanf` or `fgets` fails to read a string.

3. Modify the hash table code to implement a hash table where you store strings and integers. The string will be the key and the integer will be its associated value. Your main routine should read lines using `fgets` and read the text again using `sscanf` to get a string and a number. If no number is read, `sscanf` returns 1), then look for the string in the hash table and print its value if it there or else print an error message. If there is a string and a number (`sscanf` returns 2), then add the string or update the string's value in the hash table. Your code should exit when `fgets` fails to read a string

4. Implement a binary tree of strings and use it to read a file of text using `fgets` and then print the lines of text in alphabetical order.

Chapter 16
High performance assembly

In this chapter we discuss some strategies for writing efficient x86-64 assembly language. The gold standard is the efficiency of implementations written in C or C++ and compiled with a good optimizing compiler. The author uses gcc to have it produce an assembly language file. Studying this generated code may give you some ideas about how to write efficient assembly code.

16.1 Efficient use of cache

One of the goals in high performance computing is to keep the processing units of the CPU busy. A modern CPU like the Intel Core i7 operates at a clock speed around 3 GHz while its main memory maxes out at about 21 GB/sec. If your application ran strictly from data and instructions in memory using no cache, then there would be roughly 7 bytes available per cycle. The CPU has 4 cores which need to share the 21 GB/sec, so we're down to about 2 bytes per cycle per core from memory. Yet each of these cores can have instructions being processed in 3 processing sub-units and 2 memory processing sub-units. Each CPU can complete 4 instructions per cycle. The same is true for the AMD Bulldozer CPUs. It requires much more than 2 bytes per cycle to keep instructions flowing in a modern CPU. To keep these CPUs fed requires 3 levels of cache.

I performed a short test to illustrate the effect of main memory access versus cache on a Core i7 CPU. The test consisted of executing 10 billion exclusive or operations on quad-words in memory. In the plot below you can see that the time depends heavily on the array size. With an array of size 8000 bytes, the time as 1.5 seconds. The time steadily grows through the use of the 8 MB of cache. When the size is 80 million bytes the cache is nearly useless and a maximum of about 5.7 seconds is reached.

183

Time to Compute XOR

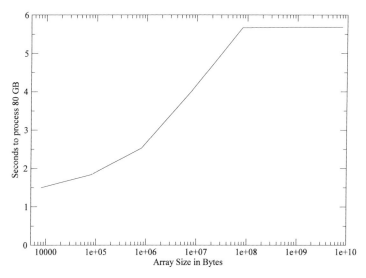

A prime example of making efficient use of cache is in the implementation of matrix multiplication. Straightforward matrix multiplication is $O(n^3)$ where there are n rows and n columns of data. It is commonly coded as 3 nested loops. However it can be broken up into blocks small enough for 3 blocks to fit in cache for a nice performance boost. Below are MFLOPs ratings for various block sizes for multiplying 2 2048x2048 matrices in a C program. There is considerable room for improvement by using assembly language to take advantage of SSE or AVX instructions.

MFLOPs for Matrix Multiplication

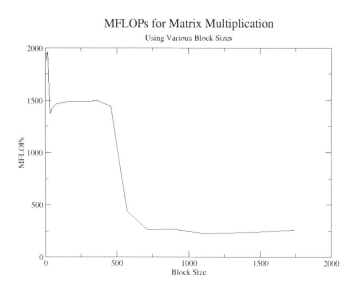

16.2 Common subexpression elimination

Common subexpression eliminations is generally performed by optimizing compilers. If you are to have any hope of beating the compiler, you must do the same thing. Sometimes it may be hard to locate all common subexpressions. This might be a good time to study the compiler's generated code to discover what it found. The compiler is tireless and efficient at its tasks. Humans tend to overlook things.

16.3 Strength reduction

Strength reduction means using a simpler mathematical technique to get an answer. It is possible to compute x^3 using pow, but it is probably faster to compute $x * x * x$. If you need to compute x^4, then do it in stages:

```
x2 = x * x;
x4 = x2 * x2;
```

If you need to divide or multiply an integer by a power of 2, this can be done more quickly by shifting. If you need to divide more than one floating point number by x, compute $1/x$ and multiply.

16.4 Use registers efficiently

Place commonly used values in registers. It is nearly always better to place values in registers. I once wrote a doubly nested loop in 32 bit mode where I had all my values in registers. gcc generated faster code by using the stack for a few values. These stack values probably remained in the level 1 cache and were almost as good as being in registers. Testing tells the truth.

16.5 Use fewer branches

Modern CPUs make branch predictions and will prepare the pipeline with some instructions from one of the 2 possibilities when there is a conditional branch. The pipeline will stall when this prediction is wrong, so it will help to try to make fewer branches. Study the generated code from your compiler. It will frequently reorder the assembly code to reduce the number of branches. You will learn some general techniques from the compiler.

16.6 Convert loops to branch at the bottom

If you code a while loop as written, there will be a conditional jump at the top of the loop to branch past the loop and an unconditional jump at the bottom of the loop to get back to the top. It is always possible to transform the loop have a conditional branch at the bottom. You may need a one-time use conditional jump before the top of the loop to handle cases where the loop body should be skipped.

Here is a C for loop converted to a do-while loop. First the for loop:

```
for ( i = 0; i < n; i++ ) {
    x[i] = a[i] + b[i];
}
```

Now the do-while loop with an additional if:

```
if ( n > 0 ) {
    i = 0;
    do {
        x[i] = a[i] + b[i];
        i++;
    } while ( i < n );
}
```

Please do not adopt this style of coding in C or C++. The compiler will handle for loops quite well. In fact the simplicity of the for loop might allow the compiler to generate better code. I presented this in C simply to get the point across more simply.

16.7 Unroll loops

Unrolling loops is another technique used by compilers. The primary advantage is that there will be fewer loop control instructions and more instructions doing the work of the loop. A second advantage is that the CPU will have more instructions available to fill its pipeline with a longer loop body. Finally if you manage to use registers with little or no dependencies between the separate sections of unrolled code, then you open up the possibility for a super-scalar CPU (most modern CPUs) to execute multiple original iterations in parallel. This is considerably easier with 16 registers than with 8.

Let's consider some code to add up all the numbers in an array of quad-words. Here is the assembly code for the simplest version:

186

```
        segment  .text
        global   add_array
add_array:
        xor      eax, eax
.add_words:
        add      rax, [rdi]
        add      rdi, 8
        dec      rsi
        jg       .add_words
        ret
```

Here is a version with the loop unrolled 4 times:

```
        segment  .text
        global   add_array
add_array:
        push     r15
        push     r14
        push     r13
        push     r12
        push     rbp
        push     rbx
        xor      eax, eax
        mov      rbx, rax
        mov      rcx, rax
        mov      rdx, rax
.add_words:
        add      rax, [rdi]
        add      rbx, [rdi+8]
        add      rcx, [rdi+16]
        add      rdx, [rdi+24]
        add      rdi, 32
        sub      rsi, 4
        jg       .add_words
        add      rcx, rdx
        add      rax, rbx
        add      rax, rcx
        pop      rbx
        pop      rbp
        pop      r12
        pop      r13
        pop      r14
        pop      r15
        ret
```

There may have been some way to use fewer callee-save registers, but the choices I made simplified the coding. In the unrolled code I am accumulating partial sums in rax, rbx, rcx and rdx. These partial sums are combined after the loop. Executing a test program with 1000000 calls to add up an array of 10000 quad-words took 3.9 seconds for the simple version and 2.44 seconds for the unrolled version. There is so little work to do per data element that the 2 programs start becoming memory bandwidth limited with large arrays, so I tested a size which fit easily in cache.

16.8 Merge loops

If you have 2 for loops iterating over the same sequence of values and there is no dependence between the loops, it seems like a no-brainer to merge the loops. Consider the following 2 loops:

```
for ( i = 0; i < 1000; i++ ) {
    a[i] = b[i] + c[i];
}
for ( j = 0; j < 1000; j++ ) {
    d[j] = b[j] - c[j];
}
```

This can easily be merged to get:

```
for ( i = 0; i < 1000; i++ ) {
    a[i] = b[i] + c[i];
    d[i] = b[i] - c[i];
}
```

In general merging loops can increase the size of a loop body, decreasing the overhead percentage and helping to keep the pipeline full. In this case there is additional gain from loading the values of b and c once rather than twice.

16.9 Split loops

We just got through discussing how merging loops was a good idea. Now we are going to learn the opposite - well for some loops. If a loop is operating on 2 independent sets of data, then it could be split into 2 loops. This can improve performance if the combined loop exceeds the cache capacity. There is a trade-off between better cache usage and more instructions in the pipeline. Sometime merging is better and sometimes splitting is better.

16.10 Interchange loops

Suppose you wish to place 0's in a 2-dimensional array in C. You have 2 choices:

```
for ( i = 0; i < n; i++ ) {
    for ( j = 0; j < n; j++ ) {
        x[i][j] = 0;
    }
}
```

or

```
for ( j = 0; j < n; j++ ) {
    for ( i = 0; i < n; i++ ) {
        x[i][j] = 0;
    }
}
```

Which is better? In C the second index increments faster than the first. This means that x[0][1] is immediately after x[0][0]. On the other hand x[1][0] is n elements after x[0][0]. When the CPU fetches data into the cache it fetches more than a few bytes and cache writes to memory behave similarly, so the first loop makes more sense. If you have the extreme misfortune of having an array which is too large for your RAM, then you may experience virtual memory thrashing with the second version. This could turn into a disk access for each array access.

16.11 Move loop invariant code outside loops

This might be a fairly obvious optimization to perform. It's another case where studying the compiler's generated code might point out some loop invariant code which you have overlooked.

16.12 Remove recursion

If it is easy to eliminate recursion then it will nearly always improve efficiency. Often it is easy to eliminate "tail" recursion where the last action of a function is a recursive call. This can generally be done by branching to the top of the function. On the other hand if you try to eliminate recursion for a function like quicksort which makes 2 non-trivial recursive calls, you will be forced to "simulate" recursion using your own stack. This may make things slower. In any case the effect is small, since the time spent making recursive calls in quicksort is small.

16.13 Eliminate stack frames

For leaf functions it is not necessary to use stack frames. In fact if you have non-leaf functions which call your own functions and no others then you can omit the frame pointers from these too. The only real reason for frame pointers is for debugging. There is a requirement for leaving the stack on 16 byte boundaries, but this only becomes an issue with functions which have local variables (on the stack) which participate in aligned 16

189

or 32 byte accesses which can either fail or be slower. If you know that your own code is not using those instructions, then neither frame pointers nor frame alignment are important other than for debugging.

16.14 Inline functions

As part of optimization compilers can inline small functions. This reduces the overhead significantly. If you wish to do this, you might be interested in exploring macros which can make your code easier to read and write and operate much like a function which has been inlined.

16.15 Reduce dependencies to allow super-scalar execution

Modern CPUs inspect the instruction stream looking ahead for instructions which do not depend upon results of earlier instructions. This is called "out of order execution". If there is less dependency in your code, then the CPU can execute more instructions out of order, allowing multiple independent instructions to execute at one (super-scalar) and your program can run more quickly.

As an example of this I modified the previous `add_array` function with unrolled loops to accumulate all 4 values in the loop into `rax`. This increased the time from 2.44 seconds to 2.75 seconds.

16.16 Use specialized instructions

So far we have seen the conditional move instruction which is fairly specialized and also the packed floating point instructions. There are many specialized instructions in the x86-64 architecture which are more difficult for a compiler to apply. A human can reorganize an algorithm to add the elements of an array somewhat like I did with loop unrolling except to keep 4 partial sums in one AVX register. Combining the 4 parts of the AVX register can be done after the loop. This can make the adding even faster, since 4 adds can be done in one instruction. This technique can also be combined with loop unrolling for additional performance. This will be explored in detail in subsequent chapters.

Exercises

1. Given an array of 3D points defined in a structure with x, y and   z components, write a function to compute a distance matrix with the distances between each pair of points.

2. Given a 2D array, M, of floats of dimensions n by 4, and a vector, v, of 4 floats compute Mv.

3. Write a blocked matrix-matrix multiplication using a C main program and an assembly function to perform the multiplication. Try various block sizes to see which block size gives the highest performance.

Chapter 17
Counting bits in an array

In this chapter we explore several solutions to the problem of counting all the 1 bits in an array of quad-word integers. For each test we use the same C main program and implement a different function counting the number of 1 bits in the array. All these functions implement the same prototype:

```
long popcnt_array ( long *a, int size );
```

17.1 C function

The first solution is a straightforward C solution:

```
long popcnt_array ( long *a, int size )
{
    int w, b;
    long word;
    long n;

    n = 0;
    for ( w = 0; w < size; w++ ) {
        word = a[w];
        n += word & 1;
        for ( b = 1; b < 64; b++ ) {
            n += (word >> b) & 1;
        }
    }
    return n;
}
```

The testing consists of calling `popcnt_array` 1000 times with an array of 100000 longs (800000 bytes). Compiling with optimization level zero (option -O0) the test took 14.63 seconds. With optimization level 1, it took 5.29 seconds, with level 2 it took 5.29 seconds again, and with level 3 it took 5.37 seconds. Finally adding `-funroll-all-loops`, it took 4.74 seconds.

The algorithm can be improved by noticing that frequently the upper bits of the quad-words being tested might be 0. We can change the inner for loop into a while loop:

```
long popcnt_array ( unsigned long *a, int size )
{
    int w, b;
    unsigned long word;
    long n;

    n = 0;
    for ( w = 0; w < size; w++ ) {
        word = a[w];
        while ( word != 0 ) {
            n += word & 1;
            word >>= 1;
        }
    }
    return n;
}
```

Using the maximum optimization options the version takes 3.34 seconds. This is an instance of using a better algorithm.

17.2 Counting 1 bits in assembly

It is not too hard to unroll the loop for working on 64 bits into 64 steps of working on 1 bit. In the assembly code which follows one fourth of the bits of each word are placed in rax, one fourth in rbx, one fourth in rcx and one fourth in rdx. Then each fourth of the bits are accumulated using different registers. This allows considerable freedom for the computer to use out-or-order execution with the loop.

```
        segment  .text
        global   popcnt_array
popcnt_array:
        push     rbx
        push     rbp
        push     r12
        push     r13
        push     r14
        push     r15
        xor      eax, eax
        xor      ebx, ebx
        xor      ecx, ecx
        xor      edx, edx
        xor      r12d, r12d
        xor      r13d, r13d
        xor      r14d, r14d
        xor      r15d, r15d
.count_words:
        mov      r8, [rdi]
        mov      r9, r8
        mov      r10, r8
```

193

```
        mov     r11, r9
        and     r8, 0xffff
        shr     r9, 16
        and     r9, 0xffff
        shr     r10, 32
        and     r10, 0xffff
        shr     r11, 48
        and     r11, 0xffff
        mov     r12w, r8w
        and     r12w, 1
        add     rax, r12
        mov     r13w, r9w
        and     r13w, 1
        add     rbx, r13
        mov     r14w, r10w
        and     r14w, 1
        add     rcx, r14
        mov     r15w, r11w
        and     r15w, 1
        add     rdx, r15

%rep 15
        shr     r8w, 1
        mov     r12w, r8w
        and     r12w, 1
        add     rax, r12
        shr     r9w, 1
        mov     r13w, r9w
        and     r13w, 1
        add     rbx, r13
        shr     r10w, 1
        mov     r14w, r10w
        and     r14w, 1
        add     rcx, r14
        shr     r11w, 1
        mov     r15w, r11w
        and     r15w, 1
        add     rdx, r15
%endrep
        add     rdi, 8
        dec     rsi
        jg      .count_words
        add     rax, rbx
        add     rax, rcx
        add     rax, rdx
        pop     r15
        pop     r14
        pop     r13
        pop     r12
        pop     rbp
        pop     rbx
        ret
```

This has an unfortunate side effect - the use of a repeat section which repeats 15 times. This makes for a function of 1123 bytes. Perhaps it was worth it to execute the test in 2.52 seconds. The object file is only 240 bytes larger than the C code with unrolled loops.

17.3 Precomputing the number of bits in each byte

The next algorithmic improvement comes from recognizing that we can precompute the number of bits in each possible bit pattern for a byte and use an array of 256 bytes to store the number of bits in each possible byte. Then counting the number of bits in a quad-word consists of using the 8 bytes of the quad-word as indices into the array of bit counts and adding them up.

Here is the C function for adding the number of bits in the array without the initialization of the count array:

```
long popcnt_array ( long *a, int size )
{
    int b;
    long n;
    int word;

    n = 0;
    for ( b = 0; b < size*8; b++ ) {
        word = ((unsigned char *)a)[b];
        n += count[word];
    }
    return n;
}
```

This code took 0.24 seconds for the test, so we have a new winner. I tried hard to beat this algorithm using assembly language, but managed only a tie.

17.4 Using the popcnt instruction

A new instruction included in the Core i series processors is popcnt which gives the number of 1 bits in a 64 bit register. So on the right computers, we can employ the technique of using a specialized instruction:

```
        segment .text
        global  popcnt_array
popcnt_array:
        xor     eax, eax
        xor     r8d, r8d
        xor     ecx, ecx
.count_more:
        popcnt  rdx, [rdi+rcx*8]
        add     rax, rdx
        popcnt  r9, [rdi+rcx*8+8]
        add     r8, r9
        add     rcx, 2
        cmp     rcx, rsi
        jl      .count_more
```

```
add     rax, r8
ret
```

We have a new winner on the Core i7 at 0.04 seconds which is 6 times faster than the nearest competitor.

Exercises

1. Write a function to convert an array of ASCII characters to EBCDIC and another to convert back to ASCII.

2. For 2 arrays of ASCII characters write a function to find the longest common substring.

Chapter 18
Sobel filter

The Sobel filter is an edge detection filter used in image processing. The operation of the filter is to process 3x3 windows of data by convolving each pixel by one 3x3 matrix to produce an edge measure in the x direction and another in the y direction. Here are the 2 matrices

$$S_x = \begin{bmatrix} -1 & 0 & 1 \\ -2 & 0 & 2 \\ -1 & 0 & 1 \end{bmatrix} \qquad S_y = \begin{bmatrix} -1 & -2 & 1 \\ 0 & 0 & 0 \\ 1 & 2 & 1 \end{bmatrix}$$

For an individual pixel $I_{r,c}$ the x edge measure, G_x, is computed by

$$G_x = \sum_{i=-1}^{1} \sum_{j=-1}^{1} (S_{x,i,j} I_{r+i.c+j})$$

where we have conveniently numbered the rows and columns of S_x starting with -1. Similarly we compute G_y using

$$G_y = \sum_{i=-1}^{1} \sum_{j=-1}^{1} (S_{y,i,j} I_{r+i.c+j})$$

Next we show how to get the magnitude of the edge measure, G,

$$G = \sqrt{G_x{}^2 + G_y{}^2}$$

18.1 Sobel in C

Here is a C function which computes the Sobel edge magnitude for an image of arbitrary size:

```
#include <math.h>

#define I(a,b,c) a[(b)*(cols)+(c)]
```

```
void sobel ( unsigned char *data, float *out,
             long rows, long cols )
{
    int r, c;    int gx, gy;

    for ( r = 1; r < rows-1; r++ ) {
        for ( c = 1; c < cols-1; c++ ) {
            gx = -I(data,r-1,c-1) + I(data,r-1,c+1) +
                 -2*I(data,r,c-1) + 2*I(data,r,c+1) +
                 -I(data,r+1,c-1) + I(data,r+1,c+1);
            gy = -I(data,r-1,c-1) - 2*I(data,r-1,c) -
                 I(data,r-1,c+1) + I(data,r+1,c-1) +
                 2*I(data,r+1,c) + I(data,r+1,c+1);
            I(out,r,c) = sqrt((float)(gx)*(float)(gx)+
                              (float)(gy)*(float)(gy));
        }
    }
}
```

This code was compiled with -O3 optimization and full loop unrolling. Testing with 1024×1024 images showed that it computed 161.5 Sobel magnitude images per second. Testing with 1000 different images to cut down on the effect of cached images, this code produced 158 images per second. Clearly the code is dominated by mathematics rather than memory bandwidth.

18.2 Sobel computed using SSE instructions

Sobel was chosen as a good example of an algorithm which manipulates data of many types. First the image data is byte data. The movdqu instruction was used to transfer 16 adjacent pixels from one row of the image. These pixels were processed to produce the contribution of their central 14 pixels to G_x and G_y. Then 16 pixels were transferred from the image one row down from the first 16 pixels. These pixels were processed in the same way adding more to G_x and G_y. Finally 16 more pixels 2 rows down from the first 16 were transferred and their contributions to G_x and G_y were computed. Then these contributions were combined, squared, added together, converted to 32 bit floating point and square roots were computed for the 14 output pixels which were placed in the output array.

Tested on the same Core i7 computer, this code produced 1063 Sobel magnitude images per second. Testing with 1000 different images this code produced 980 images per second, which is about 6.2 times as fast as the C version.

Here are the new instructions used in this code:

pxor This instruction performs an exclusive or on a 128 XMM source register or memory and stores the result in the destination register.

movdqa This instruction moves 128 bits of aligned data from memory to a register, from a register to memory, or from a register to a register.

movdqu This instruction moves 128 bits of unaligned data from memory to a register, from a register to memory, or from a register to a register.

psrldq This instruction shifts the destination XMM register right the number of bytes specified in the second immediate operand.

punpcklbw This instruction unpacks the low 8 bytes of 2 XMM registers and intermingles them. I used this with the second register holding all 0 bytes to form 8 words in the destination.

punpckhbw This instruction unpacks the upper 8 bytes of 2 XMM registers and intermingles them.

paddw This instruction adds 8 16 bit integers from the second operand to the first operand. At least one of the operands must be an XMM register and one can be a memory field.

psubw This instruction divides the second set of 8 16 bit integers from the first set.

pmullw This instruction multiplies the first set of 8 16 bit integers times the second set and stores the low order 16 bits of the products in the first operand.

punpcklwd This instruction unpacks and interleaves words from the lower halves of 2 XMM registers into the destination register.

punpckhwd This instruction unpacks and interleaves words from the upper halves of 2 XMM registers into the destination register.

cvtdq2ps This instruction converts 4 double word integers into 4 double word floating point values.

Here is the assembly code:

```
%macro  multipush 1-* ; I needed to push and pop all
    %rep  %0          ; callee save registers, so I
        push    %1    ; used macros from the yasm
        %rotate 1     ; documentation.
    %endrep
%endmacro

%macro  multipop 1-*
    %rep %0
        %rotate -1
        pop     %1
    %endrep
%endmacro

;        sobel ( input, output, rows, cols );
;        char input[rows][cols]
;        float output[rows][cols]
```

```
;           border of the output array will be unfilled
;
            segment .text
            global  sobel, main
sobel:
.cols   equ     0
.rows   equ     8
.output equ     16
.input  equ     24
.bpir   equ     32
.bpor   equ     40
            multipush   rbx, rbp, r12, r13, r14, r15
            sub     rsp, 48
            cmp     rdx, 3              ; need at least 3 rows
            jl      .noworktodo
            cmp     rcx, 3              ; need at least 3 columns
            jl      .noworktodo
            mov     [rsp+.input], rdi
            mov     [rsp+.output], rsi
            mov     [rsp+.rows], rdx
            mov     [rsp+.cols], rcx
            mov     [rsp+.bpir], rcx ; bytes per input row
            imul    rcx, 4
            mov     [rsp+.bpor], rcx ; 4 bytes per output pixel

            mov     rax, [rsp+.rows] ; # rows to process
            mov     rdx, [rsp+.cols]
            sub     rax, 2
            mov     r8, [rsp+.input]
            add     r8, rdx
            mov     r9, r8              ; address of row
            mov     r10, r8
            sub     r8, rdx             ; address of row-1
            add     r10, rdx            ; address of row+1
            pxor    xmm13, xmm13
            pxor    xmm14, xmm14
            pxor    xmm15, xmm15
.more_rows:
            mov     rbx, 1              ; first column
.more_cols:
            movdqu  xmm0, [r8+rbx-1] ; data for 1st row
            movdqu  xmm1, xmm0
            movdqu  xmm2, xmm0
            pxor    xmm9, xmm9
            pxor    xmm10, xmm10
            pxor    xmm11, xmm11
            pxor    xmm12, xmm12
            psrldq  xmm1, 1             ; shift the pixels 1
                                        : to the right
            psrldq  xmm2, 2             ; shift the pixels 2
                                        ; to the right

;   Now the lowest 14 values of xmm0, xmm1 and
;   xmm2 are lined up properly for applying the
;   top row of the 2 matrices.

            movdqa  xmm3, xmm
            movdqa  xmm4, xmm1
            movdqa  xmm5, xmm2
            punpcklbw   xmm3, xmm13 ; The low 8 values
                                        ; are now words in
```

201

```asm
    punpcklbw    xmm4, xmm14    ; registers xmm3,
                                ; xmm4, and xmm5
    punpcklbw    xmm5, xmm15    ; ready for math.
    psubw    xmm11, xmm3        ; xmm11 will hold
                                ; 8 values of Gx
    psubw    xmm9, xmm3         ; xmm9 will hold
                                ; 8 values of Gy
    paddw    xmm11, xmm5        ; Gx subtracts left
                                ; adds right
    psubw    xmm9, xmm4         ; Gy subtracts
                                ; 2 * middle pixel
    psubw    xmm9, xmm4
    psubw    xmm9, xmm5         ; Final Gy subtract
    punpckhbw    xmm0, xmm13    ; Convert top 8
                                ; bytes to words
    punpckhbw    xmm1, xmm14
    punpckhbw    xmm2, xmm15
    psubw    xmm12, xmm0        ; Do the same math
    psubw    xmm10, xmm0        ; storing these 6
    paddw    xmm12, xmm2        ; values in xmm12
    psubw    xmm10, xmm1        ; and xmm10
    psubw    xmm10, xmm1
    psubw    xmm10, xmm2
    movdqu    xmm0, [r9+rbx-1]  ; data for 2nd row
    movdqu    xmm2, xmm0        ; repeat math from
    psrldq    xmm2, 2           ; 1st row with
    movdqa    xmm3, xmm0        ; nothing added to
    movdqa    xmm5, xmm2        ; Gy
    punpcklbw    xmm3, xmm13
    punpcklbw    xmm5, xmm15    ; 2nd row
    psubw    xmm11, xmm3
    psubw    xmm11, xmm3
    paddw    xmm11, xmm5
    paddw    xmm11, xmm5
    punpckhbw    xmm0, xmm13
    punpckhbw    xmm2, xmm15
    psubw    xmm12, xmm0
    psubw    xmm12, xmm0
    paddw    xmm12, xmm2
    paddw    xmm12, xmm2

    movdqu    xmm0, [r10+rbx-1] ; data for 3rd row
    movdqu    xmm1, xmm0
    movdqu    xmm2, xmm0
    psrldq    xmm1, 1
    psrldq    xmm2, 2
    movdqa    xmm3, xmm0
    movdqa    xmm4, xmm1
    movdqa    xmm5, xmm2
    punpcklbw    xmm3, xmm13
    punpcklbw    xmm4, xmm14
    punpcklbw    xmm5, xmm15    ; 3rd row
    psubw    xmm11, xmm3
    paddw    xmm9, xmm3
    paddw    xmm11, xmm5
    paddw    xmm9, xmm4
    paddw    xmm9, xmm4
    paddw    xmm9, xmm5
    punpckhbw    xmm0, xmm13
    punpckhbw    xmm1, xmm14
    punpckhbw    xmm2, xmm15
```

202

```
        psubw    xmm12, xmm0
        paddw    xmm10, xmm0
        paddw    xmm12, xmm2
        paddw    xmm10, xmm1
        paddw    xmm10, xmm1
        paddw    xmm10, xmm2

        pmullw   xmm9, xmm9          ; square Gx and Gy
        pmullw   xmm10, xmm10
        pmullw   xmm11, xmm11
        pmullw   xmm12, xmm12
        paddw    xmm9, xmm11         ; sum of squares
        paddw    xmm10, xmm12
        movdqa   xmm1, xmm9
        movdqa   xmm3, xmm10
        punpcklwd xmm9, xmm13        ; Convert low 4
                                     ; words to dwords
        punpckhwd xmm1, xmm13        ; Convert high 4
                                     ; words to dwords
        punpcklwd xmm10, xmm13       ; Convert low 4
                                     ; words to dwords
        punpckhwd xmm3, xmm13        ; Convert high 4
                                     ; words to dwords
        cvtdq2ps xmm0, xmm9          ; to floating point
        cvtdq2ps xmm1, xmm1          ; to floating point
        cvtdq2ps xmm2, xmm10         ; to floating point
        cvtdq2ps xmm3, xmm3          ; to floating point
        sqrtps   xmm0, xmm0
        sqrtps   xmm1, xmm1
        sqrtps   xmm2, xmm2
        sqrtps   xmm3, xmm3
        movups   [rsi+rbx*4], xmm0
        movups   [rsi+rbx*4+16], xmm1
        movups   [rsi+rbx*4+32], xmm2
        movlps   [rsi+rbx*4+48], xmm3

        add      rbx, 14            ; process 14 Sobel values
        cmp      rbx, rdx
        jl       .more_cols
        add      r8, rdx
        add      r9, rdx
        add      r10, rdx
        add      rsi, [rsp+.bpor]
        sub      rax, 1             ; 1 fewer row
        cmp      rax, 0
        jg       .more_rows
.noworktodo:
        add      rsp, 48
        multipop rbx, rbp, r12, r13, r14, r15
        ret
```

Exercises

1. Convert the Sobel function into a function to perform an arbitrary convolution of an image with a 3 × 3 matrix

2. Write an assembly function to convert an image into a run-length encoded image.

3. Write a function to fill an array with pseudo-random numbers derived by using 4 separate interleaved sequences based on the formula
$$X_{n+1} = (aX_n + c) \bmod m$$
Use $m = 32$ for all 4 sequences. Use 1664525, 22695477, 1103515245 and 214013 for the values of a and 1013904223, 1, 12345 and 2531011 for the values of c.

Chapter 19
Computing Correlation

The final example of optimization is computing the correlation between two variables x and y given n sample values. One way to compute correlation is using

$$r_{xy} = \frac{\sum_{i=1}^{n}(x_i - \bar{x})(y_i - \bar{y})}{\sqrt{\sum_{i=1}^{n}(x_i - \bar{x})^2 \sum_{i=1}^{n}(y_i - \bar{y})^2}}$$

But this formula requires two passes through the data - one pass to compute averages and a second pass to complete the formula. There is a less intuitive formula which is more amenable to computation:

$$r_{xy} = \frac{n\sum_{i=1}^{n} x_i y_i - \sum_{i=1}^{n} x_i \sum_{i=1}^{n} y_i}{\sqrt{n\sum_{i=1}^{n} x_i^2 - (\sum_{i=1}^{n} x_i)^2}\sqrt{n\sum_{i=1}^{n} y_i^2 - (\sum_{i=1}^{n} y_i)^2}}$$

The computational formula requires computing 5 sums when you scan the data: the sum of x_i, the sum of y_i, the sum of x_i^2, the sum of y_i^2 and the sum of $x_i y_i$. After computing these 5 sums there is a small amount of time required for implementing the computational formula.

19.1 C implementation

The C computation is performed in the corr function given below:

```
#include <math.h>

double corr ( double x[], double y[], long n )
{
    double sum_x, sum_y, sum_xx, sum_yy, sum_xy;
    long i;
    sum_x = sum_y = sum_xx = sum_yy = sum_xy = 0.0;
    for ( i = 0; i < n; i++ ) {
        sum_x += x[i];
        sum_y += y[i];
        sum_xx += x[i]*x[i];
        sum_yy += y[i]*y[i];
```

```
                    sum_xy += x[i]*y[i];
            }
        return (n*sum_xy-sum_x*sum_y)/
                sqrt((n*sum_xx-sum_x*sum_x)*
                    (n*sum_yy-sum_y*sum_y));
    }
```

The gcc compiler generated assembly code which used all 16 of the
XMM registers as it unrolled the loop to process 4 iterations of the for
loop in the main loop. The compiler also correctly handled the extra data
values when the array size was not a multiple of four. Performing 1
million calls to compute correlation on 2 arrays of size 10000 required
13.44 seconds for the C version. This is roughly 5.9 GFLOPs which is quite
impressive for compiled code.

19.2 Implementation using SSE instructions

A version of the corr function was written using SSE instructions which
will execute on many modern computers. Here is the SSE version:

```
        segment .text
        global corr

;       rdi, rsi, rdx, rcx, r8, r9: register parameters
;
;       rdi:  x array
;       rsi:  y array
;       rcx:  loop counter
;       rdx:  n

;       xmm0: 2 parts of sum_x
;       xmm1: 2 parts of sum_y
;       xmm2: 2 parts of sum_xx
;       xmm3: 2 parts of sum_yy
;       xmm4: 2 parts of sum_xy
;       xmm5: 2 x values - later squared
;       xmm6: 2 y values - later squared
;       xmm7: 2 xy values

corr:
        xor     r8, r8
        mov     rcx, rdx
        subpd   xmm0, xmm0
        movapd  xmm1, xmm0
        movapd  xmm2, xmm0
        movapd  xmm3, xmm0
        movapd  xmm4, xmm0
        movapd  xmm8, xmm0
        movapd  xmm9, xmm0
        movapd  xmm10, xmm0
        movapd  xmm11, xmm0
        movapd  xmm12, xmm0
.more:
        movapd  xmm5, [rdi+r8]  ; mov x
```

```
movapd   xmm6, [rsi+r8]     ; mov y
movapd   xmm7, xmm5         ; mov x
mulpd    xmm7, xmm6         ; xy
addpd    xmm0, xmm5         ; sum_x
addpd    xmm1, xmm6         ; sum_y
mulpd    xmm5, xmm5         ; xx
mulpd    xmm6, xmm6         ; yy
addpd    xmm2, xmm5         ; sum_xx
addpd    xmm3, xmm6         ; sum_yy
addpd    xmm4, xmm7         ; sum_xy
movapd   xmm13, [rdi+r8+16]   ; mov x
movapd   xmm14, [rsi+r8+16]   ; mov y
movapd   xmm15, xmm13       ; mov x
mulpd    xmm15, xmm14       ; xy
addpd    xmm8, xmm13        ; sum_x
addpd    xmm9, xmm14        ; sum_y
mulpd    xmm13, xmm13       ; xx
mulpd    xmm14, xmm14       ; yy
addpd    xmm10, xmm13       ; sum_xx
addpd    xmm11, xmm14       ; sum_yy
addpd    xmm12, xmm15       ; sum_xy
add      r8, 32
sub      rcx, 4
jnz      .more
addpd    xmm0, xmm8
addpd    xmm1, xmm9
addpd    xmm2, xmm10
addpd    xmm3, xmm11
addpd    xmm4, xmm12
haddpd   xmm0, xmm0         ; sum_x
haddpd   xmm1, xmm1         ; sum_y
haddpd   xmm2, xmm2         ; sum_xx
haddpd   xmm3, xmm3         ; sum_yy
haddpd   xmm4, xmm4         ; sum_xy
movsd    xmm6, xmm0         ; sum_x
movsd    xmm7, xmm1         ; sum_y
cvtsi2sd xmm8, rdx          ; n
mulsd    xmm6, xmm6         ; sum_x*sum_x
mulsd    xmm7, xmm7         ; sum_y*sum_y
mulsd    xmm2, xmm8         ; n*sum_xx
mulsd    xmm3, xmm8         ; n*sum_yy
subsd    xmm2, xmm6         ; n*sum_xx-sum_x*sum_x
subsd    xmm3, xmm7         ; n*sum_yy-sum_y*sum_y
mulsd    xmm2, xmm3         ; denom*denom
sqrtsd   xmm2, xmm2         ; denom
mulsd    xmm4, xmm8         ; n*sum_xy
mulsd    xmm0, xmm1         ; sum_x*sum_y
subsd    xmm4, xmm0         ; n*sum_xy-sum_x*sum_y
divsd    xmm4, xmm2         ; correlation
movsd    xmm0, xmm4         ; need in xmm0
ret
```

In the main loop of this function the movapd instruction was used to load 2 double precision values from the x array and again the load 2 values from the y array. Then accumulation was performed in registers xmm0 - xmm4. Each of these accumulation registers held 2 accumulated values - one for even indices and one for odd indices

After this collection of accumulations the movapd instruction was used again to load 2 more values for x and again to load 2 more values from y. These values were used to form accumulations into 5 more registers: xmm8 - xmm12.

After completing the loop, it was time to add together the 4 parts of each required summation. The first step of this process was using addpd to add the registers xmm8 - xmm12 to registers xmm0 - xmm4. Following this the "horizontal add packed double", haddpd, instruction was used to add the upper and lower halves of each of the summation registers to get the final sums. Then the code implemented the formula presented earlier.

When tested on 1 million correlations of size 10000, this program used 6.74 seconds which is approximately 11.8 GFLOPs. Now this is pretty impressive since the CPU operates at 3.4 GHz. It produced about 3.5 floating point results per cycle. This means that more than one of the SSE instructions was completing at once. The CPU is performing out-of-order execution and completing more than one SSE instruction per cycle.

19.3 Implementation using AVX instructions

The Core i7 CPU implements a new collection of instructions called "Advanced Vector Extensions" or AVX. For these instructions an extension of the XMM registers named ymm0 through ymm15 is provided along with some new instructions. The YMM registers are 256 bits each and can hold 4 double precision values in each one. This allowed a fairly easy adaptation of the SSE function to operate on 4 values at once.

In addition to providing the larger registers, the AVX instructions added versions of existing instructions which allowed using 3 operands: 2 source operands and a destination which did not participate as a source (unless you named the same register twice). The AVX versions of instructions are prefixed with the letter "v". Having 3 operand instructions reduces the register pressure and allows using two registers as sources in an instruction while preserving their values.

Here is the AVX version of the corr function:

```
        segment .text
        global corr
;
;       rdi:  x array
;       rsi:  y array
;       rcx:  loop counter
;       rdx:  n
;
;       ymm0: 4 parts of sum_x
;       ymm1: 4 parts of sum_y
;       ymm2: 4 parts of sum_xx
;       ymm3: 4 parts of sum_yy
```

```
;       ymm4: 4 parts of sum_xy
;       ymm5: 4 x values - later squared
;       ymm6: 4 y values - later squared
;       ymm7: 4 xy values

corr:
        xor     r8, r8
        mov     rcx, rdx
        vzeroall
.more:
        vmovupd   ymm5, [rdi+r8]            ; mov x
        vmovupd   ymm6, [rsi+r8]            ; mov y
        vmulpd    ymm7, ymm5, ymm6          ; xy
        vaddpd    ymm0, ymm0, ymm5          ; sum_x
        vaddpd    ymm1, ymm1, ymm6          ; sum_y
        vmulpd    ymm5, ymm5, ymm5          ; xx
        vmulpd    ymm6, ymm6, ymm6          ; yy
        vaddpd    ymm2, ymm2, ymm5          ; sum_xx
        vaddpd    ymm3, ymm3, ymm6          ; sum_yy
        vaddpd    ymm4, ymm4, ymm7          ; sum_xy
        vmovupd   ymm13, [rdi+r8+32]        ; mov x
        vmovupd   ymm14, [rsi+r8+32]        ; mov y
        vmulpd    ymm15, ymm13, ymm14       ; xy
        vaddpd    ymm8, ymm8, ymm13         ; sum_x
        vaddpd    ymm9, ymm9, ymm14         ; sum_y
        vmulpd    ymm13, ymm13, ymm13       ; xx
        vmulpd    ymm14, ymm14, ymm14       ; yy
        vaddpd    ymm10, ymm10, ymm13       ; sum_xx
        vaddpd    ymm11, ymm11, ymm14       ; sum_yy
        vaddpd    ymm12, ymm12, ymm15       ; sum_xy
        add       r8, 64
        sub       rcx, 8
        jnz       .more
        vaddpd    ymm0, ymm0, ymm8
        vaddpd    ymm1, ymm1, ymm9
        vaddpd    ymm2, ymm2, ymm10
        vaddpd    ymm3, ymm3, ymm11
        vaddpd    ymm4, ymm4, ymm12
        vhaddpd   ymm0, ymm0, ymm0          ; sum_x
        vhaddpd   ymm1, ymm1, ymm1          ; sum_y
        vhaddpd   ymm2, ymm2, ymm2          ; sum_xx
        vhaddpd   ymm3, ymm3, ymm3          ; sum_yy
        vhaddpd   ymm4, ymm4, ymm4          ; sum_xy
        vextractf128 xmm5, ymm0, 1
        vaddsd    xmm0, xmm0, xmm5
        vextractf128 xmm6, ymm1, 1
        vaddsd    xmm1, xmm1, xmm6
        vmulsd    xmm6, xmm0, xmm0          ; sum_x*sum_x
        vmulsd    xmm7, xmm1, xmm1          ; sum_y*sum_y
        vextractf128  xmm8, ymm2, 1
        vaddsd    xmm2, xmm2, xmm8
        vextractf128  xmm9, ymm3, 1
        vaddsd    xmm3, xmm3, xmm9
        cvtsi2sd  xmm8, rdx                 ; n
        vmulsd    xmm2, xmm2, xmm8          ; n*sum_xx
        vmulsd    xmm3, xmm3, xmm8          ; n*sum_yy
        vsubsd    xmm2, xmm2, xmm6          ; n*sum_xx - sum_x*sum_x
        vsubsd    xmm3, xmm3, xmm7          ; n*sum_yy - sum_y*sum_y
        vmulsd    xmm2, xmm2, xmm3          ; denom*denom
        vsqrtsd   xmm2, xmm2, xmm2          ; denom
        vextractf128  xmm6, ymm4, 1
```

```
vaddsd     xmm4, xmm4, xmm6
vmulsd     xmm4, xmm4, xmm8    ; n*sum_xy
vmulsd     xmm0, xmm0, xmm1    ; sum_x*sum_y
vsubsd     xmm4, xmm4, xmm0    ; n*sum_xy - sum_x*sum_y
vdivsd     xmm0, xmm4, xmm2    ; correlation
ret
```

Now the code is accumulating 8 partial sums for each required sum. The vhaddpd instruction unfortunately did not sum all 4 values in a register. Instead it summed the first 2 values and left that sum in the lower half of the register and summed the last 2 values and left that sum in the upper half of the register. It was necessary to use the "extract 128 bit field", vextractf128, instruction to move the top half of these sums into the lower half of a register to prepare for adding the 2 halves.

When tested with one million calls to compute correlation on 10000 pairs of values, the AVX version used 3.9 seconds which amounts to 20.5 GFLOPs. This is achieving an average of 6 floating point results in each clock cycle. The code had many instructions which did 4 operations and the CPU did an excellent job of out-of-order execution. The use of 2 sets of accumulation registers most likely reduced the inter-instruction dependency which helped the CPU perform more instructions in parallel.

Exercises

1. Write an SSE function to compute the mean and standard deviation of an array of doubles.

2. Write a function to perform a least squares fit for a polynomial function relating two sequences of doubles in 2 arrays.

Appendix A
Installing ebe

There are basically 2 choices for installing ebe: either install a pre-compiled binary package or install from source. Installing binary packages requires a compatible binary package. There has been a need for different packages for different Linux distributions which could be frustrating. Generating an OS X binary package still requires installing the Qt libraries. On the other hand installing from source is fairly easy and easy to keep up to date.

Installing from binary packages

You can find Linux binary packages at the qtebe sourceforge site: `https://sourceforge.net/projects/qtebe/files/Linux`. There will be some recent files for a few versions of Linux. My Linux computer is running Ubuntu, so the Ubuntu files are most likely to be up-to-date. These packages are installation programs prepared with Inno Setup. To install, you download the file and execute it. The installer is fairly normal looking GUI and selecting the defaults at each step are adequate.

The binary installation packages for OS X are also at sourceforge at `https://sourceforge.net/projects/qtebe/files/OS X`. The binary install package for OS X is a gzipped tar archive. You should use

```
tar xvf mac-ebe-2.3.4.tgz   # use the proper version number
```

to extract the files. This will create a directory named "ebc.d". To install ebe you would run the install script using

```
cd ebe.d
bash install
```

This will install ebe in `/usr/local/bin`, but you can also specify a directory for the installation using

```
bash install directory
```

Installing from source on Linux

Installing from source on Linux is not too difficult. The basic idea is to install the programs and libraries required to compiler ebe, download the source code and compile. The examples are for Qt 4, but ebe is also compatible with Qt 5.

Installing the required packages for Ubuntu

The required packages (as defined by Ubuntu 14.04) are astyle, g++, gfortran, git, qt4-dev-tools and yasm. These can be installed under Ubuntu using

```
sudo apt-get install astyle g++ gfortran git qt4-dev-tools
yasm
```

It is also possible to install them using separate git commands for each package. Many of these packages will depend on other packages which will also be downloaded and installed with the ones listed. The package names may differ on another version of Linux and the contents and dependencies may also differ. It may be necessary to install gdb which was installed along with g++.

You could use GUI tools to install these packages, but Muon and the Ubuntu Software Center will not make the task any easier. It is far simpler to just type in the apt-get command.

Installing the required packages for Fedora

With Fedora the tool to use to install packages is yum and the required packages have different names. Use

```
sudo yum install astyle
sudo yum install gcc-c++
sudo yum install gcc-gfortran
sudo yum install git
sudo yum install qt-devel
sudo yum install qtwebkit-devel
sudo yum install qtwebkit-devel
```

The names of the tools we need all have "-qt4" appended to them in /usr/bin so that you can have Qt 4 and Qt 5 on the same computer. The simplest alternative is to place the directory where these tools are installed into the PATH variable. This can be done on the command line or in your .bash_profile file in your home directory:

```
export PATH=/usr/lib64/qt4/bin:$PATH
```

Downloading the source code

The git program is used to copy the source code from sourceforge using

```
git clone git://git.code.sf.net/p/qtebe/code ebe
```

This will create a directory named ebe which contains all the source code. Git is a source code management system which makes it possible to update the source code using "git pull" from the ebe directory in the future. It will download only the changes.

Compiling ebe and installing

There is a shell script in the ebe directory named "rebuild" which performs all the commands needed to build ebe. You can invoke it using

```
cd ebe
bash rebuild
```

This will compile dozens of C++ files. After building ebe you need to install it by

```
sudo cp ebe *.qm /usr/local/bin
```

The *.qm files are files used to allow you to select a different language for the ebe GUI. You can choose from Chinese, French and several other languages. If you do change the language you will need to exit ebe and restart it to see the effect.

Installing from source on OS X

To build ebe on OS X requires getting g++, gdb, astyle, gfortran, git, yasm and Qt on the computer. The Xcode package provides g++ and gdb. The MacPorts package provides the rest.

Installing Xcode from the Apple App Store

Installing Xcode is the first step for installing MacPorts detailed at https://www.macports.org/install.php. They suggest using either the Apple Developer Site or the Apple App Store. I suggest using the App Store menu choice under the Apple menu at the top left of your screen to get to the App Store and then search for Xcode. It is a free download from Apple.

Next you should install the Xcode command line tools using

```
xcode-select -install
```

Most likely you will get a message telling you that the package doesn't exist. You can ignore that message. Apparently Xcode now includes the command line tools. You can verify this by entering "g++" and "gdb -v" from the command line. Those are the tools we need.

Installing MacPorts

Using the MacPorts installation guide, you need to download the proper package file for your operating system. For my computer running Mavericks it was `MacPorts-2.3.0-10.9-Mavericks.pkg`. Click on this package file after it downloads to install MacPorts.

MacPorts is a command line tool which gives you access to thousands of free programs. To search for versions of vim you would enter

```
sudo port search gimp | more
```

You should see `gimp` listed first with a lot of optional features after it. You can install `gimp` using

```
sudo port install gimp
```

This is meant as an example and `gimp` is not needed to run ebe.

Installing tools needed by ebe

Having MacPorts installed you can then use MacPorts to install the tools needed to build and run ebe using

```
sudo port install astyle
sudo port install g95          # substitute for gfortran
sudo port install git
sudo port install qt4-mac
sudo port install yasm
```

It is not necessary to install g95 if you don't want to use FORTRAN, but if you want to use FORTRAN it is simplest to link g95 as gfortran using

```
sudo ln -s /opt/local/bin/g95 /opt/local/bin/gfortran
```

After installing these tools the steps for downloading, building and installing are similar to those for Linux.

Downloading the source code

The git command is identical

```
git clone git://git.code.sf.net/p/qtebe/code ebe
```

Building and installing ebe

The steps for building and installing are identical except for suggesting installing in /opt/local/bin

```
cd ebe
bash rebuild
sudo cp ebe *.qm /opt/local/bin
```

Appendix B
Using ebe

This book has introduced ebe a little at a time, as needed, to help students progress through increasing assembly mastery. Most of the discussion of ebe so far has been about debugging. Here we discuss editing, projects, debugging and more.

Major features

Beyond the basic issues of successfully starting and ending ebe, it is important to learn how to find help within the program. The first learning tool is a set of tooltips. Next is the help system accessible from the menu. The third learning tool is the set of keystrokes visible within the menu system. However possibly the greatest aid to learning is curiosity.

Tooltips

Move the mouse over the various subwindows and items within the subwindows and wait about a half second and ebe will popup tooltips. The tooltips are pretty persistent. If you are editing use the mouse to set the editing cursor and move the mouse cursor to the open space in a title bar to make the tooltip disappear. Tooltips will help as you get used to the program, but they will become an annoyance after you've memorized what they say. You can turn off the tooltips in the menu by unchecking the "Tooltips" option in the "View" menu.

Help

The help system operates by clicking "Help" in the main menu and then clicking on one of the help options. Each help file is displayed in a different window and can be dismissed in the normal manner for windows on your computer.

Menu

The menu system contains nearly everything which can be done in the program. Nearly all the menu options have keyboard shortcuts. Use the menu to figure out what all can be done and learn some keyboard tricks as you progress. A few things like using control with the arrow keys, home and end are not in the menu, so experiment.

Movable toolbars

There are a collection of 4 toolbars in ebe: the file toolbar, the edit tool bar, the debug toolbar and the template toolbar. Each of these has icons to perform common actions and each has a "grab point" on the left or top which can be used with a left click to move the toolbar. You can move a toolbar out of the program to make it a separate window. You can also right click on the grab point to select which toolbars are visible. Below the debug toolbar is shown as it appears as a separate window.

Ebe remembers the configuration of the ebe main window, the toolbars and its subwindows using the file ".ebe.ini", so you can relocate the toolbars as you wish to make using ebe more convenient. There is a separate ".ebe.ini" in each directory where you use ebe, so you can customize the appearance for different languages or projects.

Movable subwindows

In addition to have movable toolbars ebe has a collection of movable or dockable subwindows: data, register, floating point register, terminal, project, toy box, bit bucket, backtrace and console windows. Ebe keeps track of the visibility and location of these subwindows in ".ebe.ini" to make it easy to customize. Below we see ebe with a few of the windows in their "docked" location.

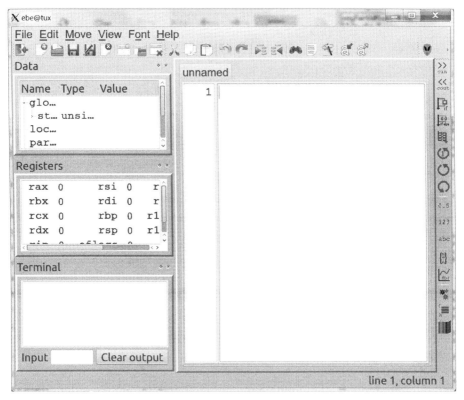

Between each of the docked windows is a "resize bar" which can be used with a left click to adjust the division of space allotted to the docked windows. There is also a resize bar between the docked windows and the source window which can be used to adjust the width of the docked windows.

Each docked window has a "title bar" at the top. There are 2 tiny icons on the right of each title bar which can be used to make the window stand-alone or to make the window disappear. You can also use a right click on a title bar to pop up a menu allowing you to select with dock windows and toolbars are visible. Visibility can also be controlled using the View menu.

You can use a left click on a dock window title bar to drag it around. You can drag it out of ebe to make it stand-alone or to a different vertical position in the dock area. You will notice a gray area in the dock area where the window will drop when you release the left button. You can even drag a dock window to the right of the ebe window or the bottom to use 2 different dock areas. Finally you can drag a dock window on top of another one to create a collection of tabbed dock windows. Perhaps you would like to be able to switch easily between the data, register and floating point register windows. Below we see a dock window with 3 tabs at the bottom for these 3 windows and the terminal window below.

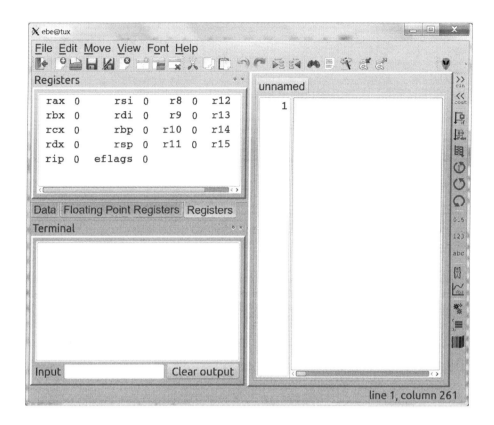

Editing

Editing in ebe uses the mouse and keyboard in mostly normal ways for editors. Special keys like Delete and Enter work as expected. For many of these normal keys an additional action is invoked using the Control key and the normal key. Most editing actions are available in the menu system which will also show the shortcut keys for the actions.

For simplicity the discussion of editing in ebe refers to using the Control key to invoke shortcuts. On OS X this is usually done using the Apple key. Fortunately the menu system displays the proper shortcuts. In addition the shortcuts are based on normal editing shortcuts obtained from Wikipedia:

`http://en.wikipedia.org/wiki/Table_of_keyboard_shortcuts`.

Navigation

Scrollbars There are vertical and horizontal scrollbars which can scroll through the file. Scrolling can also be done using the mouse wheel.

Arrow keys Moving 1 character at a time is done using the left and right arrow keys on the keyboard. Up and down arrows move up or down one line at a time.

Control + Arrow keys Control-Right moves 1 word to the right. Control-Left moves 1 word to the left.

Home/End Home moves to column 1 on the current line. End moves to the end of the current line.

Control + Home/End Control-Home moves to column 1 of line 1. Control-End moves to the end of the file.

PageUp/PageDown These keys move up/down one screenful at a time.

Control-T/Control-B Control-T (top) moves to column 1 of the top line currently on the screen. Control-B (bottom) moves to column 1 of the last line currently on the screen.

Control-M Control-M scrolls the screen until the current line is at the middle of the screen.

Control-L Control-L will pop up a dialog where you can enter a line number to go to.

Cut, copy and paste

The first step in cutting or copying is to select the text to copy or cut.

Left mouse Dragging with the left mouse button held down can be used to mark a section of text. Double clicking with the left mouse button will select a word of text.

Select all You can select all of the text using Control-A or the Edit menu option.

Select none You can cancel any select using Control-0 (zero) or the Edit menu option.

Selected text can be cut, copied and pasted using either options in the Edit menu or the normal shortcuts: Control-X for cut, Control-C for copy, or Control-V for paste. The edit toolbar also has buttons for cut, copy and paste.

Undo/redo

Control-Z will undo an edit operation. Insertions will be undone basically one line at a time. Shift-Control-Z will redo an edit operation. You can also do undo/redo using the menu system or the edit toolbar. The editor keeps track of a large number of editing steps which allows undoing a lot of changes.

Find and replace

Use Control-F to pop up the Find/Replace dialog. There is a text entry box there for entering a string to find. The focus is ready for you to type the search string when the dialog starts. If you simply want to find, then enter either Enter, Control-F or the Find button as many times as you wish. If you wish to change the string, then use Tab to move to the text entry box for the replacement field and enter a string. To replace the string, use Control-R or the Replace button. You can end the Find/Replace dialog using the Cancel button.

Deleting text

Backspace will delete the character to the left of the cursor while Delete will delete the character to the right of the cursor. Control-Backspace will delete the word to the left of the cursor and Control-Delete will delete the word to the right of the cursor.

Using tabs

Entering a tab character will enter enough spaces to move to the next tab stop. Tabs are at columns 5, 9, 13, ... - indenting 4 characters for each tab. Control-Tab will delete space characters to the left of the cursor to position to the previous tab column. The tab spacing value can be changed by editing ".ebe.ini" or by using "Edit settings" from the Edit menu.

Auto-indent

The editor will automatically enter spaces so that a new line will be indented just the same as the previous line. Ebe will indent the next line after a line ending in "{". Likewise it will unindent when a line begins with "}". Adjusting indentation for a new line can be done using Tab or Control-Tab.

Prettify

Ebe will call the external program astyle to format C and C++ programs if you use the "Prettify" option under the Edit menu or the "magic wand" icon on the edit toolbar. You can change the options used for astyle or even replace the program with another by editing ".ebe.ini" or using the "Edit settings" option under the Edit menu.

Indent/unindent

After marking a group of lines you can indent it one tab stop at a time using Control-> which resembles the C right shift operator (>>). You can shift the text left (unindent) using Control-<. There are also menu options for indent/unident and edit toolbar icons.

Comment/uncomment

Control-K will comment out the current line or a range of lines if some text is selected. Control-U will uncomment either the current line or a range of lines. Ebe will use comment syntax for the appropriate language.

Word/number completion

Ebe keeps track of words and numbers to simplify entering/re-entering longer words. It starts with the a collection of keywords and adds words and numbers as you edit. When you enter some text ebe will pop up a list of words to the right of where you are editing. Simply select the desired word (or number) and press "Enter" to accept the suggested completion or enter additional characters to narrow down the choices.

Editing multiple files

It is possible to maintain several open files in ebe. You can open multiple times using the File menu or possibly you could use a project which consists of multiple files. The various files will be accessible as tabbed windows in the source subwindow of ebe.

If you are not using a project ebe will compile or assemble only the currently selected file from those opened. This might be useful if you are working on a few similar programs or if you want to prepare a data file for your program to access. If you are using a project, then ebe will build the program using the source files in the project. Once again it is possible to have a data file as part of a project.

Debugging

The debug toolbar is shown below. There are 4 icons or buttons which are used to control debugging. Each time you click on the Run button the program saves your source code, runs the compiler and/or assembler and then starts running your program in the debugger. Most likely you will want to set a breakpoint before clicking Run. Do this by clicking to the left of a source code line where you would like to have the program stop and inspect things. Then you can click Run and Next/Step to step through your program 1 line at a time. Use Next to stay within the same function or subroutine. Use Step if you wish to debug inside a function or subroutine. You can skip past a bunch of statements using Continue which will execute until it reaches the next breakpoint. The Stop button will end the debugging process.

Run Next Step Continue Stop

Breakpoints

A breakpoint is a point in your source code which will cause the debugger to stop executing your program when it runs your program. If you set a breakpoint on line 10 of your code, the debugger will execute all lines up to line 10 when you click the Run button. Line 10 will not be run until you take another action like using one of the Next, Step or Continue buttons.

Every line of source code has a line number in the line numbers column to the left of the source code. A breakpoint is visually identified in the source code window by using a red background for the line number for the line with a breakpoint.

You set or clear a breakpoint using a left click on a line number. The first click with set the breakpoint and the second will clear it. A right click will pop up a menu allowing management of breakpoints inclucing an option to delete them all.

Running a program

The first step is to set a breakpoint on the line where you want your program to stop. Left click on the line number and you will see the line number for the line change to a bright red background. Click again if this is the wrong line.

After setting one or more breakpoints, you need to click on the Run button. This button will save your source code file, run the proper compiler for your code and then start the gdb debugger on the compiled program. When the program reaches a line with a breakpoint, it will stop and ebe will highlight the line using a pastel blue-green background. The highlighted line will be the next line to execute.

Terminal window

The terminal window is one of the dock windows which supports terminal input and output. It does not include a real terminal emulator. Instead all input is done using a text input box and the text displayed is all printed by the program plus the input echoed to make it all look more normal. The picture below shows the terminal window in a program being tested.

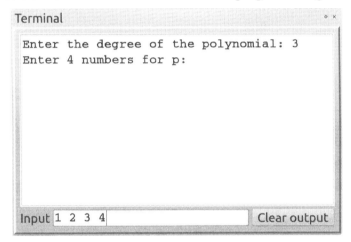

In the previous session one input operation has been done and one is in progress. The first input, 3, was typed into the Input box and after pressing Enter 3 was echoed in the terminal window. The next input is in progress. Four numbers have been typed into the Input box, but Enter has not been pressed which would complete the input.

It is possible to use Control-D or Control-Z in the Input box to send an end of file indication into the program. However this only works if the EOF is signaled before the input operation is performed. This is abnormal, but it works fine if you are single-stepping. Then you enter Control-D prior to executing the scanf call (or another form of read).

Next and step

Both the Next and Step buttons will step through your code, line by line. The difference is that Next will stay in the current function or subroutine, while Step will step into a function if one is called on the highlighted line. You generally only want to use the Step button to step into a function in the same source file or another file in the project.

Continue

The Continue button will resume normal execution of the program and it will only stop if it encounters a breakpoint. You probably would use this to rapidly step past some debugged code to reach a breakpoint in some code which currently has an error.

Data window

The data window displays variables in your program. For high level language this includes global variables, parameters to functions, local variables and user-defined variables. The globals includes a stack display which by default shows the top 6 values on the stack.

For assembly language the variables must be user-defined. The debugger is aware of the address of static variables, but not their type which makes it impossible to display them properly as globals. Below is a picture of the data window while debugging a program.

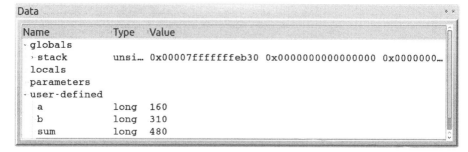

You can see that 3 local variables have been defined with type long and their values are displayed.

Defining variables

You can define variables using either the name of a variable in the editor or using the address of a variable shown either in the data window or the register window. User-defined variables are displayed automatically in the data window each time control is returned to ebe from debugging.

To define a variable by name, you can mark the variable first and then use a right click to bring up a dialog to define a variable. In this dialog you can edit the format and the size of data items as needed. The first and last values are used as array indices for the variable being defined. If this is not an array, leave the array checkbox unchecked. If this is an array, check the array checkbox and set the indices as you wish. Remember that the first index is 0.

You will notice that the name has been provided along with the address which uses the C address-of operator. You can select the type from char, unsigned char,signed char, short, unsigned short, int, unsigned int, long, unsigned long, float, double and bool. Depending on the type you can select appropriate formats. For integer types you can select decimal, hexadecimal or binary. For floating point types you can select a normal floating point display or

a nice collection of formats which can display the various fields of a floating point number. This can be quite helpful in understanding how a computer stores floating point values.

To define a variable by address, you can mark the address (a left click works) in one of the value fields in the register window and then use a right click to bring up a dialog to define a variable with the selected address.

You can use a right click on a variable in the data window to either edit or delete the variable. The edit option pops up the same dialog used to create a variable and allows choosing from the same types and formats.

For an array (or a struct in C or C++) there will be ">" to the left of the name (as in the stack variable in the previous data window picture). Clicking on the ">" pops up a window to select indices for an array or shows the fields of a C/C++ struct. Once you have selected the first and last indices (starting with 0 as the first index) clicking on OK will display the array entries one per line.

Register window

The register window provides a live display of the 16 general purpose registers, the instruction pointer and the CPU flags. Here is a sample

Registers							
rax	480	rsi	0x7fffffffeb38	r8	0x400cca		
rbx	0x0	rdi	0x1	r9	0x0		
rcx	0xffffffffffffffff	rbp	0x7fffffffea50	r10	0x1		
rdx	0x7fffffffeb48	rsp	0x7fffffffea40	r11	0x246		
rip	0x400c33	eflags	IF				

Registers r12-r15 have been left out so that the rest of the registers could be displayed using larger characters. You can change the format of a register (other than rip) by right clicking on its name. This will pop up a form allowing you to choose decimal or hexadecimal for that register or for all the registers. The flags which are currently set are displayed. In the sample the interrupt flag is set. Some interrupts can be ignored if IF is set while there are other non-maskable interrupts which are beyond software control.

Floating point register window

The floating point registers are displayed in a separate dockable window. Here is an example

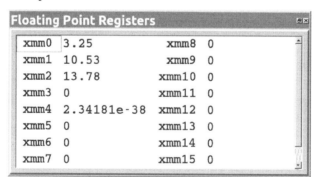

The floating point registers can be used to hold floats, doubles, packed floats, packed doubles and a variety of packed integers of various sizes. Using AVX instructions doubles the number of packed floats or doubles in each register. This makes it important to be able to select the format for the floating point registers. Right clicking on a register or its content will pop up a menu for selecting formatting one register or all. Then you get to select from all the possible interpretations of the registers.

Projects

A program in ebe is generally managed using a project file to keep track
of the source code files in the program. The name of a project is the name
of the program with ".ebe" appended to the name. Thus to build a program
named "hello", you would use a project file named "hello.ebe".

It is not necessary to use a project file with programs consisting of a
single source code file. Ebe starts execution with no known project name
(if not given on the command line). As long as there is no known project
name, it is assumed that there is only 1 source file. Creating a project or
opening a project will change the state so that ebe will be aware of having
a project file. After that point ebe will keep track of the files using the
project file.

Viewing the project window

You may need to check the Project checkbox in the View menu in order to
display the project window. The project window is one of several optional
windows which are intitially placed to the left of the source window. You
can see an empty project window below. You can move the window to be a
"floating" window by left clicking in the title bar of the project window and
dragging it until it is outside of the main window of ebe.

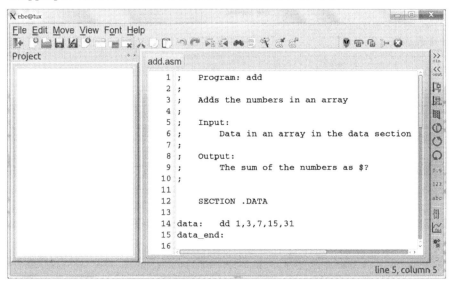

For the project window right clicking will allow you to add or delete
files from the project.

Creating a new project

You can create a new project using the "New project" option under the File menu. This option will allow you to navigate to a new directory and specify the name of the new project file. After creating the project file, any open source files will be closed and the project will be empty. Any changes to the project will be written automatically so there is no need to save a project file.

Opening a project

You can open an existing project using the "Open project" option under the File menu. This option will allow you to navigate to a new directory and open a file with the ".ebe" extension. After opening the project file, any open source files will be closed and the first file in the project will be opened in the editor.

Adding files to a project

A right click in the project window will pop up a menu which will allow you to remove the selected file from the project, open the selected file in the ebe editor, or add a file to the project. A project is simply a file with a collection of file names – one per line, so it is also possible to edit a project file with a text editor.

Closing a project

If you close the active project ebe will return to the default mode of not using a project. It will close all open files.

Toy box

The ebe toy box is a dockable subwindow which allows experimentation with expressions in C/C++ or Fortran. The basic idea is to place variable definitions in one table and expressions in expressions in a second table. A variable definition includes a name, a type and a value. The types are selected from a list of simple types in the language. The names and values must be entered.

The second table has expressions in the first column. After you enter an expression you click on the "do it" button to the right and ebe generates a program in the selected language, compiles it and executes it. From the program's output it determines the type of the expression and its value which are added to the table. Then you can choose a variety of formats depending on the type. For the integer types you can choose decimal, hexadecimal or binary. For the floating point types you can choose decimal, hexadecimal, binary, binary floating point, or fields. In the toy box window below I have included several expressions which help in understanding floating point to integer conversion and floating point format.

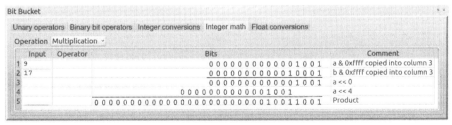

Bit bucket

The ebe bit bucket is a lower level educational tool. It is targeted primarily at assembly language students. It allows you to experiment with a variety of computer operations. It allows you to observe how binary operations like and, or, exlusive or, addition and multiplication work. It shows the steps in converting a decimal number to binary or hexadecimal. It illustrates how to convert a floating point number like 1.625 into its internal representation as a float. Here is an example illustrating multiplication.

You can see that there are 5 tabs in the bit bucket. I have selected "Integer math". After that I used the pull down list to the right of "Operation" to select "Multiplication". Initially there were 2 "Input" boxes to enter 2 numbers and a "*" in the "Operator" column on row 3. After the first clicking of "*" it converted the 2 numbers to binary in column 3. Then I clicked the "*" again and it filled in row 3 and moved the "*" to row 4. After a couple more steps the product was presented on row 5.

The 5 tabs include a large number of illustrations. An assembly language student should find the bit bucket a great tool for learning how a computer works.

Backtrace window

The backtrace window displays the information gleaned from stepping backward through the stack and examining the stack frames for each function invoked. The gdb command for this is "backtrace" or simply "bt". In the picture below we see that the function in the top stack frame is time and the program is stopped at line 18 of "testcopy.c". Next we see that time was called from the test function at line 26. The values of the parameters to test are displayed as well. Last we see that test was called from main at line 47.

```
Back Trace                                                            ○ ×
#0   time () at /home/seyfarth/asm/testcopy.c:18
#1   0x0000000000400dea in test (name=0x401197 "rep movsb",
     copy=0x400f80 <copy_repb>, a=0x2aaaab8b6010 "", b=0x2aaaac240010 "",
     count=10) at /home/seyfarth/asm/testcopy.c:26
#2   0x0000000000400f10 in main (argc=1, argv=0x7fffffffeb38)
     at /home/seyfarth/asm/testcopy.c:47
```

Console

The ebe console provides a way to access gdb directly while debugging. In its text window it displays all the communication with gdb. There is also a command entry box where you can issue a gdb command. After you press "Enter" it executes the command and the results are visible in the text window. I executed "p $rip" to print the instruction pointer register. The next instruction to execute is at 0x400ed1 which is located in main.

```
Console                                                    ◆ ×
0x7fffffffeb38: 140737488350534
(gdb)
0x7fffffffed46: "/home/seyfarth/asm/testcopy"
(gdb)
0x7fffffffeb40: 0
(gdb)
$34 = (void (*)(void)) 0x400ed1 <main+50>
(gdb)


gdb command p $rip
```

Ebe settings

Using the "Edit settings" under the Edit menu will pop up a form with a lot of adjustable features about ebe. Here is how it looks when set for a gray color scheme.

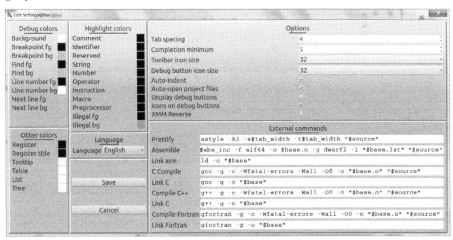

All these settings are stored in ".ebe.ini" in a very simple format, so it is possible to edit the file successfully. However the settings dialog is easier to manage.

Note that there is a "Language" option which is set to "English". Ebe can also operate in Arabic, Chinese, Danish, French, German, Hindi, Indonesian, Japanese, Portuguese, Russian, Spanish and Swedish. I have had excellent assistance for a few languages, but some of these are the direct result of using Google Translate. Some of the translations might be comical. I hope that none are offensive.

Appendix C
Using gdb

The gdb debugger is a product of the Free Software Foundation whose web site is http://www.gnu.org. It supports a variety of languages including C, C++, FORTRAN, and assembly. The debugger seems best suited for C and C++, and debugging code from yasm is less than ideal.

Gdb keeps track of source code lines quite well for yasm programs. Its primary shortcoming (at this point) is that yasm doesn't provide type information for variables. It does provide the address of variables which allows the user to do type casts to examine variables adequately though this requires more effort than if the assembler provided complete type information.

One saving feature of gdb is its macro facility. It is possible to create macros which transparently perform type casts and make debugging easier.

More extensive documentation can be found at http://sourceware.org/gdb/current/onlinedocs/gdb.

Preparing for gdb

In order for gdb to be cognizant of source code and variables, your code must be compiled with special options which add debugging symbol information to the object code. With gcc or gpp the -g option is used to enable debugging support. With yasm you also use -g but you must specify a debugging format which can be either dwarf2 or stabs for Linux or cv8 for Microsoft Visual Studio. The dwarf2 option provides the most complete compatibility using Linux while macho64 is the choice for OS X.

Starting

The typical way to start gdb is

```
gdb program
```

where `program` is the name supplied in the -o option when the program was linked.

Quitting

The command to quit is `quit` which can be abbreviated as q. If you have started running your program and the program is still running, gdb will inform you that the program is still running and ask if you wish to kill the process. Enter "y" to kill the process and exit.

Setting break points

You can set a breakpoint using the "breakpoint" command which can be abbreviated as "b". You can either set the breakpoint using a label from the source code or using a line number of the file.

```
b main
b 17
```

Running

You start the execution of a program in gdb using "run" which can be abbreviated as "r". If you are in the middle of running your program, gdb will prompt you for confirmation before killing the process and starting over.

If you have set a break point, the debugger will execute statements up to the break point and then return control to the debugger. At this point you can examine registers, examine memory, step through lines of code, or do any gdb command. If you have not set a break point, the program will run to completion or until it experiences a fault. This can sometimes be a convenient way to learn about problems like segmentation faults.

While debugging you have several options for continuing execution. The first option is to continue execution until completion or another break point is reached. This is done using the "continue" command which can be abbreviated as "c".

Another possibility is to "single step" through your program. Here there are 4 options. First you can either execute one source code statement or one machine instruction. In C/C++ you probably would prefer not to step one machine instruction at a time. You can also debug only within the same function or step into other functions when they are called. Single stepping in the same function is done using "next" or "nextinstruction". With assembly code the two instructions do the same thing. These can be abbreviated as "n" and "ni". If you use "next" the debugger will execute all calls to functions without returning to the debugger until returning from the functions.

The alternative choice is to use the "step" or "stepinstruction" command. These commands execute either one source code statement or one machine instruction and allow debugging inside a called function. They can be abbreviated as "s" and "si". The two commands have the same effect with assembly code. If you write your own functions, you would probably prefer using "step" to debug your called functions. However, you might wish to use "next" to step "through" a call to a function like printf.

Printing a trace of stack frames

It's fairly common to have programs die while executing. Below is a fairly typical occurrence.

```
seyfarth@tux:~/teaching/asm$
./testcopy
 Segmentation fault
```

A segmentation fault is generally a error in coding where your program tries to access memory which it has not mapped into the program. This could be caused by going past the end of the array. Here is a sample from running gdb with the testcopy program.

```
Reading symbols from ~seyfarth/asm/testcopy
...
(gdb) run
 Starting program: ~seyfarth/asm/testcopy
 Program received signal SIGSEGV,
 Segmentation fault. copy_repb () at copy.asm:12
12          rep     movsb
(gdb) bt
#0   copy_repb () at copy.asm:12
#1   0x000000000040097e in test
     (argc=<value optimized out>,
      argv=<value optimized out>) testcopy.c:27
```

```
#2   main (argc=<value optimized out>,
     argv=<value optimized at testcopy.c:45
```

Once again we get the segmentation fault, but immediately we see that the program died in the `copy_repb` function on line 12 of the file `copy.asm`. It was executing `rep movsb`. The "bt" command (`backtrace`) goes backwards through the stack frames for function calls. It reports that `copy_repb` was called by the `test` function which was called from `main`. The optimization level was high enough that there were variables which the `backtrace` command could not follow. I recompiled with `-O1` rather than `-O3` and got more interesting results:

```
(gdb) run
Starting program: ~seyfarth/asm/testcopy
 Program received signal SIGSEGV,
 Segmentation fault. copy_repb () at copy.asm:12
12          rep       movsb
(gdb) bt
#0  copy_repb () at copy.asm:12
#1  0x00000000004006d8 in test
    (name=0x400b7d "rep movsb", copy=0x400930 <copy_repb>,
    a=0x7ffff7ed2010 "", b=0x7ffff7953010 "",      count=100)
at testcopy.c:27 #2  0x00000000004008d5 in main
    (argc=<value optimized out>, argv=<value optimized out>)
    testcopy.c:45
```

At this point it is possible to print the values of variables and list code from `copy.asm`. We can also use the "up" command to move up the stack frame to the previous function.

```
(gdb) up
#1  0x00000000004006d8 in test (name=0x400b7d "rep movsb",
    copy=0x400930 <copy_repb>, a=0x7ffff7ed2010 "",
    b=0x7ffff7953010 "",      count=100)
at testcopy.c:27 27        copy(a,b,10000000);
(gdb) p a
$1 = (unsigned char *) 0x7ffff7ed2010 ""
```

Now we are debugging the `test` function of `testcopy.c`. The third parameter to `copy` was 10000000 while the array sizes were 1000000. Frequently you can gain a lot of insight from the stack frame trace.

Examining registers

You can use the "info registers" in gdb to print the integer registers. This can be abbreviated as "i r":

```
(gdb) i r
rax             0x0  0
rbx 0x64 100
rcx             0x891690 8984208
rdx 0x989680 10000000
rsi             0x7ffff7a4b000 140737348153344
```

```
rdi             0x7ffff7fca000    140737353916416
rbp             0x7fffffffe6a0    0x7fffffffe6a0
rsp 0x7fffffffe690    0x7fffffffe690
r8              0x64 100
r9 0x0   0
r10             0x7fffffffe3f0    140737488348144
r11 0x206       518
r12             0x7ffff7ed2010    140737352900624
r13             0x400930 4196656
r14             0x64 100
r15 0x3   3
rip             0x40093f 0x40093f <copy_repb+15>
eflags 0x10206    [ PF IF RF ]
cs              0x33 51
ss 0x2b 43
ds              0x0  0
es              0x0  0
fs 0x0   0
gs              0x0  0
```

This prints out all the general purpose registers, the flags register, the instruction pointer, the flags register and the 6 segment registers. This book has basically ignored segment registers since they aren't needed in 64 bit coding.

You can print these plus the floating point registers using "info all" (or "i all"). This would take up many lines and has not been illustrated.

More commonly you might wish to examine one register. You can do this using "print $rcx" to print register rcx. You can abbreviate "print" as "p".

(gdb) **p $rcx**
$1 = 8984208

The default print format is decimal. Use "p/x $rcx" to print in hexadecimal:

(gdb) **p/x $rcx**
$2 = 0x891690

Examining memory

Gdb also has an "examine" command (abbreviated as "x") which can be used to examine multiple memory locations. You enter the command like "x/100 &x" to print 100 locations of the x array. After the number you can append a format letter. Using x for the format letter means hexadecimal, c means character, b means binary and s means string. The examine command needs an expression evaluating to a memory location. You need to take the address of the variable as in a command like "x/100x &x". Last you can append a size letter to change the way examine interprets the memory. Unfortunately the size letters so not match what you would prefer based on using yasm. The letters used are b, h, w and g which stand for "byte", "halfword" (2 bytes), "word" (4 bytes) and "giant" (8 bytes). So you could dump data from an array of doubles using "`x/10fg &data`".

Appendix D
Using scanf and printf

The simplest method for input and output is using the C library's `scanf` and `printf` functions. These functions can handle virtually all forms of text input and output converting to/from integer and floating point format.

It may be that modern programmers are familiar with C++ I/O and not with C. It would not be simple to call C++ I/O facilities, while it is simple to call C functions. So there is probably a need for a slight introduction to the 2 basic workhorses of C I/O: `scanf` and `printf`. These are sufficient for the I/O needs for learning assembly language. Practical uses of assembly language will likely be writing computational or bit manipulating functions with no requirement for I/O. Therefore this appendix will stick to the basics to facilitate writing complete programs while learning assembly programming.

scanf

The simplest way of explaining how to use `scanf` is to show C calls, followed by assembly equivalents. `scanf` is called with a format string as its first parameter. Depending on the format string there can be an arbitrary number of additional parameters. Within the format string are a series of conversion specifiers. Each specifier is a percent character followed by one of more letters defining the type of data to convert. Here are the basic format specifiers:

format	data type
%d	4 byte integer (int)
%hd	2 byte integer (short)
%ld	8 byte integer (long)
%f	4 byte floating point (float)
%lf	8 byte floating point (double)
%s	character array (C string)

So if we wish to read a double followed by a character string we could use the format string "%lf %s".

Each additional parameter for scanf is an address of the data location to receive the data read and converted by scanf. Here is a sample C call:

```
double x;
char s[100];
n = scanf ( "%lf %s", &x, s );
```

scanf will return the number of items converted. In the call above it will return 2 if a number and a string are successfully entered. The string will be placed in the array s with a 0 at the end of the string.

Here is how to do the same thing in assembly:

```
        segment .data
x       dq      0.0
n       dd      0
s       times   100 db 0
fmt     db      "%lf %s",0
        segment .text
        lea     rdi, [fmt]
        lea     rsi, [x]
        lea     rdx, [s]
        xor     eax, eax ; no floating point params
        call    scanf
        mov     [n], eax
```

There are a couple of pitfalls possible. First the format string needs a 0 at the end and it can't be enclosed in the double quotes. Second there are no floating point parameters - &x is a address parameter and it is stored in rsi so rax must be set to 0 before the call.

printf

printf allows printing in a wide variety of formats. Like scanf its first parameter is a format string. The format string contains characters to print along with conversion specifiers like scanf. Data printed with printf is likely to be stored in a buffer until a new-line character is printed. In C, the new-line character can be represented as \n at the end of the format string. Yasm does not support C escape characters in strings, so it is necessary to explicitly add new-line (0x0a) and 0 bytes.

Here is a C printf call

```
char name[64];
int value;
printf ( "The value of %s is %dn", name, value );
```

Here is the same printf call in assembly

```
        segment .data
value dd      0
name  times   64 db 0
fmt   db      "The value of %s is %d",0x0a,0
        segment .text
        lea     rdi, [fmt]
        lea     rsi, [name]
        mov     edx, [value]
        xor     eax, eax
        call    printf
```

printf can have floating point parameters, so be careful to count them and set rax appropriately.

Appendix E
Using macros in yasm

Yasm provides both single line macros and multi-line macros. Both of these can be used to provide abbreviations with meaningful names for commonly used instructions. While these might obscure the mechanisms of assembly language while learning the language they can be of significant utility in practical situations.

Single line macros

A single line macro uses the `%define` preprocessor command. Let's suppose you are tired of seeing 0x0a for the new-line character. You could define a macro for this as

```
%define newline 0x0a
```

From that point forward you could simply use `newline` and get 0x0a inserted in replacement for the macro.

Single line macros can have parameters. Let's suppose you wanted to define a while loop macro. You might wish to compare a value in a register against a value and if a condition is satisfied jump to the top of the loop. Here is a possible `while` macro:

```
%define while(cc,label) jmp%+cc label
```

The %+ allows concatenation of tokens. After this definition we could use code like

```
        cmp rax, 20
        while(l,.more)
```

Multi-line macros

Using a multi-line macro can simply our `while` macro to include the required `cmp` instruction:

```
%macro  while 4
        cmp %1, %3
        j%2 %4
%endmacro
```

The number 4 on the `%macro` line suggests that 4 parameters are expected. You can access each parameter as %1, %2, etc. You can also access the number of parameters as %0.

Now this definition leaves the fairly pleasant feel of creating an instruction, since the macro invocation does not use parentheses:

```
        while rax, 1, 20, .more
```

Admittedly this creates an instruction with 4 parameters which must be learned, but it simplifies things a little bit.

How about the standard production of a stack frame:

```
%macro function 2
        global  %1
    %1: push    rbp
        mov     rbp, rsp
        sub     rsp, %2
%endmacro
```

We might as well simplify the ending of a function:

```
%macro return 1
        mov     rax, %1
        leave
        ret
%endmacro
```

Now we can write a simple program using both macros:

```
        function main, 32
        xor eax, eax
.loop   inc rax
        while rax, 1, 10, .loop
        return 0
```

A fairly useful pair of macros from the yasm manual are `multipush` and `multipop`. These were used earlier in the Sobel example. It makes sense to have a pair of macros to push and pop all callee-save registers for use in register intensive functions.

```
%macro pushsaved
        push rbp
        push rbx
        push r12
        push r13
        push r14
        push r15
```

```
%endmacro

%macro popsaved
        pop r15
        pop r14
        pop r13
        pop r12
        pop rbx
        pop rbp
%endmacro
```

Now these by themselves don't preserve 16 byte stack alignment, so perhaps a better choice would be needed for some functions. Maybe you could combine the creation of a stack frame with pushing the rest of the registers and subtracting from the stack pointer to achieve alignment and room for local variables.

Preprocessor variables

Yasm allows defining preprocessor variables which can be used in macros using %assign. You could assign a variable i in one spot and modify it later:

```
%assign i 1
. . .
%assign i i+1
```

For more information about yasm macros visit the yasm web site at http://www.tortall.net/projects/yasm/manual/html/index.html which discusses topics like looping and string length.

Appendix F
Sources for more information

yasm user manual

`http://www.tortall.net/projects/yasm/manual/html/index.html` is the location of the yasm user manual. This is quite extensive and a good reference for learning more about yasm.

nasm user manual

Look at `http://www.nasm.us/doc/` for the nasm user manual. This is the software which nasm is based on and the documentation is fairly similar to the yasm manual.

Stephen Morse's 8086/8088 primer

Stephen P. Morse is the architect of the 8086 Intel microprocessor. He has a primer on the 8086/8088 at

   `http://www.stevemorse.org/8086/index.html`.

Dr. Paul Carter's free assembly book

Dr. Carter has prepared an excellent book on 32 bit x86 programming which can be downloaded at http://www.drpaulcarter.com/pcasm/.

64 bit machine level programming

Drs. Bryant and O'Hallaron of Carnegie Mellon have provided an excellent treatise dissecting how gcc takes advantage of the x86-64 architecture in a document located at

`www.cs.cmu.edu/~{}fp/courses/15213-s07/misc/asm64-handout.pdf`

GDB manual

You may find a need to learn more about gdb. Send your browser to `http://www.gnu.org/software/gdb/documentation`.

Intel documentation

Intel provides excellent documentation about their processors at `http://www.intel.com/products/processor/manuals/`.

You should probably review the architecture in "*Intel 64 and IA-32 Architectures Software Developer's Manual, Volume 1: Basic Architectures*".

The instructions are described in great detail in "*Volume 2A: Instruction Set Reference, A-M*" and "*Volume 2B: Instruction Set Reference, N-Z*". These manuals are quite helpful, but some categorization of instructions would help. There are a bewildering number of instructions and looking through the alphabetized list can be overwhelming.

Index

using jmp, 92
syscall, 147, 148
system call, 146
    32 bit Linux, 146
    64 bit Linux, 147
    64 bit OS X, 147
System V ABI, 111
text segment, 28
TLB, 43
translation lookaside buffer, 43
two's complement, 15, 16
ucomisd, 140
ucomiss, 140
ulimit, 29
ungetc, 160
unrolling loops, 186
unsigned, 15
unsigned integer, 15
vaddpd, 137

vaddps, 137
virtual address, 41
vmoupd, 136
vmovups, 136
vsubpd, 137
vsubps, 137
while, 96, 100
while loop, 96, 97
Windows, 1, 2, 44, 111, 112, 114
word, 19
write, 148, 150
x86-64, 47
xor, 62, 77
yasm, 6, 19, 114
    listing, 19
zero flag. *See* ZF
zero page, 30
ZF, 48, 58, 59, 62, 69, 71